D1547891

VOLUME II

THE PROCESS OF ADMISSION
TO ORDAINED MINISTRY

The meaning of episcopal and presbyteral ministry and the structuring of the Church which is revealed in the procedures of installation or ordination to the episcopacy (bishop, superintendent, ecclesiastical inspector, etc.) and to the presbyterate (priest, pastor, etc.) in the Roman Catholic Church and certain Lutheran, Reformed, Anglican and Methodist Churches in Western Europe and in the United States.

James F. Puglisi, S.A.

VOLUME II

THE PROCESS OF ADMISSION
TO ORDAINED MINISTRY

The First Lutheran, Reformed, Anglican, and Wesleyan Rites

A Comparative Study

Translated from the French by

Mary Misrahi

Preface by Paul F. Bradshaw

A PUEBLO BOOK

The Liturgical Press   Collegeville, Minnesota

A Pueblo Book published by the The Liturgical Press

Design by Frank Kacmarcik

© 1998 by The Order of St. Benedict, Inc., Collegeville, Minnesota. All rights reserved. No part of this book may be reproduced in any form or by any means, electronic or mechanical, including photocopying, recording, taping, or any retrieval system, without the written permission of The Liturgical Press, Collegeville, Minnesota 56321. Printed in the United States of America.

Library of Congress Cataloging-in-Publication Data
Puglisi, J. F.
    [Etude comparative sur les processus d'accès au ministère ordonné.
English]
    The process of admission to ordained ministry : a comparative
study / James F. Puglisi ; translated by Michael S. Driscoll and Mary Misrahi.
    p. cm.
    "A Pueblo book."
    Based on the author's thesis (doctoral)—Université de Paris (Sorbonne).
    Includes bibliographical references and index.
    Contents: v. 1. Epistemological principles and the Roman Catholic rites.
    ISBN 0-8146-6128-9   (vol. I)
    ISBN 0-8146-6129-7   (vol. II)
    1. Ordination—History of doctrines.   2. Ordination (Liturgy)—History.
I. Title.
BV664.5.P8413   1996
262'.1—dc20   96-14468
                                                     CIP

To my religious community,
the Society of the Atonement,
on its
100th anniversary of foundation
(1898–1998)

"Ut omnes unum sint"

Contents

NOTE TO THE READER   xvii

PREFACE   xix

S E C O N D   P A R T
The Meaning of the Ordained Ministry and the Structure of the
Church According to Several Liturgies of Ordination or Installation
from the Reformation

CHAPTER 1: LITURGIES OF LUTHERAN INSPIRATION   3

A. THE *AGENDA* OF WITTENBERG (1537/1539)—
    MARTIN LUTHER   4

   1. Date of the First Ordinations and Formulation of the First Rite of
      Ordination by Luther   4

   2. Ordination of Ministers of the Word   6
         a. Structure of the Formulary   6
         b. The Nucleus: the Imposition of Hands and the Prayer   10
         c. Prayer of Ordination   11
              α) Biblical Images Employed   12
              β) Qualities Requested for the Ordinand   13
              γ) Gifts Received by the Ordinand   13

   3. Installation of a Bishop   14
         a. Structure of the Formulary   14
         b. The Nucleus: the Imposition of Hands and the Prayer   14
         c. Prayer of Installation   15

   4. Relationship Between the Ministry of Pastor
      and That of Bishop   15

5. Later Influence of the Formulary of the *Agenda*   23
    a. Reception of the Formulary of Ordination
       as Installation   24
    b. Ordination or Installation?   26

6. Conclusion: Structuring of the Church
   and the Substance of Ordained Ministry   27
    a. Structure of the Church   27
    b. Substance of the Pastoral and Episcopal Ministries   29

B. THE *ORDINATIO ECCLESIASTICA* (1537)—
JOHANNES BUGENHAGEN   30

1. Relationship to the Formulary of Luther   31

2. Ordination of a Pastor   32
    a. Structure of the Formulary   32
    b. The Nucleus: the Imposition of Hands and the Prayer   33
    c. Prayer of Ordination   33

3. Ordination of a Bishop *[Superintendens]*   34
    a. Structure of the Formulary   34
    b. The Nucleus: the Imposition of Hands and the Prayer   35
    c. Prayer of Ordination   36
        α) Biblical Images Employed   36
        β) Qualities Requested for the Ordinand   37
        γ) Gifts Received by the Ordinand   37

4. Relationship Between the Ministry of Pastor
   and That of Bishop   37

5. Later Influence of the Formulary of the
   Ordinatio Ecclesiastica   38

6. Conclusion: Structuring of the Church
   and the Substance of Ordained Ministry   38
    a. Structure of the Church   38
    b. Substance of the Pastoral and Episcopal Ministries   39

C. *DE ORDINATIONE LEGITIMA* (1549)—
MARTIN BUCER (OR BUTZER)   39

1. Relationship to the Formulary of Luther   40

2. Ordination of a Pastor   41

a. Structure of the Formulary   41

b. The Nucleus: the Imposition of Hands and the Prayer   45

c. Prayer of Ordination   46

   α) Biblical Images Employed   47

   β) Qualities Requested for the Ordinand   48

   γ) Gifts Received by the Ordinand   49

3. Installation of a Bishop   49

4. Relationship Between the Ministry of Pastor
and That of Bishop   50

5. Later Influence of the Formulary of Bucer   51

6. Conclusion: Structuring of the Church
and the Substance of Ordained Ministry   51

   a. Structure of the Church   51

   b. Substance of Pastoral and Episcopal Ministries   53

D. THE *KYRKOORDNING* (1571)—LAURENTIUS PETRI   53

1. Relationship to the Formulary of Luther   54

2. Ordination of a Priest   54

   a. Structure of the Formulary   54

   b. The Nucleus: the Imposition of Hands and the Prayer   57

   c. Prayer of Ordination   57

      α) Biblical Images Employed   57

      β) Qualities Requested for the Ordinand   58

      γ) Gifts Received by the Ordinand   58

3. Ordination of a Bishop   58

   a. Structure of the Formulary   58

   b. The Nucleus: the Imposition of Hands and the Prayer   60

   c. Prayer of Ordination   60

4. Relationship Between the Ministry of Priest
and That of Bishop   60

5. Later Influence of the Formulary of Petri   61

6. Conclusion: Structuring of the Church
and the Substance of Ordained Ministry   62

   a. Structure of the Church   62

   b. Substance of the Pastoral and Episcopal Ministries   63

E. OVERALL CONCLUSIONS   64

   1. Elements Usually Included in Each Formulary   64
      a. The Election   64
      b. The Ordination or the Liturgical Act Whereby the Elect Is
         Instituted/Installed in His Office   64
      c. The Sending Forth, or the Mission, to a Concrete Ministry,
         Most Often in a Parish or in a Wider Territory Such
         as a Diocese That Includes Several Reformed
         Communities   65

   2. Actors Involved in the Process   65
      a. The Community Concerned   65
      b. The Newly Ordained   66
      c. The Holy Spirit   66
      d. The Heads of the Neighboring Communities   67

   3. Substance of the Ordained Ministry   67

   4. Structure of the Ordained Ministry   68

   5. The Meaning of Ordination   69

**CHAPTER 2: FORMULARIES INSPIRED BY THE
CALVINIST REFORMATION   71**

A. THE *ZÜRICHTER PRÄDICANTENORDNUNG*—1532   71

   1. Analysis of the Text   72
      a. Examination   72
      b. Presentation and Election   72
      c. Ordination   73

   2. Formula or Prayer of Ordination   73
      a. Biblical Images Employed   74
      b. Qualities Requested for the Ordinand   74
      c. Gifts Received by the Ordinand   74

   3. Conclusion: Structuring of the Church
     and the Substance of Ordained Ministry   74
      a. Structure of the Church   74
      b. Substance of the Pastoral Ministry   75

B. THE *FORMA AC RATIO* (1550)—JAN ŁASKI   75

   1. Description of the Rite   76
      a. Election   76
      b. The Assessment of the Results, and the Examination   78
      c. Ordination   79

   2. Prayer of Ordination   80
      a. Biblical Images Employed   82
      b. Qualities Requested for the Ordinand   82
      c. Gifts Received by the Ordinand   82

   3. Later Influence of the Formulary of Jan Łaski   82

   4. Conclusion: Structuring of the Church
     and the Substance of Ordained Ministry   83
      a. Structure of the Church   83
      b. Substance of the Pastoral Ministry   84

C. THE *BUKE OF DISCIPLINE* (1560)—JOHN KNOX   85

   1. Description of the Rite   86
      a. Election   86
      b. Examination and the Commitment of the People   88
      c. Blessing   89

   2. Prayer of Blessing (or of Ordination)   91
      a. Biblical Images Employed   92
      b. Qualities Requested for the Ordinand   93
      c. Gifts Received by the Ordinand   93

   3. Later Influence of the Formulary of the *Buke of Discipline*   93

   4. Conclusion: Structuring of the Church
     and the Substance of Ordained Ministry   94
      a. Structure of the Church   94
      b. Substance of the Pastoral Ministry   94

D. THE FORMULARY OF MIDDLEBURGH (1586/1602)   95

   1. Description of the Rite   96
      a. Election   97
      b. Presentation and Examination   97
      c. Ordination   98

2. Prayer of Ordination   98
    a. Biblical Images Employed   99
    b. Qualities Requested for the Ordinand   100
    c. Gifts Received by the Ordinand   100

3. Later Influence of the Middleburgh Formulary   100

4. Conclusion: Structuring of the Church
   and the Substance of Ordained Ministry   100
    a. Structure of the Church   100
    b. Substance of the Pastoral Ministry   101

E. OVERALL CONCLUSIONS   101

1. Elements Usually Found in Each Formulary   102
    a. Election   102
    b. Ordination   103
    c. Missioning   105

2. Actors Involved in the Process   105
    a. The Congregation Concerned   105
    b. The Newly Ordained   106
    c. The Holy Spirit   107
    d. The Neighboring Communities   108

3. Substance of the Ordained Ministry   108

4. Permanence in the Superintendency Is Not Evident in the Texts
   We Have Examined   108

CHAPTER 3: THE FIRST ORDINALS OF THE CHURCH OF
ENGLAND   111

A. THE ORDINALS OF 1550 AND 1552   112

1. Author of the Ordinal of 1550   112

2. Structure of the Ordinations   112
    a. Priest   114
        α) Liturgy of the Word   114
        β) Preliminaries   115
        γ) Ordination   118
        δ) Communion   119

    b. Bishop   119
        α) Liturgy of the Word   120
        β) Preliminaries   120
        γ) Consecration   122
        δ) Communion   122

  3. Prayers of Ordination (or Consecration)   123
    a. Priest   123
        α) Biblical Images Employed   125
        β) Qualities Requested for the Ordinand   125
        γ) Gifts Received by the Ordinand   125
    b. Bishop   126
        α) Biblical Images Employed   127
        β) Qualities Requested for the Ordinand   127
        γ) Gifts Received by the Ordinand   127

  4. Relationship Between the Priesthood and the Episcopacy   127

  5. Later Influence of the Ordinals   128

  6. Conclusion: Structuring of the Church
    and the Substance of Ordained Ministry   128
    a. Structure of the Church   128
    b. Substance of the Ministries of Priest and Bishop   130

B. THE ORDINAL OF 1661   131

  1. Structure of Ordination and Consecration   136
    a. Priest   136
    b. Bishop   139

  2. Relationship Between the Priesthood and the Episcopacy   140

  3. Conclusion: Structuring of the Church
    and the Substance of Ordained Ministry   141
    a. Structure of the Church   141
    b. Substance of the Ordained Ministry   141

C. OVERALL CONCLUSIONS   141

  1. Elements Usually Included in Each Formulary   142
    a. Election   142
    b. Ordination   143
    c. Mission   144

2. Actors Involved in the Process   144
    a. The Local Church   144
    b. The Newly Ordained   145
    c. The Holy Spirit   145
    d. The Neighboring Bishops   146

3. Substance of the Ordained Ministry   146

4. Permanence of the Ordained Ministry   146

CHAPTER 4: FIRST FORMULARY OF THE METHODIST CHURCH   147

A. THE *SUNDAY SERVICE* (1784)—JOHN WESLEY   147

1. Author: Relationship with the Rituals of the Church of England   147

2. Structure of the Ordinations of the *Sunday Service*   152
    a. Elder   152
    b. Superintendent   154

3. Prayers of Ordination   155

4. Relationship Between the Presbyterate and the Superintendency   155

5. Later Influence of the Ordinal of the *Sunday Service*   157

6. Conclusion: Structuring of the Church and the Substance of Ordained Ministry   159
    a. Structure of the Church   159
    b. Substance of the Ministries of Elders and Superintendents   160

CHAPTER 5: THEOLOGICAL REFLECTION   163

A. IMAGES MOST FREQUENTLY USED IN THE RITUALS   163

B. THE ORDAINED MINISTER AS A PERSON AND THE QUALITIES THAT ARE REQUIRED OF HIM   166

C. FUNCTIONS OF THE ORDAINED MINISTERS   168

D. USE OF THE CATEGORY OF PRIESTHOOD   172

E. ESCHATOLOGICAL MEANING OF THE INDIVIDUAL
    MINISTRY   175

F. PNEUMATOLOGICAL MEANING OF THE ORDAINED
    MINISTRY: CHARISM AND FUNCTION   177

G. THE QUESTION OF THE DIRECTION OF THE CHURCH   182

H. STRUCTURING OF THE CHURCH AND ORDINATION   184
    1. The Lutheran-Reformed Model   185
    2. The Anglican Model   189

I. FRAMEWORK OF ORDINATION   193

BIBLIOGRAPHY   199

1. ABBREVIATIONS   199

2. SOURCES   204

3. STUDIES   212

INDEX   225

Note to the Reader

Two kinds of footnote numeration are used in this study: the numbers refer to footnotes; the numbers preceded by an asterisk (*) refer to the liturgical texts that are reproduced in a separate volume.

On October 3, 1990, the two Germanies were reunified. This event brought about a revision of the ecclesiastical structures of the Churches of Germany. In September 1990, the parallel organizations of RDA and RFA (East and West Germany) decided to fuse. In this study I have maintained the distinction between East and West in the third volume of the analytical study and the fourth volume of liturgical texts, because these texts were created by the individual Churches and denote a historical and often theological stage in the evolution of the liturgy in the Churches involved.

Concerning the Catholic Church, I have designated the Western part, the only one taken into consideration in my work, as Latin Catholic, especially when it deals with the Churches of the Latin rite which have produced the Gallican, Frankish, or Romano-German rites. I have reserved the adjective Roman for the rituals of the Church of this city, all the while being conscious of their progressive reception in the Latin Church. Concerning the conjunction of the adjectives Catholic and Roman, see the enlightening research of Y. CONGAR, "Romanité et catholicité. Histoire de la conjonction changeante de deux dimensions de l'Eglise," *RSPT* 71, 2 (1987) 161–190.

A final aid for the reader not familiar with certain technical terms is a small glossary found at the end of the third volume. It is accompanied by a list of some Churches with their equivalent in English.

Preface

In his introduction to the first volume of this work, Hervé Legrand expressed his admiration for the qualities inherent in all the volumes and the importance of the service to church and academy which the author has rendered by his careful efforts. I do not intend to repeat those comments here, but merely want to add my own assent to them. The subject of ordination has traditionally been a much neglected area within the field of liturgical studies, and insufficient attention has been paid to the significant contribution that analysis of the actual texts of historical rites can make to our understanding of the doctrines of church and ministry. Even for those who wished to penetrate further into this relatively unknown jungle, the task was made more difficult by the serious lack of accessible editions of some of the key documents and of translations into the English language. This was especially true of some of the sixteenth-century rites treated in this particular volume. James Puglisi has done a great deal here to remedy these various deficiencies, for which we may be grateful. By laying out the rites before us and offering rich insights into their interpretation, he has provided an invaluable guide for students of liturgy, systematic theologians, and ordinary Christians who want to understand better the meaning of ordination and ministry within the Church.

To attempt any generalizing comments on the rich variety of rites discussed in this volume, coming as they do from different time periods and from widely diverse ecclesiastical traditions, is a dangerous, if not foolhardy, exercise. There are many significant differences between them, which the reader must take care to note if he or she is not to distort the historical picture unfairly. Yet one may perhaps legitimately point out certain trends that run through many of the rites with which we are concerned. These are admittedly more developed and more clearly articulated in some cases than they are in others. But even their lack of prominence in some rites does not always spring from a difference of theological conviction in the minds of the compilers. One should be conscious that, especially in the earlier rites of the sixteenth century, Reformers were sometimes compelled by the situation in which they found themselves to compromise and adopt practices that they would not have wished to adopt in more ideal circumstances and that were not always fully consistent with their doctrines of church and ministry.

Fundamental, of course, to all efforts to draw up rites of ordination for the churches of the Reformation was the desire to return to what was seen as the New Testament basis for ordained ministry. But the Reformers' vision of this scriptural model was profoundly affected by two major factors. The first was the absence of the sort of critical biblical scholarship which most Christians of the late twentieth century take for granted. Nor did they know as much as we do today about the history of Christianity in the second and third centuries and of the emergence then of patterns of ministry and methods of appointment to ministry that might have helped them make better sense of the scattered and ambiguous references to such things in the New Testament. The second factor was their own experience of ordained ministry as it was practiced in the Catholic Church of their time. Their consciousness of what they perceived to be abuses in the current system strongly colored the way that they read the scriptural evidence. In the light of this, they are perhaps more to be applauded for how far they did succeed in understanding what the New Testament had to say than to be criticized for the ways in which they failed to grasp it properly.

Nowhere is the conjoint influence of these two factors more apparent than in their attitudes towards episcopacy. It is true that those who rejected bishops in the sixteenth century did so in part because they rightly perceived that the evidence of the New Tesament did not explicitly support the hierarchical structures which had subsequently grown up in the Church, and that theologians from Jerome to the scholastics had not been convinced that bishops constituted an order distinct from the presbyterate. But they were also affected by episcopacy as they personally had experienced it, with bishops being not just princes of the church but ranked as persons of autocratic power within the structures of society. It was this abuse of the episcopal office as they saw it that led them to interpret the ambiguities of the biblical evidence negatively and to side with those theologians who had questioned the status of the episcopate rather than with those who had defended it. Thus some Reformers simply wanted to have a different sort of bishop in the church, one more in line with what they understood to have been the apostolic model, sometimes preferring to substitute the non-scriptural title "superintendent" for "bishop" because of the negative connotations of the traditional name; but others solved the problem by eliminating episcopacy altogether and espousing the doctrine of the parity of all ministers as what they believed the New Testament to have taught.

Similarly, the tendency among the Reformers to distinguish between the interior sense of vocation and the external call to ministry, to which Puglisi rightly draws attention, also arose from their personal observation of the pattern of ordination in the Catholic church of their day. They were convinced that many of those who were being ordained were not truly called to ministry, for they failed to display what the Reformers thought were the qualities of a person with a divine vocation. While some of them attacked the external call of the church as being defective in certain respects—especially the absence of a true election by the people—which thereby allowed unsuitable candidates to gain admission to the ordained ministry, others dealt with the problem by drawing a distinction between the external call, which might have been rightly carried out, and a true inner call from God to the candidate, which they judged to be lacking.

Indeed, two of the great Reformation recoveries of the ordination theology and practice of the early church were brought about less by historical knowledge of what had once been done and more in reaction against what they perceived as the failure of the medieval church to ensure that only those truly called by God received ordination. These two insights were that ordination is ultimately an act of God rather than just an action of the church, and that in calling someone to ministry God works through the whole church and not just through the bishop alone. They called for the involvement of lay people in the whole process of ordination—from election to the public celebration of the rite—not simply because that was what had happened in the early centuries of Christianity but because they believed that this reform would put a stop to the wrong people being ordained. This also helps to explain the emphasis laid on a new feature in Reformation ordination rites not derived from primitive Christianity, the public examination of the candidates, in which they were usually questioned not only about their orthodox beliefs but also about their sense of vocation, their character, and their intentions. And it illuminates the stress generally placed in the prayer texts themselves on the need for God to bestow appropriate personal qualities on the ordinands in place of the tendency in medieval rites to accentuate the bestowal of certain powers. While in taking this line the Reformers were reverting to what had been the dominant note in ancient ordination prayer texts, their motivation was less antiquarian than doctrinal: ordained ministry was for them less about the exercise of particular powers and functions and more about placing in positions of leadership men whose whole character and conduct of life would be exemplary to their congregations.

The Reformers' lack of precise and detailed knowledge about early Christian practice accounts for the quite remarkable diversity of prayer patterns that we find in the rites of the various ecclesiastical traditions. Faced with the competing scholastic theories as to what constituted the essential "matter" and "form" of ordination—anointing, vesting, the handing over of the instruments of office, and so on—they quite naturally reverted to the New Testament elements of prayer and imposition of hands as the only essential features of the rite (though in Scotland even the use of the imposition of hands came under suspicion for a while as perhaps connoting a transmission of power that the Reformers did not wish to perpetuate—a further example of the thesis that I have been advancing that it was not Scripture alone which determined Reformation practice). But the New Testament did not prescribe the place of prayer within the rite nor the sort of prayer that was to be used, and hence the various compilers came up with quite different arrangements. Some provided a formal ordination prayer of the classical kind; others followed Luther in making the Lord's Prayer the central oration within the rite; and still others believed that it was sufficient as long as the commissioning of the candidates took place within the general context of public prayer. In some cases the imposition of hands accompanied the prayer itself (as in ancient times, though this was usually unknown to the compilers themselves); in other cases prayer preceded the laying on of hands; and occasionally the laying on of hands preceded the prayer.

Perhaps the strangest feature of Reformation ordination practice to modern eyes, however, and especially to those living in a culture where Church and state are strictly separated, is their tendency to involve the civil authorities in the process. But we must remember that most of them did not have a vision of a gathered congregation as constituting the Church but of a Christian nation state, in which the civil and the ecclesiastical authorities constituted two arms of God's rule on earth, and might often involve some of the same individuals in both administrations. In rejecting papal authority, most Reformers had no intention of abandoning the idea of a common locus of authority that would bind together the separate congregations and individual ecclesiastical ministers as one body. Hence the civil authorities were the natural choice as representing the wider church in the ordination practice of local regions.

What then may we learn from these rites mostly produced in a situation of conflict and reaction to centuries of distortion and abuse and in conditions of less historical knowledge than we now possess? They have their limitations: this we must frankly acknowledge. But they also have considerable value in offering a counterbalance to certain unhelpful ways of thinking about ordination and the Church, and in recovering—albeit often more by accident than design—insights that had once abounded in primitive Christianity and then been overlaid with other ideas and emphases. Their solutions may not always be our solutions, but the questions and challenges to our own ecclesiology that they pose are ones that we must address if we hope to arrive at a wholeness in the vision of our different ecclesiastical traditions and a mutual recognition of one another's ministries within the one body of Christ. May this book contribute to that ecumenical goal.

Paul F. Bradshaw
Professor of Liturgy
University of Notre Dame

Second Part

The Meaning of the Ordained Ministry and the Structure of the Church According to Several Liturgies of Ordination or Installation from the Reformation

Chapter 1

Liturgies of Lutheran Inspiration

The Reformation in Europe brought about a series of progressive changes in the worship of the Catholic Church, starting with the most common rites in the life of the Church, as, for example, the celebration of the Lord's Supper.[1] Those rites in use for the ordination of ministers were changed more slowly. A number of historians of the Lutheran Reformation hold that the ordination of new ministers was not a matter of any urgency, since there were Catholic priests who had joined the movement and taken over some of the Reformed parishes. However, once this first generation of ministers no longer sufficed at a time when the number of Reformed parishes was increasing, the Reformed authorities were forced to lend the matter more thought.[2] This may account for the fact that we do not see new

---

[1] Several collections of Eucharistic texts that came out of the Reformation have been published in a number of languages. As an example, one will find the reforms made in all the Churches (Lutheran, Reformed, Anglican, etc.) in I. PAHL (ed.), *Coena Domini I. Die Abendmahlsliturgie der Reformationskirchen im 16./17. Jahrhundert* (Fribourg: Universitätsverlag, 1983). According to this collection, the first such texts date from 1521/1522.

[2] See, for example, J.H.P. REUMANN, *Ministries Examined: Laity, Clergy, Women, and Bishops in a Time of Change* (Minneapolis: Augsburg Publishing House, 1987) 25–29 (+ bibliography); L. OTT, *Le sacrement de l'Ordre*, trans. from the German [*Das Weihesakrament*] by M. Deleporte (Paris: Cerf, 1971) 286; B. D. SPINKS, "Luther's Other Major Liturgical Reforms: 2. The Ordination of Ministers of the Word," *Liturgical Review* 9, 1 (1979) 20 f.; and P. R. NELSON, *Lutheran Ordination in North America, The 1982 Rite* (Ann Arbor, Mich.: University Microfilms International, 1987) 239–247. It seems likely that there was another reason the Reformers

rites of ordination immediately appearing. Moreover, for Martin Luther there were other, more pressing matters than the reform of ordinations.[3]

In the paragraphs that follow we shall study the early rites established by Luther himself (between 1535 and 1539[*239–*252]) and by other reformers who drew their inspiration from him: J. Bugenhagen (Denmark, 1537[*253–*269]), M. Bucer (Strasbourg, 1549[*270–*293]), and L. Petri (Sweden, 1571[*294–*322]). We will be paying particular attention to the structure of the rite (its elements, the order in which they occur, the participants, and the procedures), as well as to the substance of the ministries themselves.

A. THE *AGENDA* OF WITTENBERG (1537/1539)— MARTIN LUTHER

1. DATE OF THE FIRST ORDINATIONS AND FORMULATION OF THE FIRST RITE OF ORDINATION BY LUTHER

The first ordination conferred by Luther was that of Georg Rörer in the parish church of Wittenberg on May 14, 1525. Even though there

---

did not immediately ordain ministers: doing so was not, doctrinally, an urgent priority, for "first the sovereignty of the Gospel had to be restored, as well as the free nature of salvation in Jesus Christ, a salvation that was a gift of the power of the Holy Spirit conveyed through the Word and the sacraments. It was only later that attention was paid to the ministry which is at the service of this Gospel," A. BIRMELE, "Le ministère dans les Eglises de la Réforme," *Positions luthériennes* 29, 3 (1981) 192.

[3] "The emphasis was put on values such as conscience, Scripture, faith, the Word of God. The ministry has apparently lost all primacy. The rejection of even papal primacy is only the result of the devaluation that affected every ministry as such. Obedience to the authority of the minister was no longer a matter of conscience," D. OLIVIER, "La question des ministères au sein des Eglises de la Réforme protestante durant la seconde moitié du XVIe siècle," in *Eglises, sociétés et ministères. Essai d'herméneutique historique des origines du christianisme à nos jours* (Paris: Centre Sèvres, 1986) 94. The theological conflicts described by O. H. Pesch are similar: ecclesiological questions such as the relationship between the pope and the council, the specific nature of episcopal ministry, the relationship between the proclamation of the Word and the administration of the sacraments as functions of ecclesiastical ministry, the meaning of the sacraments in the life of the Church, and the very essence of the Church occupied theologians in the late Middle Ages: see O. H. PESCH, "Luther und die Kirche," *Lutherjahrbuch* 25 (1985) 113–139, esp. 115f.

are no records of the specific rite used, tradition has it that Luther introduced Rörer into his function as minister of the Word with prayers and the laying on of hands.[4] It was not until 1535 that the Prince-Elector John Frederick of Saxe established within his Electorate the procedure of admission to the ministry (the examination, the call, and the ordination of candidates). It is apparently in 1536–1537 that Luther drew up the rite of ordination, following what constituted the heart of apostolic tradition: the Word of God, the laying on of hands, and the prayer.[5] This revised text is found in the *Agenda* of Wittenberg of 1539.[6] Luther replaced the great prayer of ordination of the medieval pontificals with the Lord's Prayer, followed by a prayer elaborating on its three parts. With the passage of time, a *"Vollzugsformel"* (prayer of conferral or of transmission of office) was added as well. This last existed side by side with the prayer, in the rite of some Churches.

Only one rite of ordination has come down to us directly from the pen of Luther. This may be due to the fact that he referred to the ordained ministers as "bishops, that is to say, preachers and pastors,"[242] in line with the interchangeability of the terms "bishop" and "presbyter" found in the New Testament; in line as well with the medieval debate on the sacramentality of the office of bishop. Even in the Confession of Augsburg (art. XXVIII) the "episcopal ministry" to which one is ordained is rightly called *pastor seu episcopus*, whereas the title of the prayer of ordination composed by Luther himself is *ordinatio ministrorum verbi*.

[4] H. LIEBERG, *Amt und Ordination bei Luther und Melanchthon* (Göttingen: Vandenhoeck & Ruprecht, 1962) 182.

[5] H. LIEBERG, *Amt und Ordination . . .*, 191–207.

[6] The text "Das deutsche Ordinationsformular" is found in three columns in the Weimar edition: *D. Martin Luthers Werke. Kritische Gesamtausgabe* (Weimar: Hermann Böhlaus Nachfolger, 1883) t. 38, 423–431 (quoted as WA followed by the number of the tome, the page number, and the line number; English translation found in *Luther's Works*, American edition, J. PELIKAN and H. T. LEHMANN [eds.], [St. Louis/Philadelphia: Concordia Publishing House/Fortress Press] vol. 53, 122–126 [hereafter *LW* followed by the volume and page number]). The three texts taken are: the Hamburg codex (**H** = 1535), the Fribourg codex (**F** = 1538), and the Agenda of Wittenberg (**R** = 1539). See WA 38, 411 for a description of all the manuscripts.

Nevertheless, we possess a rather sketchy description (somewhat of an apologia) of Luther's consecration of Nikolaus von Amsdorf in 1542 as "Christian bishop" of Naumburg.[7] It contains a description of what a good Christian bishop does, as well as a justification of the act itself of ordaining Amsdorf after having refused the candidature of Julius Flug, duly elected by the chapter of the cathedral. Luther emphasizes the fact that the entire canonical procedure was followed: an election took place (including the involvement of representatives of the people, as was correct); the notary authenticated the legal records; the candidate possessed the necessary qualities (which, for Luther, were a good knowledge of Scripture, a just life and good conduct, and, in Amsdorf's case, celibacy); the consecration took place in the medieval cathedral of Naumburg and was performed by an ordaining minister (that is, someone who was himself duly ordained—in this case, Luther himself) assisted by three other bishops (Dr. Nicholas Medler, the curate and superintendent of Naumburg, the Magister Georges Spalatin, curate and superintendent [= "*Pfarherr und Super-attendent*"] of Aldenburg, the Magister Wolffgangus Stein, curate and superintendent of Weissenfels); and it was performed in the presence of the faithful as well as the princes and Protectors of the Church. For the description of the ritual, see below, paragraph 3.

2. ORDINATION OF MINISTERS OF THE WORD
(= *Das deutsche Ordinationsformular*)[*239–*252]

a. *Structure of the Formulary*
This formulary is divided into several sections (cf. Table I.3 of vol. IV) that can be described as follows: the election, the ordination (the Word, the admonition, the laying on of hands, and the prayer), and the mission. The entire action takes place in the context of the celebration of the Lord's Supper which follows the ordination (a fact which explains the second chanting of the Our Father by the ordi-

---

[7] *Exempel, einen rechten christlichen Bischof zu weihen* (1542), WA 53, 231–260, esp. 257. See also the reconstruction made by P. BRUNNER, *Nikolaus von Amsdorf als Bischof von Naumburg* (Gütersloh: Verlagshaus Gerd Mohn, 1961) and the commentary of R. F. SMITH, *Ordering Ministry. The Liturgical Witness of Sixteenth-Century German Ordination Rites* (Ann Arbor, Mich.: University Microfilms International, 1988) 202–224. Cf. Table I. 4 (found in vol. IV).

nand[8]). We note that the congregation plays an important role, particularly in the choice of the elect, for only the congregation can testify as to his qualifications; and, as in the *Apostolic Tradition,* the congregation prays that the will of God be done and that the mission of the Church be extended.[239] God is seen as the primary actor, not the Church. We see, in the act of ordination, a distinction between the author of the gifts and the role of the Church[9] (represented by the ordaining minister): this distinction is reinforced by the prayer to the Holy Spirit which follows the presentation of the elect. It is not clear what hymn Luther wanted to be sung, because he replaced the usual hymn prescribed by the pontificals *(Veni creator spiritus)* with the *Veni sancte spiritus (et emitte coelitus,* the sequence for the Feast of Pentecost) or with the *Veni sancte Spiritus (reple tuorum corda fidelium,* a verse of the alleluia of *in festo pentecostes).* The hymn is followed by the collect[10] of the Feast of Pentecost.

Obviously, the proclamation of the Word occupied a central place in Luther's work of reform. The readings for this rite are: 1 Timothy 3:1-7, and Acts 20:28-31. Manuscript H has the readings follow an admonition based on 1 Timothy 4:4f., in which the ordinands hear:

"St. Paul says: 'Every creature of God is good . . . for it is sanctified by God's word and by prayer' [I Tim 4:4-5]. You are not only good creatures, sanctified by the Word and the sacrament of baptism, but in a second sanctification you have also been called to the holy and divine ministry, so that many others may be sanctified and reconciled to the Lord through your word and work. This goes to show how devoutly and worthily you ought to hold your office so that you may be sound in faith, pure in word, irreprehensible in conduct, and that

---

[8] Cf. the "German Mass" (1525/1526) of Luther, in I. PAHL (ed.), *Coena . . .,* 36–39 (= WA 19, 72–113 = *LW* 53, 61–90).

[9] Cf. P. F. BRADSHAW, "An Act of God in the Church: A Reformation Understanding of Ordination," *Liturgy* 24, 3 (1979) 22f.

[10] The text is found in WA 35, 554. The second hymn, *Veni sancte spiritus (reple tuorum . . .),* in its German translation, was written by Luther around 1524; cf. WA 35, 448f., and, for the music, WA 35, 510–512, no. 20; for these texts and music in English, see *LW* 53, 266–277. See P. BRUNNER, "Beiträge zur Lehre von der Ordination unter Bezug auf die geltenden Ordinationsformulare," in R. MUMM and G. KREMS (eds.), *Ordination und kirchliches Amt* (Paderborn/Bielefeld: Verlag Bonifatius-Druckerei/Luther-Verlag, 1976) 71, who identify the pentecostal character *("Die Ordination bekommt einen pfingstlichen Charakter")* of ordination.

you may be found good stewards in word and deed of the mysteries
of God and useful ministers of Christ in the day of the Lord, as St.
Paul teaches, I Timothy 3 . . ."[11]

[11] Cf. *241 (= WA 38, [ms. **H**] 424.23–425.18 = LW 53, 124). P. Brunner has this
comment to offer on this text: "Für die zum Amt Berufenen gibt es außer der
Heiligung, die ihnen als Glieder des priesterlichen Gottesvolkes bereits zuteil
geworden ist, noch eine andere, die durch die Berufung in das Ministerium verbi
Ereignis wird. Diese Heiligung besteht keineswegs in einem neuen Heiligungs-
grad der Berufenen, sondern darin, daß durch den Dienst der so Berufenen andere geheiligt werden, also durch Wort und Taufe Glieder des priesterlichen
Gottesvolkes werden. Der Diener selbst wird durch sein Wirken im *sanctum et divinum ministerium* zu einem Mittel dafür, daß am Menschen jener Übergang voll-
zogen wird, durch den er vor Gott gute, für ihn geheiligte Kreatur wird. Die so
Geheiligten werden durch die Verbindung des göttlichen Wortes mit dem
amtlichen Wirken des Dieners zu einem 'Gewinn' für den Herrn gemacht, sie
werden ja sein Eigentum. Es klingt hier etwas an von dem paulinischen Verständ-
nis des Apostelamtes in Röm 15, 16, zumal wenn wir diesen Text nach der Vul-
gata lesen: *(gratia) data est mihi a Deo, ut sim minister Christi Jesu in Gentibus:
sanctificans Evangelium Dei, ut fiat oblatio Gentium accepta et sanctificata in Spiritu
sancto"* ("For those who are called to the ministry there exists, besides the sanctification that they have received as members of the priestly people of God, another
sanctification that is effected by the call to the *'ministerium verbi.'* This latter does
not consist of a new degree of holiness, but rather it enables them to work for the
sanctification of others: they will become members of the priestly people of God
through the Word and by baptism. As for their servant, through his actions in the
sanctum et divinum ministerium, he becomes an instrument through which humanity is transformed into a goodly creature before God and the ministerial action of
the servant is carried out. Those who are thus sanctified 'belong' to the Lord, they
are his 'property.' This recalls to mind the Pauline conception of the apostolic
ministry found in Romans 15:16, especially if we read this text in the Vulgate:
'(the grace) that God has given me to be a minister of Jesus Christ among the pagans, consecrated to the ministry of the Gospel of God, so that the pagans might
become an acceptable offering sanctified by the Holy Spirit'"), P. BRUNNER,
"Beiträge zur Lehre . . .," 77.

This text will be taken up by Bugenhagen; cf. *264. A. C. Piepkorn (a Lutheran),
in his contribution to the bilateral Lutheran-Catholic dialogue on the Eucharist
and ordained ministry in the United States (1970), used this text among others to
show that in the Symbolic Books the sacred ministry is nowhere presented as deriving from the universal priesthood of the faithful: see A. C. PIEPKORN, "The
Sacred Ministry and Holy Ordination in the Symbolical Books of the Lutheran
Church," in P. C. EMPIE and T. A. MURPHY (eds.), *Lutherans and Catholics in Dialogue.* Vol. IV: *Eucharist and Ministry,* reprint [1st ed. 1970] (Washington, D.C./
Minneapolis: USCC/Augsburg Publishing House, 1979) 107f.

As we take another look at these readings, we see that their central context is, naturally, the ministry, but seen primarily from the point of view of the personal qualities required of the minister, and then in terms of the primary responsibility of safeguarding the faith. The first reading emphasizes the *good conduct* that the bishop must demonstrate: he must be a blameless person. The second reading speaks more of the *vigilance* that the minister must show in the face of the dangers that can threaten the flock that has been entrusted to him. So the two primary functions of the bishop as they emerge from these readings are those of watchman *(episkopē)* and shepherd *(poimainein)*.

The meaning of these terms is made more explicit in the exhortation and the question addressed to the elect.[242] Here we see that Luther understands the word "bishop" to mean ministers who are "preachers and pastors" *(Prediger und Pfarrer)*, and that feeding the flock means to nourish it with the Word of God both through preaching and through the example of a blameless Christian life. The question which follows will become the basis for one of the questions that we will find in almost all the other rites of ordination. Manuscript F contains another version, longer this time, of the same exhortation, and it provides us with two further illuminations: God calls *("berufen")* through institutions (the Church and the secular authorities *["weltliche Obrickeit"]*), and the elect should not only be acceptable to the congregation, but he should also have the approval of the civil authorities (cf. 1 Tim 3:7).

After this all the "presbyters" impose their hands, while the ordaining minister recites the Our Father. At the end there is an optional prayer.

Next, the ordinands are given their mission (cf. 1 Pet 5:2-4), which is basically a reminder of the founding of their ministry, emphasizing once more its pastoral and evangelical dimensions.

Each ordinand is then blessed, and, after having sung a hymn to the Holy Spirit (it should be noted that a prayer to the Spirit is found both at the beginning and at the end of the ritual), all proceed to the celebration of the Supper with the singing of the Our Father.

Several elements should be noted:

—the simplicity of this ritual when contrasted with the medieval rites;

—the central position of the Word of God in the entire celebration;
—the various roles of the actors on the scene, namely, the active participation of the faithful, the civil authorities, and the other members of the ministerial body;
—the pneumatological context created by the framing of the entire rite within two prayers to the Holy Spirit (thus providing a pentecostal context);
—the fact that the words "bishop," "preacher," and "pastor" are all interchangeable;[12]
—the emphasis on the "episcopal" substance of the ordained ministry (the pastoral and prophetic functions);
—the fact that the traditional gesture of the imposition of hands and the prayer have been restored to a place of central importance.

b. *The Nucleus: the Imposition of Hands and the Prayer*

The heart of the act of ordination remains the imposition of hands and the prayer. As early as 1523 these elements were emphasized by Luther in the consultation that he gave to the faithful of Bohemia. In fact, he enumerated the steps in the choice of new ministers by the congregation: choosing (by vote) one or more men from among those who are qualified; presenting them to the entire congregation while confirming them (we will see that the concept of "consecration" will gradually give way to that of "confirmation") with the prayer and the imposition of hands (done by those who are more competent [*"potiores"*]); and then acknowledging and honoring them as bishops and ministers rightfully established.[13] In this process the relationship between what one can call the local Church, that is, the congregation,

---

[12] For example, *Von den Konziliis und Kirchen* (1539), WA 50, 632f. (= "On the Councils and the Church," *LW* 41, 154–156); The Smalcald Articles [1537], IInd part, art. 4, *Die Bekenntnisschriften der evangelisch-lutherischen Kirche* (Göttingen: Vandenhoeck und Rupert, 1986) 430; hereafter cited *BSLK* followed by page number (= *The Book of Concord. The Confessions of the Evangelical Lutheran Church*, trans. and ed. by T. G. TAPPERT [Philadelphia: Fortress, 1959, p. 300; hereafter cited *BC* followed by page number]); *Das deutsche Ordinationsformular*, WA 38, 427.15–19 (*LW* 53, 125 and = *242).

[13] *De instituendis ministris Ecclesiae* (1523), WA 12, 191.23–193.35ff. (= "Concerning the Ministry," *LW* 40, 37–40). Lieberg notes that the first ordination performed by Luther in 1525 included the imposition of hands and the prayers in the context of the divine service; cf. H. LIEBERG, *Amt und Ordination . . .*, 182.

and the minister or ministers elected and ordained is strongly emphasized, and we see the action of God in the participation of all in the act of election, as well as in the acts of ordination and mission. This is precisely what Luther intended, namely, that the process be guided and carried out by God.[14]

The prayer consists of the Our Father, which could be followed by a commentary on its three parts.[*246–*249] This choice is surprising: this prayer is, of course, very important in Christian tradition, but in itself it does not contribute anything specifically pertinent to the ministry or to the rite that is being carried out. This lack of specificity could be explained by the fact that at this time there was a strong reaction against everything that could lead to divisions among the baptized—that might cause an *injuria baptismi*—a negative pall over the grace of baptism, deleterious to the evangelical community (WA 6, 561–564 = LW 36, 107–113). Thus the new minister is "confirmed" in his ministry, rather than "admitted" or "empowered." Nevertheless, P. F. Bradshaw seeks an explanation in the fact that for several of the Reformed Churches "it was thought sufficient for the ordination simply to take place within the general context of prayer."[15]

c. *Prayer of Ordination*

Here is the text in English:

"Merciful God, heavenly Father, you have said to us through the mouth of your dear Son our Lord Jesus Christ: 'The harvest is truly plenteous, but the laborers are few. Pray therefore the Lord of the

---

[14] *De instituendis . . .*, WA 12, 191.25 (= LW 40, 37): *"indubitata fide credendo, a deo gestum et factum esse, quod hac ratione gesserit et foecerit consensus communis fidelium . . ."* (". . . believing beyond a shadow of a doubt that this [i.e., prayer and the laying on of hands] has been done and accomplished by God. For in this way the common agreement of the faithful . . . is realized and expressed"). See also W. ELERT, *The Structure of Lutheranism*. Vol. 1, *The Theology and Philosophy of the Life of Lutheranism Especially in the Sixteenth and Seventeenth Centuries*, trans. from the German [*Morphologie des Luthertums*] by W. A. Hansen (St. Louis: Concordia Publishing House, 1962) 347.

[15] P. F. BRADSHAW, "The Reformers and the Ordination Rites," *Studia Liturgica* 13, 2–4 (1979) 103 (= *Ordination Rites*. Papers Read at the 1979 Congress of *Societas Liturgica*, eds. W. Vos & G. Wainwright [Rotterdam: Liturgical Ecumenical Center Trust, 1980]).

harvest, that he will send forth laborers unto his harvest' [Matt 9:37-38]. Upon this your divine command, we pray heartily that you would grant your Holy Spirit richly [reichlich] to these your servants, to us, and to all those who are called to serve your Word so that the company of us who publish the good tidings may be great (cf. Ps 68:11), and that we may stand faithful and firm against the devil, the world and the flesh, to the end that your name may be hallowed, your kingdom grow, and your will be done. Be also pleased at length to check and stop the detestable abomination of the pope, Mohammed, and other sects which blaspheme your name, hinder [zerstören] your kingdom, and oppose your will. Graciously hear this our prayer, since you have so commanded [geheissen], taught, and promised even as we believe and trust through your dear Son, Jesus Christ our Lord, who lives and reigns with you and the Holy Spirit, world without end. Amen."

α) *Biblical Images Employed*. The prayer of ordination is a commentary on the three parts of the Lord's Prayer.[16] The prayer, which is addressed to the Father, begins with a quotation from Matthew 9:37 and following, where the Lord sends the disciples out to preach the gospel. By using this text Luther gives an eschatological dimension to the ministry, because the interpretation that Matthew gives to the Lord's Prayer is clearly eschatological inasmuch as it expresses the longing for the coming of the Kingdom,[17] which is realized in the growing number of the faithful who have heard the gospel preached to them. Moreover, in the ordination prayer the context of Matthew 9 imparts missionary overtones to the whole prayer: the name of the

---

[16] Ms. **H** gives simply: ". . . *dicat ordinator 'pater noster' etc. cum oratione: Barmhertziger himlicher vater . . ."*[244]

[17] P. BRUNNER, "Ein Vorschlag für die Ordination in Kirchen lutherischen Bekenntnisses," *Theologische Literaturzeitung* 100, 3 (1975) 183. He points out that Luther did not use the Our Father, as was traditional, but rather followed his own inspiration. This shows that through the service of the ministers God has "an eschatological hold" on the world; along the same lines; cf. id., "Beitrage zur Lehre . . .," 110. For the eschatological context of the Our Father in the Gospel of Matthew, see J. L. MC KENZIE, "The Gospel According to Matthew," in R. E. BROWN, J. A. FITZMYER and R. E. MURPHY (eds.), *The Jerome Biblical Commentary*. T. 2, *The New Testament and Topical Articles* (Englewood Cliffs, N.J.: Prentice-Hall, Inc., 1968) 73f.

Lord is sanctified by the act of sending workers out into his vineyard.

Next follows the epiclesis, in which it is asked that the Holy Spirit be given "to these your servants, to us, and to all those who are called to serve your Word . . ."[18] It is the Holy Spirit who makes possible the proclamation of the gospel, for the company of the ministers grows[19] with the ministers who remain faithful in the fight against the devil, the world, and the flesh (which are in fact forces which slow down the growth of the Kingdom of God) so that the will of God be done.

Lastly, the petition "Deliver us from evil" is elaborated with the request "to check and stop the detestable abomination of the pope, Mohammed, and other sects." The image of the Good Shepherd who protects the flock of the Lord is clearly expressed here (cf. the reading of Acts 20:28-31).

β) *Qualities Requested for the Ordinand.* This prayer concerns not just the ordinand alone, but the entire body of the servants of the Word (meaning, of course, the ministers ordained within the community). The prayer asks that the gospel be proclaimed so that the will of God might be done. So it is the Spirit who gives all that is necessary for the accomplishment of this goal: the Spirit calls worthy individuals, sends them forth, keeps them faithful, and gives everything needed for the building up of the Kingdom of God, which is founded on the preaching of the gospel.

γ) *Gifts Received by the Ordinand.* The prayer does not contain any explicit reference to these gifts. However, we do see, at the sending forth which follows the prayer, a reference to the reward promised to the ministers who remain faithful to their post: the crown which does not wilt (1 Peter 5:4).

---

[18] F. Schulz sees in the "we" of the invocation not only the ordaining minister and his assistants, but also the entire assembly of the faithful who are "co-ordinants" (*"mitordinierende"*) as was true, in his opinion, in the early Church; cf. F. SCHULZ, "Evangelische Ordination. Zur Reform der liturgischen Ordnungen," *JLH* 17 (1972) 43 and 51. Cf. the commentaries of Luther on this subject in his Sermon of 9 June 1535, WA 41, 204–215 (= *LW* 13, 329–334).

[19] Compare Ps 68 (67), v. 10 f., where the goodness of God restores to the psalmist his inheritance. The image employed there is that of "the rain," a symbol also used for the Spirit (in the hymn to the Holy Spirit).

3. INSTALLATION OF A BISHOP

The term "installation" merits a brief discussion. Even though Luther employed the words *"weihen"* (= to consecrate) and *"ordinieren"* (= to ordain) throughout the document that we are considering, the words *"Einführung"* and *"Einsetzung"* (= installation), among others, will become those classically used in Lutheran tradition to describe the liturgical office of the installation of a bishop. We shall see below (5, b) some further distinctions made in Lutheranism on the subject of "ordination" and "installation."

a. *Structure of the Formulary*

We have only a description of the installation of a bishop; no liturgical composition from the hands of Luther has come down to us. According to this description, it seems that the office was very close to that of the ordination of ministers of the Word. What follows is the description, from Luther, of an installation that he himself performed on January 20, 1542, the installation of Nikolaus von Amsdorf.

The principal elements are the election, the confirmation by the civil authorities, the consecration by the imposition of hands and the prayer, carried out with the assistance of the bishops of the neighboring communities; everything takes place in the presence of the community, the princes and the Protectors.[20] There is no reference to the texts used in this office.

b. *The Nucleus: the Imposition of Hands and the Prayer*

It is noteworthy that Luther specifically mentions the two elements of the imposition of hands and the prayer. These are the two biblical elements which are to occupy the place given in the medieval pontificals to the anointing and all the secondary rites. Moreover, he notes the presence of the bishops (clearly, of the Reformed Churches) who have come from neighboring towns. We have already seen the capital importance of their presence for the early Church in the first part of this study (see vol. I, pp. 3 ff). We should note this fact, for it points

---

[20] *Exempel, einen rechten . . .*, WA 53, 257. From a remark that Luther made at the beginning of the treatise, we know that explanatory rites such as, for example, the anointing, did not take place (ibid., 231). Cf. P. BRUNNER, *Nikolaus von Amsdorf . . .*, 61ff.

up Luther's express desire that everything be done according to the ancient canons (". . .*Wie der alten Kirchen brauch gewest und die alten Canones leren . . .*").[21] More cannot be said on the subject of these two elements, for lack of documentary evidence.

c. *Prayer of Installation*

Unfortunately, we do not possess any texts composed by Luther himself. All we have are certain indications that show the similarity between the function of the bishop and that of the ministers of the Word. According to Scripture, the duties of a bishop are that he live a holy life, that he preach, baptize, remit or retain sins, comfort souls and help them to reach eternal life (1 Tim 3:2; Titus 1:7, 9). We can compare these duties to those of the ministers of the Word.[241]

4. RELATIONSHIP BETWEEN THE MINISTRY OF PASTOR AND THAT OF BISHOP

The first element of the relationship between the two ministries—their similarity—may be discerned in the affirmation of J. Pelikan that "Luther had been urging a congregational polity as a substitute for an episcopal polity, but was willing to agree to a presbyterian polity if congregationalism seemed too extreme a solution for the problem of continuity of structure."[22] For Luther, the office of preaching is the most exalted, so he saw very few differences between the two ministries,[23] for baptismal priesthood permits little distinction among the baptized. Elsewhere Luther does distinguish the functions of the bishops, who are to visit the parishes, see to the correct preach-

---

[21] *Exempel, einen rechten . . .*, WA 53, 257.

[22] J. PELIKAN, *Spirit versus Structure: Luther and the Institutions of the Church* (N.Y.: Harper & Row, 1968) 37.

[23] Luther used the terms "bishop" and "pastor" as synonyms: for example, *Von den Konziliis . . .*, WA 50, 632–633.35ff. (= *LW* 41, 154f.). See B. LOHSE, "The Development of the Offices of Leadership in the German Lutheran Churches: 1517–1918," in I. ASHEIM and V. R. GOLD (eds.), *Episcopacy in the Lutheran Church? Studies in the Development and Definition of the Office of Church Leadership*, American trans. of the German [*Kirchenpräsident oder Bischof? Untersuchungen zur Entwicklung und Definition des kirchenleitenden Amtes in der lutherischen Kirche*] (Philadelphia: Fortress Press, 1970) 53.

ing of the Word,[24] install the pastors,[25] and encourage friendly relations between parishes.[26]

Three terms are essential for a description of ordained ministry in the thinking of Luther: the minister is to watch over his flock, feed it (with the pure gospel and the sacraments), and give a good example. These are the images present in the rite established by Luther. All the ministers of the Word are to exercise their ministry in the light of these concepts.

We cannot draw too many conclusions from the rite of ordination; but Luther spoke elsewhere of the functions of the ministers of the Word, of the bishops, and of the "emergency bishops" (Notbischöfe). They are called "emergency bishops" precisely because after the break with Rome a vacuum opened up that Luther did not have an adequate ecclesiology to respond to. We must note here his distinctions in order to understand the evolution that will take place later in the history of Lutheranism. This subject could constitute an entire field of research in itself (the bibliography is huge), but we can only present in this study a few facts and considerations.[27]

[24] On the importance of preaching, cf. *Predigten von 1519 bis 1521*, WA 9, 415.30f. As for the functions of the bishops, see WA 26, 196.3–9 (= LW 40, 269f.). Later on he thought that the bishop should also supervise the teaching and the conduct of the pastors; see, below, n. 44.

[25] *Das ein christliche Versammlung oder Gemeine Recht und Macht habe, alle Lehre zu urtheilen und Lehrer zu berufen, ein- und abzusetzen, Grund und Ursach aus der Schrift* (1523), WA 11, 413.28–414.5 (= "That a Christian Assembly or Congregation has the Right and Power to Judge all Teaching and to Call, Appoint, and Dismiss Teachers, Established and Proven by Scripture," LW 39:310f.) and *Unterricht der Visitatoren an die Pfarrherrn im Kurfürstentum Sachsen* (1528), WA 26, 235.7–13 (= "Instructions for the Visitors of Parish Pastors in Electoral Saxony," LW 40, 313).

[26] *De instituendis . . .*, WA 12, 194.14–18 (= LW 40, 41).

[27] We shall mention here only a few studies on the subject of Luther and his theology of the ministry: J. AARTS, *Die Lehre Martin Luthers über das Amt in der Kirche. Eine genetischsystematische Untersuchung seiner Schriften von 1512 bis 1525* (Helsinki: Hämeenlinna, 1972) esp. 57–81; W. BRUNOTTE, *Das geistliche Amt bei Luther* (Berlin: Lutherisches Verlagshaus, 1959); W. ELERT, *The Structure of Lutheranism . . .*, esp. 339–385; J. H. ELLIOTT, "Death of a Slogan: From Royal Priests to Celebrating Community," *Una Sancta* (N.Y.) 25, 3 (1968) 18–31, and id., *The Elect and the Holy. An Exegetical Examination of 1 Peter 2:4-10* (Leiden: E. J. Brill, 1966); J. HEUBACH, *Die Ordination zum Amt der Kirche* (Berlin: Lutherisches Verlagshaus, 1956); P. MANNS, "Amt und Eucharistie in der Theologie Martin Luthers," in P. BLÄSER, S. FRANK, P. MANNS et al., *Amt und Eucharistie* (Pader-

One precaution must be voiced at the very outset: we must not try to find perfect consistency or a strict systematization in the voluminous writings of Luther on the subject of the ministry, for he was not a systematic theologian, but, rather, an exegete and a prophetic spirit reacting to the problems of his time; sometimes his views are lacking in coherence even among themselves.[28] However, certain principles do emerge: the importance of the gospel announcing the justification of humankind, and the restoration of the importance of the "common" priesthood of the faithful.

The first principle is the supremacy of the Word of God, the sole *"regula fidei"* and the only power underpinning the Church,[29] for it is

___

born: Bonifatius-Druckerei, 1973) 68–173; D. OLIVIER, *La foi de Luther* (Paris: Beauchesne, 1978) 213–222; J. H. PRAGMAN, *Traditions of Ministry. A History of the Doctrine of the Ministry in Lutheran Theology* (St. Louis: Concordia Publishing House, 1983); J.H.P. REUMANN, *Ministries Examined . . .*; E. SCHLINK, *Theology of the Lutheran Confessions*, trans. from the German [*Theologie der lutherischen Bekenntnisschriften*, 3rd ed.] by P. F. Koehneke and H. J. Bouman (Philadelphia: Fortress Press, 1961) esp. 226–268.

[28] H. LIEBERG, *Amt und Ordination . . .*, 13; and A. GREINER, "L'ecclésiologie de Martin Luther," *Positions luthériennes* 25, 3 (1977) 156. In his work, J. Pragman spoke of the necessity of viewing Luther in the context of the battles that he fought for the cause of his "rule of faith," that is, the defense of the Word of God in its purity, against the attacks and the errors of the enthusiasts *("Schwärmer")* and some positions of the papists that he understood as violations of the biblical understanding of the ministry: see J. H. PRAGMAN, *Traditions of Ministry . . .*, 13 and 20. Some writers, as, for instance, L. GREEN, "Change in Luther's Doctrine of the Ministry," *Lutheran Quarterly* 18, 2 (1966) 173–188, tried to trace the evolution of Luther's thinking on the subject of the ministry. These attempts at reconstructing such an evolution are criticized precisely because such intuitions as are deemed "new" after a point in time could be identified in Luther's thinking at an earlier time; see J.H.P. REUMANN, *Ministries Examined . . .*, 27–29. We can also add B. Lohse, who presented four stages of evolution in the thought of Luther; see B. LOHSE, "Zur Ordination in der Reformation," in R. MUMM and G. KREMS (eds.), *Ordination und kirchliches Amt* (Paderborn/Bielefeld: Bonifatius-Druckerei/Luther Verlag, 1976) 13f. Reumann was a member of the Lutheran commission for the dialogue between Lutherans and Catholics in the United States. His presentation is quite balanced, since he gives an account of all the currents in Lutheranism. This chapter was written for a session of the Lutheran-Catholic commission, and was published in P. C. EMPIE and T. A. MURPHY (eds.), *Lutherans and Catholics . . .*, IV, 227–282.

[29] For example, see *De captivitate Babylonica ecclesiae praeludium* (1520), WA 6, 560f. (= "The Babylonian Captivity of the Church," *LW* 36, 106ff.); *Ad librum eximii Magistri Nostri, Magistri Ambrosii Catharini, defensoris Silvestri Prieratis acerrimi,*

from the gospel that humanity learns of the justification of the sinner through grace alone, by means of faith, as the central feature of the plan of God. Everything else Luther has to say about the various ministries revolves around this central point. For example, he speaks of the manifestation of the Church through certain signs, which are the true preaching of the only Word, the sacraments, faith, and the confession of faith.[30] For Luther the Church is a holy congregation of the faithful (WA 7, 742) in which the only power is the one that brought the Church into existence; the Church is interior, hidden, a spiritual communion of souls through faith, the Word, and the Spirit. The Church cannot, then, be defined in terms of laws and by her exterior, worldly ordering, but by the love of God.[31]

---

responsio (1521), WA 7, 721.12f.: ". . . *tota vita et substantia Ecclesiae est in verbo dei* . . ." (". . . the whole life and essence of the Church is in the Word of God . . ."); *De abroganda missa privata Martini Lutheri sententia* (1521), WA 8, 419f. (= "The Misuse of the Mass," *LW* 36, 143–145); *Aus das überchristlich, übergeistlich und überkünstlich Buch Bocks Emfers zu Leipzig Antwort. Darin auch Murnarrs seines Gesellen gedacht wird* (1521), WA 7, 633.9f. (= "Answer to the Hyperchristian, Hyperspiritual and HyperLearned Book by Goat Emser in Leipzig - including some Thoughts Regarding his Companion, the Fool Murner," *LW* 39, 157).

[30] *Von dem Papstum zu Rome widder den hochberumpten Romanisten zu Leipzig* (1520), WA 6, 297 (= "On the Papacy in Rome against the Most Celebrated Romanist in Leipzig," *LW* 39, 70f.); *Eine kurze Form der zehn Gebote, eine kurze Form des Glaubens, eine kurze Form des Vaterunsers* (1520), WA 7, 219. Cf. Y. CONGAR, *L'Eglise de saint Augustin à l'époque moderne* (Paris: Cerf, 1970) 352– 360. But we should not overlook the fifth note of the Church that Luther recognizes, namely, the ecclesiastical ministries; see *Von den Konziliis . . .*, WA 50, 632.35–633 (= *LW* 41, 154f.).

[31] Cf. *Ad librum . . .*, WA 7, 742.34, 735, 745.8ff., 762.11ff.; *Von dem Papstum . . .*, WA 6, 292f. (= *LW* 39, 64–67); Y. CONGAR, *L'Eglise . . .*, 354; M. LIENHARD, *L'Evangile et l'Eglise chez Luther* (Paris: Cerf, 1989) 120–130, and id., "La doctrine des deux règnes et son impact dans l'histoire," *Positions luthériennes* 24, 1 (1976) 25–41 but esp. 25–33 where the author discusses the nuance this doctrine finds in Luther and its application by Melanchthon and other Lutherans. In a very interesting little book, L. Newbigin criticizes the use of the oppositions exterior/interior and visible/invisible, writing: "by substituting for the truly biblical dialectic between saint and sinner a false and non-biblical dialectic between exterior and interior, visible and invisible, Luther himself contributed significantly to the confusion of the teachings coming out of the Reformation." Newbigin goes on to show how these categories altered the truth of the Bible which "insists on a real and visible community. The problem stems from the fact that what is purely spir-

Luther spiritualized the Church, attempting to go beyond the medieval synthesis which saw two powers at work in the governance of the state: the *sacerdotium,* which brings the universal Church to salvation, and the *imperium,* the temporal power of the Christian princes, the power which oversees the wealth of the city.[32] The categories he used are the two kingdoms found in the Augustinian dialectic of the two Cities. The very framework of his treatise on "Christian freedom"[33] is the opposition between the exterior (a synonym for what is corporeal and visible, for reason, *res, loca, corpus,* political rights, *leges et disciplina,* etc.) and the interior (a synonym for what is spiritual and invisible, faith, rebirth through baptism, vocation, Word, Spirit, etc.). The Law is in the service of grace, says E. Fincke, because the working of salvation is free and depends only on the call of grace. The symbolic, liberating act of Luther was his burning of the bull of his excommunication on December 10, 1520, in Wittenberg, along with the whole of the canonical collections which, for him, belonged to the exterior order of the Church. In this way he symbolically "spiritualized" the Church.[34]

---

itual can become purely private. We no longer discern the spirits and we enter into spiritual communion among ourselves entirely on the basis of our sensory experience: sight, hearing, and touch. And if we are deprived of them, we quickly become prisoners of our own blinders. Now, the one body of which we read in the New Testament is not the opposite of the one Spirit, but its consequence. To radically oppose the two is fatal for an authentic doctrine of the Church"; see L. NEWBIGEN, *L'Eglise. Peuple des croyants, Corps du Christ, Temple de l'Esprit* (Neuchâtel/Paris: Delachaux & Niestlé, 1958) 72 and 74.

[32] On the development of the "theory" of the two swords during the Middle Ages and its influence on ecclesiology, see Y. CONGAR, *L'Eglise . . .,* 142–155. For the context that Luther confronted, see B. COOKE, *Ministry to Word and Sacraments. History and Theology* (Philadelphia: Fortress Press, 1976) esp. 481 and 579; and M. LIENHARD, *L'Evangile . . .,* 107–119.

[33] For example, *Epistola Lutheriana ad Leonem Decimum summum pontificem. Tractatus de libertate christiana* (1520) WA 7, 50.5f. and 13ff.; 56.15ff.; 59.24ff.; 60.5ff., etc. (= "The Freedom of a Christian," *LW* 31, 344f., 353f., 358ff.); and also Y. CONGAR, *L'Eglise . . .,* 353–355 on the use of Augustine's oppositions.

[34] H. STROHL, "La notion d'Eglise chez les Réformateurs," *RHPR* 16, 3–5 (1936) 268; E. FINCKE, "Le ministère de l'unité," in W. STÄLIN et al., *Eglises chrétiennes et épiscopat: vues fondamentales sur la théologie de l'épiscopat,* trans. from the German by Sister Willibrorda (Paris: Mame, 1966) 66.

This permitted him to break with the Catholic episcopate and recognize the temporal powers of the princes. In fact, in 1528, he gave the charge of *episkopē* to the princes themselves, calling them *"Notbischof."* He could do this because he had determined that the *sacerdotium* was "common to all the faithful" (if an individual exercises it, it is because he has received the mandate from others);[35] what is more, in his eyes the episcopacy was not sacramental, following here the opinion of St. Jerome and the majority of medieval thinkers on the subject; and, lastly, in the face of the serious disorders of that period, the prince was considered a principal member of the Church (*"praecipium membrum ecclesiae"*),[36] and for this reason he was called upon to maintain order.

[35] *Von dem Papstum . . .*, WA 6, 285–324 (= LW 39, 55–104); *An den christlichen Adel deutscher Nation von des christlichen standes besserung* (1520), WA 6, 407f. (= "To the Christian Nobility of the German Nation Concerning the Reform of the Christian Estate," *LW* 44, 127–130).

[36] G. SIEGWALT, "Point de vue protestant sur le ministère d'unité," *Positions luthériennes* 25, 3 (1977) 129f., writes to this point: "It [the Lutheran Reformation] did not adopt or introduce the various forms of the ministry of unity for theological or ecclesiological reasons, *but for purely empirical considerations.* Since the Catholic bishops had remained reticent as regards the Reformation, the Church was entrusted to the princes, who in effect became emergency bishops holding administrative and disciplinary powers. Moreover, Luther installed visitators, and, certainly at the end of his life, some bishops, but without having sufficiently reflected on the latter's ministerial status, and this is the reason this ministry disappeared so quickly. As for the doctrinal ministry, it was taken up by the universities, especially the theological faculties . . . The Lutheran Reformation—especially the way in which it evolved in different regions and countries—did not really pay serious attention on a theological level to the close organic relationship that exists between the question of the organization of the Church (that is, its structure as a Church) and the question of legitimate authority in the Church. For this reason Lutheranism suffered from a lack of a solid sense of its essence as a Church" (italics ours). See also: J. H. LERCHE, "La charge épiscopale dans l'Eglise évangélique," in W. STÄHLIN et al., *Eglises chrétiennes . . .*, 49, and for Jerome's opinion, 41f. For the establishment of the prince as "emergency bishop," see *Unterricht der Visitatoren . . .*, WA 26, 197.19ff. (= LW 40, 271), and the comparison between Melanchthon and Luther on the rights of the princes as the *praecipua membra ecclesiae* found in W. ELERT, *The Structure of Lutheranism . . .*, 379–385. The author concludes: "No theocracy came into being. Instead, there was government of the church by the sovereigns. In the end the power of the church became an appendage of the sovereignty of the princes, and the church became a department of the state," here p. 383.

The second principle was Luther's new emphasis on the "common" priesthood of all the baptized (*"allgemeines Priestertum"*—a formula not used by Luther, who said, rather, that we are all consecrated priests [WA 6, 407f. = *LW* 44, 127–130]).[37] Studies of Luther's conception of the ministry have shown that he bases his thinking on two cardinal points. Firstly, Luther wants to emphasize the common priesthood of all the baptized: "We are all priests, as many of us as are Christians. But the priests, as we call them, are ministers chosen from among us. All that they do is done in our name; the priesthood is nothing but a ministry."[38] He was combating the sacerdotalization of the ministry and the disqualification of the laity. Secondly, Luther stresses the public character of the office of the ministers: "It is true that all Christians are priests, but not all are pastors. For to be a pastor one must be not only a Christian and a priest but must have an office and a field of work *(Kirchspiel)* committed to him."[39] Luther was distancing himself here from the "enthusiasts" *(Schwärmern)* who rejected all structures and institutionalizing of ministerial office.

In Lutheran tradition we find two theories of the basis of public ministry. Either it derives its legitimacy from the principle of the priesthood of all the baptized, or else it is legitimized by divine insti-

[37] For the use of this expression and its variants in Luther, see P. MANNS, "Amt und Eucharistie . . .," 121f. For the problem of coherence in the vocabulary of Luther, see the comments of W. BRUNOTTE, *Das geistliche Amt . . .*, 51. On the contexts and uses of this exegetical discovery of Luther, there is an excellent summary in J. H. PRAGMAN, *Traditions of Ministry . . .*, 14–34. Lastly, for an exegetical study of the texts used by Luther as the basis of his thinking on this subject, see the two works of J. H. ELLIOTT cited in n. 27.

[38] *"Sacerdotes vero quos vocamus ministri sunt ex nobis electi, qui nostro nomine omnia faciant, et sacerdotium aliud nihil est quam ministerium,"* De captivitate . . ., WA 6, 564.11–12 (= *LW* 3, 113).

[39] *Der 82. Psalm ausgelegt* (1530), WA 31/I, 211.17–19 (= "Psalm 82," *LW* 13, 65). According to Reumann the question is not to determine Luther's real position in this debate, but to ask oneself how we can explain the intervention of God in and through humankind. Quoting R. H. Fischer, Reumann shares his opinion: "The ambiguity often stems from the two uses of the expression 'ministry of the word,' as (1) 'the church's (the priesthood's) task of proclaiming the gospel,' (2) 'the public office in the church; the clergy are the special ministers of the church, around whom the church's order is built,'" J.H.P. REUMANN, *Ministries Examined . . .*, 28; the quotation is from R. H. FISCHER, "Another Look at Luther's Doctrine of the Ministry," *Lutheran Quarterly* 18, 3 (1966) 270.

tution. Both ideas are to be found in the thinking of Luther. In the first case, the risk lies in seeing public ministry as an office whose power is conferred by the congregation: the minister could be seen as a mere bureaucrat chosen by the congregation. This is the "delegation theory" (*Übertragungstheorie*). In the second case, if the office of the ministry is instituted directly by God through Christ, the danger is that the role of the faithful could be reduced to that of passive audience. This is the "theory of divine institution."[40]

There is thus some ambiguity in the thinking of Luther, which can be found in Lutheran tradition. For H. Dombois (a Lutheran), the movement of the Reformation could therefore be seen as incapable of acknowledging the concrete diversity of various charisms and functions within the unity of the whole body. Both the common priesthood and the particular ministries have become equivocal concepts. This opinion, however, is not shared by others writers. P. Manns (a Catholic), for example, states that Luther was referring to 1 Corinthians 12:12 and Romans 12:4 at the beginning of his exegetical research "to show that membership in the one body and the equality that flows from membership do not exclude the possibility of a particular ministry or the specific work of each member."[41] Another writer, a Lutheran, has found a way to express the articulation of these realities in Luther's work without over-systematizing his thought or eliminating the tension that exists between the priesthood of all the baptized and the office of the public ministry: "It is inadequate to say that 'ministry and priesthood exist together in the Church as complementary vehicles of the Word.' The ordained ministry exists in the

---

[40] T. G. WILKENS, "Ministry, Vocation and Ordination: Some Perspectives from Luther," *Lutheran Quarterly* 29, 1 (1977) 71f. Examples include: "All Christians are truly of the spiritual estate," *An den christlichen Adel . . .*, WA 6, 407.13ff. and 22–23 (= LW 44, 127), 408.11 (= LW 44, 128); for the divine institution of the ministry, *An den christlichen Adel . . .*, WA 6, 441.24–26 (= LW 44, 176f.) and *Von den Konziliis . . .*, WA 50, 633.3 (= LW 41, 154); for the tyranny of the clergy over the laity, *De captivitate . . .*, WA 6, 561–564 (= LW 36, 107–113). For an evaluation of the theory of delegation, see E. SCHLINK, *Theology of . . .*, 244f.

[41] P. MANNS, "Amt und Eucharistie . . .," 91, and in a note to p. 128 he refers to the treatise *An den christlichen Adel*. For the opinion of H. DOMBOIS, *Das Recht der Gnade. Ökumenisches Kirchenrecht*, I, 2nd ed. (Witten: Luther Verlag, 1969) 251f.

Church, the priesthood does not; the latter *is* the Church. The Church *is* a priesthood; it *has* an ordained ministry"[42] (italics ours).

All of this explains the distinction that Luther sees between the ministry of the bishop (or superintendent) and that of pastor. The primary task of a superintendent is to ensure that the Word is correctly taught and preached;[43] next, he is to visit the parishes, install the pastors, and also watch over their conduct.[44]

5. LATER INFLUENCE OF THE FORMULARY OF THE *AGENDA*

Luther's formulary met with great success, and was soon widespread throughout Lutheran Germany.[45] Its acceptance by the Churches of Württemberg and Hesse is important, for this was the basis for the new tradition of ordination in the evangelical Church, or

---

[42] R. H. FISCHER, "Another Look . . .," 270. See *Aus das überchristlich . . .*, WA 7, 628; *De instituendis . . .*, WA 12, 180 (= LW 40, 80); *De captivitate . . .*, WA 6, 566, 564 (= LW 36, 116, 113); and *Predigt am 21. Sonntag nach Trinitatis (16.Oktober)* [1524], no. 55, WA 15, 721. Lieberg also explains that for Luther public ministry took place *"coram ecclesiae"* (before the Church) and *"in nomine ecclesiae"* (in the name of the Church), H. LIEBERG, *Amt und Ordination . . .*, 71.

[43] *Unterricht der Visitatoren . . .*, WA 26, 235.9–11 (= LW 40, 313).

[44] *Unterricht der Visitatoren . . .*, WA 26, 196.3–9 (= LW 40, 270); *Das ein christliche Versammlung . . .*, WA 11, 413.28–414.5 (= LW 39, 311f.); *De instituendis . . .*, WA 12, 194.14–18 (= LW 40, 41); *Unterricht der Visitatoren . . .*, WA 26, 235.7–13 (= LW 40, 313), to compare with *Das ein christlich Versammlung . . .*, WA 11, 409.10–11 and 20–22 (= LW 39, 306) where he attributed doctrinal judgment to the congregations. See *Exempel, einen rechten . . .*, WA 53, 253.6ff. for a general description of episcopal ministry, including that of pastors, and J. H. LERCHE, "La charge épiscopale . . .," 42. For a discussion of the relationship between the ministry of building up (the Word and the sacraments) and that of unity, see G. SIEGWALT, "Point de vue . . .," 127–131.

[45] The formularies that were based on Luther's are enumerated in the following studies: P. GRAFF, *Geschichte der Auflösung der alten gottesdienstlichen Formen in der evangelischen Kirche Deutschlands. I: Bis zum Eintritt der Aufklärung und des Rationalismus* (Göttingen: Vandenhoeck & Ruprecht, 1937) 387–390; F. SCHULZ, "Evangelische . . .," 1–4; R. W. QUERE, "The Spirit and Gifts are Ours: Imparting or Imploring the Spirit in Ordination Rites?," *Lutheran Quarterly* 27, 4 (1975) 327f.; for contemporary rites: F. SCHULZ, "Documentation of Ordination Liturgies," in ROMAN CATHOLIC/LUTHERAN JOINT COMMISSION, *The Ministry in the Church* (Geneva: Lutheran World Federation, 1982) 35–43. If a particular formula comes from Luther's formulary, this will be noted in our discussion of the texts.

"installation." These formularies have been studied by F. Schulz, and his conclusions will be presented below.[46]

a. *Reception of the Formulary of Ordination as Installation*

In Württemberg the formula of ordination appears as the office of installation in the first parish in which the ordained was to serve. The formulary provided for this ceremony was only used once, precisely on the occasion of the minister's first entrance into service. What Luther called "ordination" in his formulary becomes "first installation" (as ordination) in Württemberg in 1547. In the eventuality of a minister's changing parishes, he is not reordained, but simply presented to the congregation with the first prayer of the formulary for the so-called installation.[47] However, a juridical formula of transmission of office was added *(Vollzugsformel)*, pronounced along with the imposition of the right hand. This formula echoes the prayer that was just recited over the elect, and contains the following declaration: ". . . I ordain and confirm and attest you by order of our almighty and gracious prince and lord whose legitimate and Christian authority is given by God . . ."[48] The emphasis is certainly placed on the fact that the person thus ordained has been duly called and installed according to the established order. In this sense ordination is seen as

[46] See F. SCHULZ, "Evangelische . . .," 4–9, and id., "Die Ordination als Gemeindegottesdienst. Neue Untersuchungen zur evangelischen Ordination," *JLH* 24 (1979) 2–19.

[47] Cf. F. SCHULZ, "Evangelische . . .," 4. The first is found in the synodal Ordinance of Württemberg of 1547, A. L. RICHTER, (ed.), *Die evangelischen Kirchenordnungen des sechzehnten Jahrhunderts,* anastatic reprint [1st ed. 1846] (Nieuwkoop, 1967), t. II, 94f. (cited as RICHTER followed by the number of the tome and the page), and the second further on (RICHTER II, 95). This tradition is received by other Churches; see F. SCHULZ, "Die Ordination . . .," 2. As a result, even the Churches in which Luther's formulary had been in force adopted the Ordinance of Württemberg for the installation of pastors already ordained in a parish (for examples, see ibid.).

[48] We reproduce here the German text taken from the KO of Pfalz: ". . . ordne, konfirmiere und bestätige ich dich aus Befehl des Allmächtigen und unseres gnädigsten Landesfürsten und Herrn als der ordentlichen, christlichen und von Gott gegebenen Obrigkeit . . .," E. SEHLING (ed.), *Die evangelischen Kirchenordnungen des XVI. Jahrhunderts,* anastatic reprint [1st ed. 1902–1913] (Tübingen, 1955) t. XIV, 242 (cited as SEHLING, followed by the number of tome and page); see F. SCHULZ, "Evangelische . . .," 6; cf. RICHTER II, 95 for the Württemberg text.

an act of confirmation of a received vocation. The imposition of hands is thus emptied of its meaning by becoming an act of authentication.

The clear opportunity for rooting the process of ordination deeply within the community is lost here. Luther's rediscovery of the common priesthood finds no application, for what we have here is an eclipse of the sacramental aspect of the process of election-ordination, as a reaction against the "oversacramentalization" of ordination among Catholics. This occurred when the category of the priesthood supplanted that of the ministry, and when absolute ordinations multiplied at a time when the powers of order and jurisdiction were separating. We can surmise from the subtitle of the synodal Ordinance of 1547 that this rite was soon to replace the former papal consecration and ordination. At this time, too, the Latin Church was debating the question of what was the essential element in the rite of ordination; from this fact it is possible to conclude that the indicative prayers (*"accipe potestatem,"*[109] and *"accipe Spiritum Sanctum"*[115]) had some influence on the Lutheran prayer, at least in its form and context, if not in its content.

Lastly, the acceptance of the formulary of Luther led certain evangelical theologians of the nineteenth century to think that it was necessary to reintroduce ordination, because they thought that installation alone existed in the evangelical Church. They had lost sight of the original meaning of installation as ordination, which originated in the tradition of Württemberg.[49]

As for the Church of Hesse, it blended together the formulary of installation of the tradition of Württemberg with that of Luther. In contrast with the tradition of the former, the formulary of Hesse of 1566 is called "ordination" (Sehling VIII, 203). The ordination was to be conferred in Marburg, or else near the seat of the superintendent, or during the installation in the first parish where the new pastor was to exercise his ministry.

In a third instance, that of the installation of a pastor already ordained, the prayer of conferral (*Vollzugsformel*) accompanied by the imposition of hands was omitted. In the case of an installation in a first parish, the liturgy of Hesse of 1574 took as its model that of

[49] Cf. F. SCHULZ, "Die Ordination . . . .," 10f.

installation/ordination found in Württemberg with its shortened prayer and the imposition of hands. F. Schulz concludes that in this way we have a prayer parallel in form and in content to that of Württemberg; however, he goes on, "The juridical act of the prince in Württemberg corresponds to a 'highly ecclesiastical' juridical act in Hesse, an idea foreign to the evangelical conception of Luther's formulary of ordination, running the risk of reducing the service of ordination to the ritual prayer of transmission alone."[50]

This development will explain the subsequent choices made within the various Churches between ordination and installation, following the debate within the German Reformed community regarding these two terms, and even regarding the imposition of hands itself during an ordination/installation.[51]

b. *Ordination or Installation?*

The two concepts existed together at the heart of early Lutheranism. One could say that the concept of "ordination" taken from Luther by the Lutheran Churches of northern Germany illustrates the Protestant concern to underscore the central importance of the Word of God and of the prayer. The imposition of hands was seen as a blessing; it was not a matter of transmitting powers, but of confirming a vocation already received.

The ceremony of installation included a strictly juridical element that was missing in the original formula of Luther: all the classical forms were to be respected. The spiritual dimension of the ministry held only a secondary place. Nevertheless, the link between the ministry and the community regained the importance it had lost over the centuries. Yet, because of the lack of a true understanding of Luther's thought on the common priesthood, the individual ministry was not able to express the relationship between the ministerial nature of the entire Church and the gifts of the Spirit any better than did the medieval Church. The reason for this failure lies with the premises underlying all reflection on the ministry, which takes as its point of departure the priesthood of priests, in its absolute sense. Thus the medieval Church and the Churches of the Reformation meet here,

[50] F. SCHULZ, "Evangelische . . .," 9, and also id., "Die Ordination . . .," 5–7.
[51] On this point see the explanation of the context in F. SCHULZ, "Die Ordination . . .," 1f. and 22f.

as Dombois affirms, at the very heart of the same framework of thought.[52]

However, the distinction between ordination and installation will actually effect very few changes. We see a change only in the case of a second installation (e.g., in a new parish or for a different ministry). In this case there will be neither an imposition of hands nor the prayer that was reserved for first installations, except, most often, in the case of the installation of a bishop or a superintendent, which will include the imposition of hands. In general, installation is the act of taking up certain functions, in the context of a concrete community.

6. CONCLUSION: STRUCTURING OF THE CHURCH AND THE SUBSTANCE OF ORDAINED MINISTRY

a. *Structure of the Church*

We can discern a certain structuring of the Church in our examination of the various roles of the constellation of actors involved in the ceremony of ordination or installation. The process involves the civil authorities, the other ministers, and the congregation. We see that responsibility for the life of the Church is a shared one, as witness must be borne to the orthodoxy of the elect (assured by the examination carried out by the ministers charged with this task), the quality of his Christian life (attested by his sisters and brothers in the community— he is indeed worthy), and the regularity of his civil life (no objection on the part of the civil authorities).[*239] In this context the election is the same thing as the vocation: we can also see in it a pneumatological dimension.

The community is aware that it has been gathered together by the Spirit, and that what takes place is done by the inspiration of the Spirit (the hymn to the Holy Spirit and the collect that follows make this clear[*240]). The community is thus constituted by the Spirit and the Word that follows right after the invocation. The community is active also in the act of praying, having been invited to pray "for them as well as for all the ministers."[*239]

[52] Cf. H. DOMBOIS, *Das Recht . . .*, 552: "Der wesentlichste Ertrag dieser Darstellung aber ist, daß sie uns das Urteil ermöglicht, daß die reformatorische Ordinationslehre unter Bewahrung der gleichen Denkstruktur eine dialektische Umkehrung der scholastischen ist."

The ordinands are destined for particular congregations, so that their ordination is not disassociated from the communities in which they are to exercise their ministry.[250] They must express their desire to take upon themselves the service of the gospel that is being entrusted to them. Their brothers in the ministry impose hands upon them, the biblical symbol of blessing which also attests to the collegial nature of ministry in the Church. The prayer of ordination is pronounced by a pastor responsible for the ordination; we do not know, however, if he was a minister with a specific charge for this role.[53]

The Spirit is invoked once more during the prayer for the elect, but, as we have seen above, there is no true specificity in this part of the prayer. Elsewhere Luther wrote: ". . . having been born a priest through Baptism, a man thereupon receives the office . . . Out of the multitude of Christians some must be selected who shall lead the others by virtue of the special gifts and aptitude which God gives them for the office . . ."[54] The Church that appears in this rite of ordination is a Church formed by the saving act of Christ who engages in his priesthood the participation of all those who believe in him, and makes them all responsible for the primary task of the proclamation of the gospel. Within this Church God grants specific gifts to certain members for the service of the Word, so that his name may be glorified, his Kingdom increase, and his will be done.[247]

The fact that there is no significant difference between the rite of ordination of a minister of the Word and that of the installation of a bishop is significant, for by treating these two ministries identically, Luther failed to recognize the specific nature of the multiple gifts that the Spirit bestows upon the Church for her building up (Eph 4:11f.) and for the exercise of her ministry in the world. We have seen that there were a number of reasons for this omission (it was an emergency solution, it was due to the historical context, etc.). The ministry of direction in the Lutheran communities was focused in the office of the pastor, who, according to the rite of ordination, functions as a New Testament bishop (with the tasks of vigilance, preaching, and teaching—see below, b). The

[53] We saw above that it is probable that at the time Luther intended to keep the office of bishop, with one of the latter's functions being to confer ordination; cf. p. 15 and n. 22.

[54] 6. Predigt über den 110. Psalm (9. Juni) [1535], WA 41, 209.24–31 (= "Psalm 110," LW 13, 322).

fact that Luther believed it was necessary to keep the office of bishop for reasons of "good order" (and not necessarily because it was essential to the nature of the Church), coupled with his understanding of the delegation of the ministerial functions to certain persons in the community, suggests that the dialectic of the two realms (spiritual/temporal, interior/exterior, grace/law, etc.) also played in his conception of the formulation of the liturgical rite of ordination.

b. *Substance of the Pastoral and Episcopal Ministries*

The affirmation of the near equality of the ordained ministries in the rites of ordination/installation also defines the substance of these two ministries. If one takes into consideration the rite alone, it is possible to say that their functions are identical: they *watch over* the congregation (particularly in regard to correct doctrine, discipline, good conduct, and protection from false prophets), they are to *feed* the flock (with preaching and the teaching of correct doctrine), and they are to *serve*. In *Exempel, eine rechten . . .,* Luther gives an identical list of the functions of both bishop and pastor: each must live a holy life, preach, baptize, forgive or retain sins, comfort souls and help them to reach eternal life (WA 53, 253.3–8; cf. 1 Tim 3:2; Titus 1:7, 9).

However, elsewhere Luther adds to the functions of the bishop the task of vigilance over the doctrine taught in his territory, by means of parish visits (WA 26, 196.3–9 = *LW* 40, 269f.), the tasks as well of ordaining preachers (WA 11, 414 = *LW* 39, 311f.), supervising their teaching and their conduct (WA 26, 235.7–13 = *LW* 40, 313), and encouraging good relations between the parishes (WA 12, 194.14–18 = *LW* 40, 41). In the confession of Augsburg of 1530 we read: ". . . According to divine right *(de iure divino* and *nach gottlichen Rechten),* therefore, it is the office of the bishop to preach the gospel, forgive sins, judge doctrine and condemn doctrine that is contrary to the gospel, and exclude from the Christian community the ungodly . . . On this account parish ministers and churches are bound to be obedient to the bishops according to the saying in Luke 10:16, 'He who hears you hears me.'"[55] As the history of Lutheran episcopacy unfolds, this substance will be understood differently.

[55] *CA* 28, 20f. *(BC* 84). This aspect *"de iure divino"* is not always interpreted in the same way; see J. A. BURGESS, "What is a Bishop?," *Lutheran Quarterly* NS 1, 3 (1987) 313.

B. THE *ORDINATIO ECCLESIASTICA* (1537)—JOHANNES BUGENHAGEN

The author of this ordinance (Johannes Bugenhagen, known as the "Pomeranian Doctor" [1485–1558]) was a friend and close collaborator of Martin Luther. He was active mainly in northern Germany and in Denmark. Bugenhagen composed several ordinances before Luther had formulated his own.[56] At the invitation of Christian III, the first Lutheran king of Denmark, Bugenhagen collaborated in the redaction of the *Ordinatio ecclesiastica*, and in accordance with its prescriptions he ordained seven Danish bishops for the dioceses of Denmark in September 1537.[57]

[56] Thus, for example: KOs Brunswick of 1528 (SEHLING VI/1, 337ff.), Hamburg of 1529 for chaplains, pastors, and superintendents (SEHLING V, 502f.), Lübeck of 1531 (SEHLING V, 349f.) and Pomerania of 1535 (SEHLING IV, 331f.). The structure of the offices of ordination contained in these ordinances was very simple, following the Lutheran principle of accepting nothing that was not in the examples from the New Testament—in other words, the imposition of hands and the prayers. The difference between the two approaches is that Luther expected ordination to take place in a central seat such as the main Church of a region, while Bugenhagen insisted that it take place in the community where the new minister was to serve. In either case Luther's prayer was prescribed almost everywhere, and the ordinances formulated later by Bugenhagen contained Luther's formulary; see, for example, the KOs of Hildesheim of 1542–1543 (RICHTER II, 279f.) and of Wolfenbüttel of 1543 (SEHLING VI, 69ff.). For some commentaries on the liturgical connection between the formularies of Luther and those of Bugenhagen, see H. LIEBERG, *Amt und Ordination . . .*, 189–194; F. SCHULZ, "Die Ordination . . .," 11–13; J. GLENTHØJ, "Amt und Ordination bei Bugenhagen in der Reformation der dänischen Kirche," *EVANGELIUM-'euaggelion'-GOSPEL. Zweimonatsschrift für lutherische Theologie und Kirche* 13, 1 (1986) 12–28, esp. 17–19; G. KRETSCHMAR, "Die ordination bei Johannes Bugenhagen," in P. DE CLERCK and E. PALAZZO (eds.), *Rituels. Mélanges offerts à Pierre-Marie Gy, o.p.* (Paris: Cerf, 1990) 357–384, esp. 362–379; R. F. SMITH, *Ordering Ministry . . .*, 121–201; and H.J.E. BEINTKER, "Fortsetzung und Festigung der Reformation. Neuordnung in evangelischen Kirchen unter Bugenhagens Anleitung mittels seiner Braunschweiger Kirchenordnung von 1528," *Theologische Zeitschrift* 44, 1 (1988) 1–31 (the ordinance of this Church served as a model for several Churches in North Germany. We should note Bugenhagen's use of superintendents to reorganize the life of the parishes that were threatened by the instability that resulted from the rupture caused by Luther's Reform. The author emphasizes the importance of the concept of the "visitation" required by Luther [*Unterricht der Visitatoren . . .*, WA 26, 195–240 (= LW 263–320)] for maintaining order as well as for supervising the quality of preaching and the Christian life of the community).

[57] Cf. S. BORREGAARD, "The Post-Reformation Developments of the Episcopacy in Denmark, Norway, and Iceland," in I. ASHEIM and V. R. GOLD (eds.),

1. RELATIONSHIP TO THE FORMULARY OF LUTHER

Looking at Tables I.3 and I.4 (see vol. IV), we see immediately that the two rites are almost identical in structure. In Bugenhagen's rite, the structure of the ordination of superintendent is more fully elaborated than is that of priests, but, in the main, it remains close to that of Luther's, even in the similarity between the two rites of ordination. One curious thing is that, with Bugenhagen, the complete rite was composed for the ordination of a superintendent, and not for a pastor, as was the case with Luther. The quotation from Matthew 9 is retained, following the example of Luther, but what follows is a new composition, found in the Kirchenordnung (= KO) of Hamburg of 1529. The sermon has its central place in the celebration, as do the imposition and the prayer. An election (with examination) is obligatory; it must be ratified by the magistrates;[58] there has also been inserted the text of an oath of loyalty sworn to the king[253] after the prefect *(praefectus)* has received from the superintendent the documents which give the results of the election and the examination as to the correct doctrine and conduct of the elect. This order of things makes the oath and the confirmation by the representative of the king a precondition for the ordination. In everything else the same Lutheran principle was always maintained: everything takes place in the presence of the Church. With Bugenhagen the terms "presbyter," "episcopus," and "superattendens"/"superintendens" are used in the Latin text, while in the German texts the vocabulary remains rather vague: "pastores," "predicante," "seelsorger," "superattendente."

Episcopacy . . ., 116f.; and P. G. LINDHARDT, "Historisk om bispe- og præste-vielsesritualerne," in KIRKEMINISTERIETS LITURGISKE KOMMISSION, *De biskoppelige handlinger* (Copenhagen: B. Stougaard Jensen, 1978) 11–20.

[58] Cf. the preface of the king written on the occasion of the promulgation on September 2, 1537; the text is reproduced in M. S. LAUSTEN (ed.), *Kirkeordinansen 1537/39* (Copenhagen: Akademisk Forlag, 1989) 93ff.; and B. J. KIDD (ed.), *Documents Illustrative of the Continental Reformation* (Oxford: Clarendon Press, 1967) 328f., no. 132a. The text of the *Ordinatio ecclesiastica* is found in the editions of Lausten on pp. 112–115 *(Ritus instituendi ministros)* and 140–144 *(Juramentum Superintendentis* and *Hisce Caerimoniis ordinabitur publice Superintendens dominica die aut festo)*; E. FEDDERSEN (ed.), "Die lateinische Kirchenordnung König Christians III von 1537 nebst anderen Urkunden zur schleswig-holsteinischen Reformationsgeschichte," *Schriften des Vereins für schleswig-holsteinische Kirchengeschichte* 18, 1 (1934) 26–30 and 61–65; and KIDD on pp. 330–334 (= partial edition).

2. ORDINATION OF A PASTOR [*253–*258]

a. *Structure of the Formulary*

As with Luther, the entire rite is inserted into the Eucharistic celebration, and enclosed within two hymns to the Holy Spirit. The description is so sketchy that it is difficult to ascertain the participation of the laity in the worship, but the faithful are exhorted to pray for the elect, and they respond "Amen" to the collect of ordination. The text of the presentation of the elect requires categorically that he observe the principles of Lutheran Reform: the person called must possess the necessary qualities; his doctrine is examined as well as his conduct; and the minister is assigned to a particular community (there are no absolute ordinations). [*254] After the hymn and the collect, the single reading is taken from Titus (1:5-16), followed by the sermon. The suggestions for the instruction are given schematically and follow those of Luther's formulary. Lastly, the imposition of hands (by the bishop and the presbyters), the Lord's Prayer (pronounced by the bishop alone), and the collect (there is no text, but it is prescribed "that the whole congregation respond 'Amen'") precede the singing of the second hymn to the Holy Spirit. A final word is added by Bugenhagen[59] to comment on the meaning of this rite, using a quotation from Saint Paul: thus the creature is sanctified by Word and prayer. [*258]

As the next part of the document shows, the ordination is not repeated when a minister is installed in a particular parish. The procedure is as follows: the ordinand receives a letter (with the seal of the bishop) attesting his ordination; he presents it to the provost (*praepositus*) who is to install him in the congregation to which he has been assigned. But before the installation, the local civil authorities are informed that such and such a person is going to be their preacher and will be administering the sacraments. During the office that follows, the provost reads the bishop's letter so that he can bear witness that the one who is going to be installed has been properly called, examined, and ordained minister. With this the whole process concludes.

---

[59] This is the text that we will also find for the ordination of a bishop (*264), but that we have already come across in Luther in the formulary of ms. H; see *241.

As in the case of the ordination of a bishop in Luther's work, the schema of the rite contains some ambiguity. However that may be, it is clear that the ministries of bishop and presbyter are equal; but with Bugenhagen it would appear that episcopal ministry is above that of presbyter. We cannot draw too many conclusions from this fact, but it should be mentioned.

b. *The Nucleus: the Imposition of Hands and the Prayer*

Following Luther's preference, these two elements are of primordial importance in the work of Bugenhagen as well. In the ritual, freed from all sorts of extrinsic rites and gestures, the sole act of the imposition of hands by the bishop and the presbyters appears to regain its original dignity. For an understanding of the contemporary interpretation of what was being enacted during ordination, we shall refer to the words of Bugenhagen himself, at the end of the rite of the ordination of ministers: *"Ita hoc totum negotium Ordinationis perficietur, secundum dictum Pauli: 'Creatura sanctificatur per Verbum et Orationem'"* [1 Tim 4:5].*258

c. *Prayer of Ordination*

We know that the ordaining minister prays the Our Father in such a manner as to be heard, and in the vernacular, and that he adds the collect composed for the occasion *("oret aperta voce vulgariter, Pater noster; et addat collectam, ad hoc factam, sine tono . . .")*. It seems probable that this prayer is the same as for the ordination of the bishop in the same ritual;[60] the reader can refer to our commentary on the installation of the bishop.

---

[60] F. Schulz notes that Bugenhagen composed a prayer of ordination in 1529 for the KO of Hamburg; the text begins, as did Luther's, with the quotation from Matthew 9:37, but in 1537 the text of Luther's prayer replaced that of Bugenhagen. However, in the ritual of 1685 we find the same prayer for the ordination of a minister of the Word and a bishop. But the text of this prayer is the same as that of 1537, so it is probable that this prayer was also intended for the ordination of a pastor: see F. SCHULZ, "Evangelische . . .," 42f. Refer also to R. W. QUERE, "The Spirit . . .," 327f.; H. HOLLOWAY, *The Norwegian Rite* (London: Arthur H. Stockwell, 1934) 179–181. On the question of who copied whom in the use of the prayer of ordination, see H. LIEBERG, *Amt und Ordination . . .*, 192f. (without a satisfactory conclusion).

3. ORDINATION OF A BISHOP [SUPERINTENDENS] [*259-*269]

When Christian III appealed to Bugenhagen to compose a Church ordinance for the Danish Churches, he wanted to take all temporal power away from the bishops (as well as their wealth), a power claimed only by the king. What should remain in the hands of the bishop was only the staff of the gospel of the Kingdom of God.[61] Clearly, this thinking is in conformity with Luther's concept of the spiritualization of the Church.

a. *Structure of the Formulary*

We recognize some ancient elements in this rite: the celebration is to take place on a Sunday or a feast day; it takes place during the Eucharistic celebration; the presentation of the elect notes that he was elected for a particular Church;[*260] and the faithful are invited to participate in the prayer for the ordinand. In this way the entire Church is able to be present, because Sunday is the day of the principal assembling of the Church, and each Church should choose its own

---

[61] Cf. S. BORREGAARD, "The Post-Reformation . . .," 119, and the preface of the king, M. S. LAUSTEN (ed.), *Kirkeordinansen* . . ., 93f., and B. J. KIDD (ed.), *Documents* . . ., 329. Bugenhagen also formulated the coronation ritual of the king. The parallels with the ritual of ordination are striking. Bugenhagen based his composition on the medieval rituals, but he was faithful to the conception of Luther who saw the prince as the first member of the Church and *"defensor fidei."* The ritual ends with the king (who faces the people) reading the gospel with his sword in hand, for he promises to serve his subjects with the gospel and the sword; see J. GLENTHØJ, "Amt und Ordination . . .," 19f. The political situation in Germany and the Scandinavian countries was not the same. For example, the Reformation was introduced in Norway by King Christian III (a Dane) against the will of the people, and with the political and economic purpose of acquiring the wealth of the Church of the country (the Catholic bishops were for the most part wealthy princes), and of destroying its nationalist political influence. These intentions are seen in the concept of ordination that maintains Christian III's power; cf. the study of S. IMSEN, *Superintendenten. Ein studie i kirkepolitikk, kirkeadministrasion og statsutvikling mellom reformasjonen og eneveldet* (Oslo/Bergen/Troms: Universitetsforlaget, 1982) 140–143. (My thanks to Professor Roald Flemestad for having supplied me with this reference.) At first the early superintendents received only the salary of a simple laborer *("Die ersten Superintendenten wurden einfach wie Handwerker besoldet")*: J. GLENTHØJ, "Amt und Ordination . . .," 25. Lastly, the attitude of the king is also seen in his "manifesto" published October 30, 1536, in paragraph 3, as quoted in B. J. KIDD (ed.), *Documents* . . ., 334f., no. 133.

ministers. The participation of the entire community faithfully reflects this ecclesiological reality.

The structure of the two offices (of bishop and pastor) is more or less identical, except that nothing is said about the way in which the superintendent is called to his office. A paragraph that precedes the actual ritual contains the oath of the superintendent. It is, first of all, an oath of loyalty to the king, and then an oath of office in which the elect promises to respect the gospel and the sacraments, to carry out his charge in collaboration with the pastors, and, lastly, to care for the schools and for the poor.

In the rite of ordination of a superintendent, after the psalm *"Domine, Dominus noster,"* there are added a short question[*262] and a sign of the confirmation of the commitment of the elect. Three readings are provided (Titus 1:5-16; Acts 20:25-38; 2 Tim 4:1-5). These are followed by a brief admonition on the functions of this office (to preach, to baptize, to administer the Sacrament, to exhort, to comfort, etc.) and the comment that the ordination is sanctified by Word and prayer (cf. *258). Next comes a sort of justification of the institution of ordination taken from Luke 6:12, Matthew 9:37, and 1 Timothy 5:22, after which the ordaining minister, the presbyters and the elders impose their hands while the ordaining minister recites the prayer. The ordination proper ends with the second hymn to the Holy Spirit and the Mass according to the Danish ritual.

b. *The Nucleus: the Imposition of Hands and the Prayer*

We must not pass over without commentary the fact that it is not only the presbyters who participate in the imposition of hands, but also the elders *("senioribus")*. We may legitimately wonder if this means that public office derives from a ministry common to all the baptized. This would not seem to be the case, since this innovation in regard to the other ordinances prepared by Bugenhagen and even the formulary of Luther was not maintained in Danish Lutheranism. It did not pass into the Norwegian Ritual of 1685 either, and it remained an isolated case.[62] On the other hand, it is important to note that not a word is said about the title to which the ordinand is being ordained and for which the presbyters are imposing hands. We recall that

[62] Cf. H. HOLLOWAY, *The Norwegian Rite*, 206.

Luther stated categorically that the three other ministers who imposed hands over Nikolaus von Amsdorf were "superintendents"/
bishops. We know that Bugenhagen was only a priest and had not
been ordained bishop either in the Catholic Church or in the
Lutheran.[63] So it follows that the intent was to create a distinct
ministry with its own specific tasks.

The prayer that accompanies the imposition of hands is preceded,
as from now on in the Lutheran formulary, by the recitation of the
Lord's Prayer. The collect that follows is used for both offices, with
the necessary changes, of course, being made.

c. *Prayer of Ordination*

"Eternal and almighty Father, you who have taught us through
your only Son, our Master, that 'The harvest is plentiful but the
laborers are few; therefore ask the Lord of the harvest to send out
laborers into his harvest' [Matt 9:37f.]; and that the good laborers,
that is, the preachers and doctors of the churches remind us of these
words asking this of your grace through their true and faithful
prayer *(quae verba nos admonent bonos operarios, id est, praedicatores et
ecclesiarum doctores a tua gratia seria et fideli prece petendos)*. We beseech
you in your great goodness to look down with indulgence upon your
servant whom we choose *(eligimus)* for the episcopal office of the
Church, that he may be diligent in your Word to preach Jesus Christ,
our only salvation, to instruct consciences *(ad docendas conscientias)*, to
comfort, to exhort *(ad monendum)*, and to teach clearly with all patience and sound doctrine, in such a way that your holy Gospel may
always remain among us pure and without the leavening of human
doctrine and that it may bring us all the fruit of eternal salvation.
Through Jesus Christ, your Son, our Lord."[*266]

α) *Biblical Images Employed*. The prayer opens, as does Luther's, with
a quotation from Matthew 9:37, and ends with the reminder that
faithful servants, in the persons of the preachers and doctors, are
chosen by the grace of God and by prayer. The images are those of a
benevolent God generous towards his Church and the selection and
sending forth of workers into the harvest of the Lord, a concrete sign
that God hears our prayers. The gift of ministers to the Church is also
an act of God and a supreme sign of his grace; the faithful have only

[63] S. BORREGAARD, "The Post-Reformation . . .," 119f.

to receive them. What is more, the only teacher is Christ, who teaches us to pray to express our needs. We should note that a true epiclesis is missing in this prayer, although Luther has one.

β) *Qualities Requested for the Ordinand.* Next the congregation prays that the elect may have diligence (for preaching, teaching, counseling, exhorting, and defending the gospel) and patience as he applies himself to evangelical work.

γ) *Gifts Received by the Ordinand.* According to the text of the prayer, the new bishop does not receive any specific gifts, other than that received by all the faithful: the fruit of eternal salvation. We can perhaps read in this prayer that the very office of the ministry is a gift of God, for through the ministry the gospel is spread to the entire world, and thanks to the faithful exercise of the ministry, the gospel may remain pure and without the leavening of human teaching in the Church.

4. RELATIONSHIP BETWEEN THE MINISTRY OF PASTOR AND THAT OF BISHOP

Their relationship here seems similar to that seen in Luther. It is not certain that the change found in Bugenhagen, namely, the ampler development of the rite of ordination of a bishop, necessarily means that there was a clear distinction between two different orders, because he does not make any such distinction in his other ordinances. On the contrary, he begins habitually to present the one single text, with rubrics specific to the different situations (the KO of Hamburg of 1529). We know that this rite was presented to a commission before its authorization.[64] In any case, the direct influence of Luther's formulary is obvious. So for Bugenhagen one single ministry of the Word could find itself exercised differently according to the various functions, without any separation between different orders. The ministry is received through the imposition of hands and the prayer, just as was prescribed in the law of Moses, and in the same way as the apostles were chosen and sent out.[*264, §4]

Lastly, the ministry of the Word is understood as the teaching of the gospel, including the forgiveness of sins and eternal life in Christ, charity, the Cross, penance, obedience, and the sacraments.[*262] We find

[64] S. BORREGAARD, "The Post-Reformation . . .," 117 and 119; and P. G. LINDHARDT, "Historisk . . .," 11f.

that the definition of the ministry is the same here as it was in Lutheran tradition. This, then, is all that we have on the different functions of the bishop.

5. LATER INFLUENCE OF THE FORMULARY OF THE *ORDINATIO ECCLESIASTICA*

This formulary is important because it is the basis of the Danish, Norwegian, and Icelandic formularies. Norway separated from Denmark in 1814 and established its own liturgy, but its rites of ordination remained heavily indebted to the formulary of Bugenhagen. The same is true for Iceland, which remained part of Denmark until 1944.[65]

6. CONCLUSION: STRUCTURING OF THE CHURCH AND THE SUBSTANCE OF ORDAINED MINISTRY

a. *Structure of the Church*

In these texts the Church is structured according to the model of the early Church, which saw its task as the preaching of the gospel to the whole world. In order to accomplish this task, certain members of the Church are called, invested with this mission, and sent out to preach. They are chosen by God,[*254/*257/*260/*266, §2] and receive the mandate of the Church for their ministry. According to the suggested readings, these ministers are equipped by the Spirit to be the guardians of the faith and of the gospel as they nourish the faithful with the pure Word of the Lord and with the sacraments of Christ.[*263] Each minister is ordained for a particular community, and he is elected by the people[*254/*259] and confirmed by the civil authorities as is prescribed by the preface of the king; his vocation is received and confirmed by the imposition of hands and the prayer.[*258/*264, §2]

Bugenhagen elsewhere gave what could be considered a definition of ordination: ". . . the servants of the Word . . . will receive before the parish the spiritual order for which they will be called 'ad ministerium spiritus non littere,' 2 Corinthians 3 [cf. v. 6]; they will then be persons ordained to preach the Gospel of Christ."[66] The context of the beautiful quotation from Paul comes from his explanation of the

---

[65] Cf. S. BORREGAARD, "The Post-Reformation . . .," 122–124.

[66] The KO of Hamburg of 1529: ". . . erwelde denere des wordes, . . . schollen des sondages in der karcken vor der gemene entfangen den geestliken orden, dar van se mogen heten ordinati ad ministerium spiritus non littere, 2. Cor. 3. Dat is,

meaning of his ministry in the new covenant, in which he has just stated the importance of the grace of God which established him in his vocation. Here is what St. Paul says in verse 5f.: "Not that we are competent of ourselves to claim anything as coming from us; our competence is from God, who has made us competent to be ministers *(diakonous)* of a new covenant, **not of letter, but of Spirit**; for the letter kills, but the Spirit gives life." According to this context it is clear that Bugenhagen understood the act of ordination as the empowering of the minister by the grace of God, and as a sanctification, a "setting-aside" for the service (the offering) of the gospel.

b. *Substance of the Pastoral and Episcopal Ministries*

Clearly, Bugenhagen adhered quite strictly to Luther's doctrine concerning the ministries. His ritual does not attempt to add anything to it. We must acknowledge, along with Schulz, that Bugenhagen does not represent an opinion expressed in the revisions made in Württemberg according to which ordination is a juridical act within a liturgical framework.[67] The substance of the ministries is therefore emphatically spiritual and evangelical. We cannot determine that there was any great difference between the substance of the two offices. But, from the oath sworn by the superintendent, we know that the latter's ministry includes a grave responsibility to uphold his brethren the pastors. All we can affirm positively is that, as in the preface of the king, the power of the new bishops must be subject to spiritual governance. Nevertheless, we do not find this expressed explicitly in the rituals. We can say, however, that the substance of the ministries is absolutely in accord with the tradition of the Reformation: the ministries are the means of safeguarding the purity of the Word of God in the service of the community, and they are the vehicles through which the sacraments of the new covenant are administered.

C. *DE ORDINATIONE LEGITIMA* (1549)—MARTIN BUCER (OR BUTZER)

Martin Bucer (1491–1551, born in Kuhhorn) was one of the Strasbourg Reformers of importance, particularly for the reform of the

---

lude de vorordent sint, to predikende dat evangelion Christi, . . ." (SEHLING V, 502).

[67] F. SCHULZ, "Die Ordination . . .," 12.

liturgy in that city. He had his first contact with Lutheran theology during Luther's defense against his Dominican adversaries in Heidelberg in 1518, where Bucer was studying for the Dominican Order. After being dispensed from his religious vows, he joined Luther (in 1521) and moved to Strasbourg after his excommunication in 1523; he remained active there until his exile in 1549.[68]

Bucer remains a "bridging person" between the Reformed and the Lutherans due to his desire to see peace reign between the two visions of Reform, a desire shown in his intervention which concluded with the Concord of Wittenberg (1536) between the Lutherans and the Swiss Reformed. What is more, he had a profound influence on Reformers such as the Frenchman Jean Calvin, who lived in Strasbourg from 1538 to 1541.[69] During his exile in England, he played a not inconsiderable role in the revision of the *"Book of Common Prayer" (BCP)* and even, as we shall see, on the formation of the Anglican ordinal.[70] It is for this reason that we shall examine this ritual of ordination.

1. RELATIONSHIP TO THE FORMULARY OF LUTHER

The two rites share a similar structure, while Bucer's is more developed than Luther's. The readings are more numerous and longer.

[68] For the bibliography, see the two tomes of J.-V. POLLET, *Martin Bucer. Etudes sur la correspondance avec de nombreux textes inédits* (Paris: Presses Universitaires de France, 1958–1962). On the basic choices concerning the reform of the ordained ministries, three works are notable: R. BORNERT, *La Réforme protestante du culte à Strasbourg au XVIᵉ siècle (1523-1598)* (Leiden: E. J. Brill, 1981); W. VAN'T SPYKER, *The Ecclesiastical Offices in the Thought of Martin Bucer* (Leiden/N.Y./Cologne: E. J. Brill, 1996); W. P. STEPHENS, *The Holy Spirit in the Theology of Martin Bucer* (Cambridge: Cambridge University Press, 1970) who corrects certain interpretations of the historical facts made by C. HOPF, *Martin Bucer and the English Reformation* (Oxford: Blackwell, 1946).

[69] Cf. A. GANOCZY, *Calvin, théologien de l'Eglise et du ministère* (Paris: Cerf, 1964) 50–57, and for the conception of the "four ministers" and ordination, see pp. 297–327 and W. VAN'T SPIJKER, "Bucer's Influence on Calvin: Church and Community," in D. F. WRIGHT (ed.), *Martin Bucer: Reforming Church and Community* (Cambridge: Cambridge University Press, 1994) 32–44.

[70] Cf. below, ch. 3 (III, A), and on the importance of his interventions, see, among others: E. C. MESSENGER, *The Lutheran Origin of the Anglican Ordinal* (London: Burns, Oates and Washbourne, Ltd., 1934); and P. F. BRADSHAW, *The Anglican Ordinal. Its History and Development from the Reformation to the Present Day* (London: SPCK, 1971) 20–38.

As for the content, we see Bucer's concern to be more thorough in the examination of the elect: he has a number of questions where Luther only has one, which was preceded by a brief exhortation that is much more developed in Bucer. The Lord's Prayer is omitted, and a long prayer of ordination, containing in part the commentary on the three parts of the Our Father,[*290] takes its place, but does not repeat that of Luther. As in the ritual of Württemberg (and later, of Hesse),[71] we find here a formula of transmission (repeating somewhat the epiclesis of the prayer of ordination) pronounced with the imposition of hands.[*291] In relation to Luther's ritual, these changes brought about, too, a change in the understanding of the ordained ministry, which from then on revolved around the conception of the role of the Holy Spirit in the ministry.[72] Lastly, the office of ordination is celebrated during the worship service of Holy Communion.

2. ORDINATION OF A PASTOR

According to what Bucer says at the end of his ritual,[*293] there are three orders of "presbyters and curates = *presbyteri et curati*" (the bishops, the presbyters who assist them, and the deacons); the ritual he proposes is to vary in solemnity according to the case (the greatest solemnity for the bishop, and the least for the deacons). In reality this means that the rituals are identical, since he does not describe in detail the way in which this solemnity is to be expressed. All this is perfectly in accord with the conception of the ministry as elaborated in Strasbourg.[73]

a. *Structure of the Formulary*

The structure of the formulary is simple and largely conforms to that of the formularies already discussed. The framework of the ordination is that of the Reformed Eucharistic celebration, for the entire Church is to be present and is to participate in the election and ordination of the new ministers. We see here once again the elements of

[71] Cf. the KOs of Württemberg of 1547 (RICHTER II, 95) and of Hesse of 1566 (SEHLING VIII, 203).

[72] W. P. STEPHENS, *The Holy Spirit . . .*, 173. We shall have occasion to return to this work when we discuss the prayer of ordination.

[73] R. BORNERT, *La Réforme . . .*, 426ff.; J. KITTELSON, "Martin Bucer and the Ministry of the Church," in D. F. WRIGHT (ed.), *Martin Bucer . . .*, 83–94; and W. VAN'T SPIJKER, *The Ecclesiastical Offices . . .*, 169–189, 195–205, 306–343.

the election: an examination of the life and the doctrine of the future ordinands, a trial sermon, the election in the presence of representatives of the whole community, and then the ratification by the magistrates.[74]

We should, however, note one original feature in relation to Luther's structure of ordination. Six new choices of readings have been added to those found in the Lutheran rites,'[272] namely, Ephesians 4, Titus 1, and a choice between Matthew 28, John 10, John 20, or John 21. The first conforms to the conception of the organization and the basis of the ministries,[75] while the second gives a description of the functions and personal qualities required of the ministers.[76] The gospel pericopes reflect different aspects of the ordained ministry.

[74] On the role attributed to the magistrate in the Reformation in the work of Bucer, see G. HAMMANN, *Entre la secte et la cité. Le projet d'Eglise du Réformateur Martin Bucer (1491-1551)* (Geneva: Labor et Fides, 1984) 309–336. Briefly, Hammann writes that ". . . the structure of the traditional Church having been dismantled, there was no one else (i.e., other than the magistrate) who could assume that legislative and jurisdictional power that had previously been held by the bishop. The people of Strasbourg, agreeing in this matter with the other Reformers, had no theological difficulties with the idea that the responsibility for keeping watch at *the second table of the Law* (that is, morality) was the purview of the civil authorities" (p. 313). But Bucer attributed responsibility in doctrinal matters, as well, to the first table of the Law. This could happen because of the elimination of papal and episcopal authority, but, as we just saw in Luther's case, we also perceive here a dialectic opposing grace/Law, interior/exterior, the Church "ad intra"/the Church "ad extra," spiritual/carnal, as well as the august political principle of *"cuius regio, eius religio."*

[75] *Ein kurtzer warhafftiger bericht von Disputationem und gantzem handel, so zusuchen Cunrat Treger, Provincial der Augustiner, und den predigern des Evangelii zü Strassburg sich begeben hat* [1524], R. STUPPERICH (ed.), *Martin Bucers deutsche Schriften* (Gütersloh/-Paris: Verlagshaus Gerd Mohn/Presses Universitaires de France, 1962) 2, 136.38–137.3 (cited hereafter as *MBDS*), and *MBDS* 2, 136.24–30; see also the *Confessio Tetrapolitana* [1530], art. 15, *MBDS* 3, 117 (for English trans., see A. C. COCHRANE [ed.], *Reformed Confessions of the Sixteenth Century* [Philadelphia/London: Westminster Press/SCM Press, 1966] 73, hereafter cited COCHRANE, followed by page no.); *De vi et usu sacri ministerii, explicatio* (Cambridge, November 9, 1550); C. HUBERT (ed.), *Martini Buceri scripta anglicana* (Basel: Petri Pernae Officina, 1577) 567.27–31 (hereafter, *MBSA*); and W. P. STEPHENS, *The Holy Spirit . . . .*, 174–177 [*Epistolam ad ephesios* (1527), 37v.].

[76] *Von der waren Seelsorge und dem rechten Hirtendienst, wie derselbige in der Kirchen Christi bestellet und verrichtet werden solle* [1538], *MBDS* 7, 117 and 121, abridged in *Der Kürtzer Catechismus* [1543], *MBDS* 6/3, 252–254; and *Ein Sum-*

Next the presentation*273 allows the faithful the chance to intervene if they have something to say about the elect, and if not, then all proceed to the ordination, beginning with the exhortation addressed to the ordinands on the subject of the ministry and its functions.*274-*276 Here we note the following features:

—a description of the pastor, for the minister is chosen to carry out Christ's mission: to seek out the lost sheep, lead them to eternal salvation, and teach them. The flock is called variously sheep, children of God, spouse and body of Christ (oves, filii Dei, sponsa et corpus Christi);

—a teaching on the supremacy of the action of God, on our total dependence on him and on his Spirit, for certainly the dignity and responsibility of this office are great, but God is the source of all: the minister need only turn to the Spirit to receive the help that he will need; he must meditate on the Scriptures to find the pertinent exhortations in them and to draw the help that he will need to live as a Christian in this world;

—an exhortation addressed to the minister as good servant so that as a worthy steward he may put his confidence in the power of God who gives him his vocation along with the ability to fulfill it, with the help of the Holy Spirit, by sanctifying his life and the lives of his flock, with a life in conformity with the teachings of Christ.[77]

At the end of the exhortation the office proceeds to another examination of the elect to determine their attitude toward their vocation,

---

marischer vergriff der Christlichen lehre und Religion [1548], art. 13 (for an English trans., see D. F. WRIGHT, Common Places of Martin Bucer [Appleford: Sutton Courtenay Press, 1972]: "A Brief Summary of the Christian Doctrine and Religion," 83 [hereafter cited WRIGHT, followed by page no.]).

[77] These themes are found in the writings of Bucer; for example, the role of the Spirit in the ministry: Von der waren . . ., MBDS 7, 110f., and Die Berner Disputation [1528], MBDS 4, 50; the ministry is at the service of the Church: Von der waren . . ., MBDS 7, 111, to inspire faith and charity (Epistolam ad ephesios, 37); the power of the Spirit will guide the minister in his teaching: Martin Butzers an ein christlichen Rath und Gemeyn der statt Weissenburg Summary seiner Predig daselbst gethen [1523], MBDS 1, 96.36–97.5; and God acts through his ministers in the Church: De vi et usu . . ., MBSA 590, 24–31; they do not simply proclaim the forgiveness of sins, they forgive them: De vi et usu . . ., MBSA 592, 25–35; cf. De vi et usu . . ., MBSA 593, 27–33.

43

and their understanding of the basis of the ministry.[277-287] This is actually more of a ritual examination, for the canonical examination has already taken place.[78] This examination is followed by another exhortation if the ordination takes place in the community where the minister or the ministers are to assume their duties.

Next all pray in silence for the ordinands. The prayer of ordination follows, said by the principal ordainor without the imposition of hands,[289-290] but at its conclusion he imposes hands with the presbyters and says the prayer, which is a sort of benediction.[291] This prayer has taken the place of the missioning of Luther's rite and the formula of transmission that we saw in Württemberg. It is a sort of continuation of the epiclesis of the prayer of ordination, and it had great success in the Reformed offices of ordination through the work of Jan Łaski (Ioannis a Lasco) (1550) and the KO of Hesse of 1566.[79] We discern in this formula the relationship Bucer sees between the ordained ministry exercised in the heart of the community of the people of God, and the salvific activity of God, for the Lord is present in the midst of his people, and grants what is prayed for.[80] Worship continues with the profession of faith and the celebration of Holy Communion.

We will have more to say later as to the meaning of ordination, the imposition of hands, and the content of the epicletic prayer, but we

[78] For the importance of this examination, see *De ordinatione legitima ministrorum ecclesiae revocanda* [1549], *MBSA* 242, 12–15 (= "An Inquiry Concerning the Restoration of the Lawful Ordination of the Church's Ministers," WRIGHT 257f.); *De Regno Christi* [1550], ch. IIII: ". . . *In omnem horum vitam, mores et studia accuratissime est inquirendum et explorandum, quam confirmatam habeant regni Christi revocandi cum facultatem, tuam voluntatem . . .*," F. WENDEL (ed.), *Martini Buceri opera latina* (Gütersloh/Paris: C. Bertelsmann Verlag/Presses Universitaires de France, 1955) 15, 103.10–12 (hereafter *MBOL*) (". . . Their whole lives, their habits of behavior and special interests, must be inquired into and explored, to see how strong a talent and a will they have for restoring the Kingdom of Christ . . .") (= "On the Kingdom of Christ," in W. PAUCK [ed.], *Melanchthon and Bucer* [Philadelphia: Westminster, 1969] 270, hereafter cited PAUCK, followed by page no.). He has suggested a total of thirty-two questions on the life, the education, and the doctrine of the elect: *De ordinatione . . ., MBSA* 245–252 (= WRIGHT 261–268); and W. P. STEPHENS, *The Holy Spirit . . .*, 192.

[79] *934; cf. F. SCHULZ, "Evangelische . . .," 8f.

[80] *De ordinatione . . ., MBSA* 255, 17f. (= WRIGHT 270); and W. P. STEPHENS, *The Holy Spirit . . .*, 194f.

should note at the outset the importance that Bucer attributes to vocation in his ritual of ordination, as seen in the exhortation to the elect and in the Trinitarian theology which underlies the actions of the community. "We teach," he writes, "that it is the Lord's will that these his ministers should be chosen for this ministry by the whole of his congregation from among themselves, being examined by them and ordained, consecrated and instituted in his name with solemn prayer and the laying-on of hands" [Acts 1:24ff.; 6:3-6; 13:3; 14:23].[81] The minister appears as the vehicle through which the glorified Christ builds up his Church on earth.[82] The main category is that of "servant," for the minister is the servant of the Word and of the Spirit, who joins the exterior activity of the minister to the interior action of God.[83]

b. *The Nucleus: the Imposition of Hands and the Prayer*

The imposition of hands is restored to its full importance through its central position during the rites of ordination. However, Bucer does not position this act in the same place in the rite as Luther—he did not leave it in the main prayer of ordination. We do not know the reasons for this. All we know is that he did not want to diminish its importance. In a few lines written by him we see that he relates this gesture to the meaning of "the communication of the power and grace of God to the newly ordained,"[84] and that he holds that the gift of the Spirit for the exercise of the ministry is conveyed by the imposition of hands.[85] W. P. Stephens has shown that Bucer does not have a theology of the sacraments that links grace automatically to an exterior sign, but a theology that does not separate the action of the sacrament from the action of God. The act is always associated with the prayer and the Word of God. This position of Bucer was upheld by others, who noted that he gave the same meaning to the gesture

---

[81] *Ein Summarischer . . .*, art. 12 (= D. F. WRIGHT, 270).

[82] *Von der waren . . .*, MBDS 7, 110f.

[83] *Grund und ursach auss gotlicher schrifft der neüwerungen an dem nachtmal des herren, so man die Mess nennet, Tauff, Feyrtagen, bildern und gesang in der gemein Christi, wann die züsammenkompt, durch und auff das wort gottes zü Strassburg fürgenommen* [1524], MBDS 1, 253.37; cf. also *Der Kürtzer . . .*, MBDS 6/3, 252–253.

[84] *Der Kürtzer . . .*, MBDS 6/3, 253–254.

[85] *Von der waren . . .*, MBDS 7, 124.17–18: ". . . das die gabe des heiligen geists den Kirchendienst wol zü verrichten mit dem hendtufflegen der Eltisten gegeben würdt . . ."

of the imposition of hands during confirmation: "The imposition of hands signifies a disposition to assume in a holy manner a particular charge in the Church, or yet a communication of the Holy Spirit for the purpose of entering into such a function."[86] Bucer even calls the imposition of hands "a sacramental ceremony" in the KO of Kassel.[87] One last passage from Bucer shows that by the gesture of the imposition of hands we are to understand that it is the Lord himself who establishes the elect: ". . . The elect were established in their ministry by the imposition of hands, as before the Lord and by the Lord himself, and they received the guarantee that the Holy Spirit would help them to fulfill their office properly . . ."[88]

We have very little from his pen concerning the prayer of ordination itself. We know only that the ministers were ordained in the assembly of the community of God with recourse to fasting, prayer, and the imposition of hands; they are established, ordained, and consecrated with solemn prayers and the imposition of hands.[89]

c. *Prayer of Ordination*

"Almighty God, Father of our Lord Jesus Christ, we give thanks to your divine majesty and to your Son, our Lord and Redeemer, that you have given him to us to be both our Redeemer and our teacher unto the blessed life of eternity. And it has pleased you that, having accomplished our redemption by his death and taken his seat at your right hand in the heavens, the renewer of all things in heaven and earth, he should grant to us lost and wretched men, and send as you did send him, apostles, prophets, evangelists, teachers and pastors, by whose ministry he might himself gather unto you your children

---

[86] M. BUCER, *Quid de baptismate infantium* [1553], p. A VIIr: "Impositio manuum adaptatio est ad certum in Ecclesia munus sancte obeundum vel Spiritus Sancti ad eiusmodi functionem collatio," quoted by R. BORNERT, *La Réforme . . .*, 437, where he discusses the act of the imposition of hands in relationship to confirmation. See W. P. STEPHENS, *The Holy Spirit . . .*, 193–195 and 213–220 and F. SCHULZ, "Die Ordination . . .," 19f.

[87] *Ordenung der Kirchenübunge. Für die Kirchen zu Cassel, 1539, MBDS 7,* 292. See also G. HAMMANN, *Entre la secte . . .*, 257f. (ordination as a "third sacrament"), and 297–307.

[88] *Von der waren . . ., MBDS 7,* 140.15–18.

[89] *Der Kürtzer . . ., MBDS 6/3,* 253–254, and *Ein Summarischer . . .,* art. 13 (= WRIGHT 83).

scattered in the world, and having manifested you to them in himself, might regenerate and renew them unto you, to the perpetual praise of your holy name. Among whose number it has pleased your mercy that we too should be brought and regenerated to you through your same Son, and by his same holy ministry, and should form this Church as it stands here *[coram te]* before your holy face *[in tuo sancto conspectu]*. Wherefore, for these countless unspeakable benefits of your eternal goodness, and for deigning to call to the same ministry of men's salvation these your servants here, and to present them to us for ordination to the same, we give you the best thanks we can offer, and praise and adore you. And we humbly beg and beseech you through your same Son, richly to pour out your Holy Spirit in the name of your Son upon these your ministers *[ut spiritum sanctum tuum, in nomine filii tui, opulente in hos ipsos tuos ministros effundas]*, and also ever to teach and direct them that they may both faithfully and profitably perform their ministry to your people, the flock of our good Shepherd, your Son, and may also daily draw many to your glory and, once drawn, instruct and conform them more perfectly every day to all your holy will. Grant, moreover, to all for whose salvation they minister by your will, minds to receive your holy word *[da quoque illis omnibus, quorum saluti vis istos ministrare, animos verbi tui capaces]*, and to us all who here and everywhere call upon your holy name, to declare unceasingly our gratitude to you for these and all your other benefits, and daily so to advance in the knowledge and faith of you and of your Son through your Holy Spirit that through these your ministers and those to whom by your will we give them as ministers, and through us all, your holy name may be ever more fully glorified, and the blessed kingdom of your Son be more widely extended and more powerfully prevail wherever it has reached, through your same Son, our Lord Jesus Christ, who lives and reigns with you in the unity of the same Spirit, world without end. Amen.'"[*289–*290]

α) *Biblical Images Employed.* The first part[*289] treats mainly of the establishment of the Church as the culmination of Christ's mission of salvation. Our Lord has brought all things to perfection and he has sought out the lost sheep in order to reconcile the universe, for the glory of the Father who sent him. He accomplished all this through

47

his life, his death, his resurrection, his entire life through his ascension. Finally, he gave apostles, prophets, evangelists, doctors, and pastors ". . . by whose ministry he might himself gather unto you your children scattered in the world, and having manifested you to them in himself, might regenerate and renew them unto you . . ."[90] The ministers serve the mission of the glorified Christ for the building up of his body, the Church on earth; it is from within his power that they act. The eschatological dimension of the ministry is clear, for the Church is already founded on earth as the people of God gathered together by Christ into his body, and founded on the apostles; but it is still being built up (this is the theme of regeneration and ongoing renewal). At this point, and further along in the prayer, we also see the theme of growth linked to the ministry (both of Christ and of the ministers); this aspect has an eschatological dimension, because it is always the Kingdom of God which is growing, a Kingdom already established among us but not yet fulfilled in all its plenitude.

Secondly, a Eucharistic phrase gives the reason for giving thanks to God:[*290] for the generosity of his interventions in the past, for the continuation of his plan of salvation through the ministry of these men, and for the generous gift that they make of themselves to the Church—for all these things thanks are given to God.

Lastly, with the image of the flock at one with its shepherd, Christ, and its ministers, the end of the prayer asks that the name of God be glorified, that the Kingdom of his Son be extended and strengthened. The eschatological metaphor of growth is found here, as it was at the very beginning of the prayer.

β) *Qualities Requested for the Ordinand.* The required qualities are: faithfulness, obedience, and the ability to guide and to serve. Obedience, because the pastors must learn from Christ his ways, so that they may teach and govern. Faithfulness, because they must exercise their ministry with constancy. And lastly, they must follow the example of the Good Shepherd and guide, feed, and serve those who

---

[90] *289: ". . . tu eum misisti, Apostolos, Prophetas, Evangelistas, Doctores et Pastores, quorum ministerio dispersos in mundo filios tuos ipse ad te colligeret, eosque te eis, in semetipso manifesto, tibi ad perpetuam laudem nominis sancti tui, regigneret et renovaret."

are entrusted to them. The gift of the Holy Spirit is prayed for, so that the new ministers may be instruments of the ministry of Christ in the Church.

γ) *Gifts Received by the Ordinand.* In two places we find the gift that the ordinand receives mentioned: in the prayer of ordination at the point of the epiclesis, and in the prayer of benediction[*291] which follows the prayer of ordination. The epiclesis asks for the gift of the Holy Spirit so that the ordinand may teach, govern, and lead the Church. During the benediction the congregation prays for the presence of the triune God, for his protection and his guidance of the ordinand. The metaphor employed is that of the protective hand of the triune God, an image that perhaps recalls the scene of God guiding his people with his strong right hand through the Red Sea and the desert to the Promised Land. G. Hammann reminds us that Bucer saw a correlation between the people of the old covenant and the people of the new covenant, but that the Church only reached adulthood at Pentecost: "The community of the Old Testament has today ceased to be the 'ecclesia Dei,' replaced by the 'spouse of Christ,' who will live forever. From her beginnings in Jerusalem, she becomes this gathering of the elect from the whole world over, walking in the plenitude of the Spirit towards her fulfillment."[91] Comparing this idea to that expressed in the metaphor of the "strong hand of God," we can readily see in it the continuation of the blessing of the Trinity upon the one who is to act in God's name, in the heart of the community, as was true all throughout the history of the people of God. The gift of God is conferred upon the ordinand to guide him in his task of building up this people of God and to accompany it on the road to its fulfillment.

3. INSTALLATION OF A BISHOP

Bucer did not provide a separate ritual for the establishment of a bishop in his ministry. We know that he was aware of the plurality of the ministries, because he wrote that no one in the Church possesses all the gifts that are needed, and yet all the necessary gifts are provided within the ministry of the Church. Bucer had full appreciation

[91] G. HAMMANN, *Entre la secte . . .*, 145. We have already seen Bucer's position on the communication of the Spirit by the imposition of hands; cf. n. 81.

of the fact that God had so ordered human existence that we all have need of each other.[92] R. Bornert has attempted to show that in the thinking of Bucer we can discern an evolution from a dual conception of the pastoral ministry to the belief that it was essentially one. For Bucer the bishop was an *"Eltisten,"* or a presbyter, elected to preside over the body of ministers[93] and to take his part in the spiritual administration and the pastoral ministry (and, by implication, the governance and supervision), along with all the other presbyters. To the deacon was entrusted the temporal administration of the Church.

4. RELATIONSHIP BETWEEN THE MINISTRY OF PASTOR AND THAT OF BISHOP

The clearest description of the relationship between these two orders is found in the work entitled *A Brief Summary* (1548) where we read, at article 13:

"We teach that the Holy Spirit has appointed two distinct degrees in the church's ministry (1 Tim 3:1,8). The one comprises the senior pastors, whom the Holy Spirit styles overseers and elders (Tit 1:5, 7; Acts 14:23; 20:28), and to whom he entrusts the ministries of teaching, the holy sacraments, and Christian discipline, that is to say, everything concerned with the cure of souls. The other degree comprises those who are to aid the elders in all their pastoral ministry and in feeding Christ's sheep, and at the same time to be zealous in helping the needy (Acts 6:2-4)."[94]

It is clear from this description that Bucer is referring to the presbyters/bishops and the deacons. Nevertheless, the first group (the supervisors and the elders) is charged with a pastoral ministry (the cure of souls) which includes the supervision of the flock entrusted to

---

[92] Cf. *Von der waren . . .*, MBDS 7, 117.23–26, and *De vi et usu . . .*, MBSA 567, 27–31.

[93] *Von der waren . . .*, MBDS 7, 121, and *Der Kürtzer . . .*, MBDS 6/3, 253–254; see R. BORNERT, *La Réforme . . .*, 426–428. G. Hammann thinks that this thesis of Bornert is overly schematized; see his commentaries on the plurality of ministries in Bucer: G. HAMMANN, *Entre la secte . . .*, 273–276. Nevertheless, we think that Bornert means to speak only of the ordained ministers; in which case the two writers appear in agreement—see on this point the analysis of Hammann on pp. 287–291 of his study.

[94] *Ein Summarischer . . .*, art 13 (= WRIGHT 83).

them: by teaching, by celebrating the sacraments, and by governing. He makes little distinction between the members of this group: they are all pastors of higher rank. We see the same thing in the rite of ordination that he composed,[293] but with this difference, that the bishops and elders (called also "cardinals") are in charge of governing the Church. Elsewhere Bucer expresses the wish that the bishop, once he has been elected to the college of elders, may bear the care of the whole Church and, from his higher position, supervise all the ministries and affairs of the Church.[95] As for the deacons, they occupy the same place in both documents.[96] With all of this in mind, we may conclude that Bucer sees no essential difference between the presbyters and the bishops: all are charged with the pastoral ministry of governing the Church.

5. LATER INFLUENCE OF THE FORMULARY OF BUCER

Bucer's ideas will encounter fertile ground in two different areas: obviously, in England, as we shall see later, and on the continent as well, particularly in the rites of ordination prescribed by Jan Łaski (1550/1565) and in the KO of Hesse of 1566. This influence is seen primarily in the division of the offices into those of bishop, presbyter/elder, and deacon; it can also be discerned in the epiclesis and in the benediction pronounced with the imposition of hands.[97] We have provided a list of these influences in the technical notes to the ordination texts produced in the fourth volume of this study.

6. CONCLUSION: STRUCTURING OF THE CHURCH AND THE SUBSTANCE OF ORDAINED MINISTRY

a. *Structure of the Church*

The salient feature of the theology of Bucer is his conception of ordained ministry as a ministry of the Spirit. It is this concept that led him to reform the structure of the Church by transposing the

---

[95] *Von der waren . . ., MBDS* 7, 121.

[96] R. Bornert explains that later on, in Strasbourg, there was some loss of the oneness of the ministry, since the deacons did not have any real status: cf. R. BORNERT, *La Réforme . . .*, 429.

[97] Cf. H. SCHULZ, "Evangelische . . .," 8f.; and for the influence of Bucer on liturgical reform in general during the 16th century, see G. J. VAN DE POLL, *Martin Bucer's Liturgical Ideas* (Assen: Van Gorcum & Co., 1954) appendix C.

ministry from the category of "priesthood" to that of *"diakonia."*[98] The priesthood, as Luther had seen, is a reality that belongs to all the people, based on baptism;[99] it is therefore the responsibility of the entire people to take part in a decision as important as the election and ordination of their ministers, as we have seen in the rubric that opens the ritual of Bucer[*270] and the exhortations pronounced on this occasion. One could say that the community is aware that it is conferring the vocation and receiving the ministers it needs in one and the same act; the community bears witness as well to the faith of the elect and at the same time to the quality of their Christian life. It is not exactly an act of delegation that is taking place here, but rather the awareness of being able to carry out the plan of God in case of necessity. Moreover, the Eucharistic setting of the process of election/ordination and of the prayers of the faithful means that "ordination [will be] beneficial for the Church and those to be ordained."[*271]

The pastoral imagery of the great exhortation[*274-*276] is particularly interesting in that it does not conceive of the ministry in terms of superiority and inferiority, or as a state of competition between two bodies, but rather it presents it as an office of *diakonia*. The words "dignity" and "responsibility" occur several times in this exhortation. The ministers are seen as the servants of a Church which remains priestly in her entirety.

The prayer of ordination conceives of the ordained ministry as a continuation of the ministry of Christ, prolonged in that of the apostles, the prophets, etc. It is said clearly that the ministry of Christ was to carry out the Father's plan of salvation, and that the Father sent him to reconcile the world to him, and to gather the sheep into one fold, for the glory and praise of his name.

Lastly, the Trinitarian reality[100] of the ministry is evident in the prayer of benediction, where the blessing of the Trinity protects and strengthens the new ministers: it will constitute the power whereby their ministry will bear fruit. Their ministry is a means of salvation given to the Church, as well as a tool for the Church to use in her task of actualizing the plan of God.[*290]

[98] R. BORNERT, *La Réforme . . .*, 419.
[99] Cf. *Ein Summarischer . . .*, art. 11 (= WRIGHT 82f.).
[100] Cf. W. P. STEPHENS, *The Holy Spirit . . .*, 184, where he states that for Bucer the ministry is the work of the Trinity, which explains why he attributes it some-

b. *Substance of the Pastoral and Episcopal Ministries*

To recapitulate, the pastoral and episcopal ministries are the means Christ uses to build up his Church on earth:[*289–*290] "He continues to govern, to guide and to feed his flock through the intermediary of the ministry of his word."[101] Both pastors and bishops have a pastoral charge of supervision, governance, and teaching. Their guidance must also be a moral power, through the example of their Christian life.[*281–*285] One of the pastors must bear the major responsibility for the Church by seeing to her good order, her doctrine, and her affairs: this is the superintendent. But we have seen that Bucer has nothing more precise to say on the subject of this superintendent's role.

D. THE *KYRKOORDNING* (1571)—LAURENTIUS PETRI

Laurentius Petri (1499–1573), the younger brother of Olaus Petri (a pioneer Reformer in Sweden), was consecrated archbishop of Uppsala (1531–1573) by Petrus Magni (the last bishop duly elected and consecrated in Rome in 1524 as bishop of Västerås). He studied in Wittenberg where he adopted Reformed theology, but he remained a moderate, and maintained a solid balance in the application of the principles of the Reformation in Sweden. The project of putting the Church's affairs in order was entrusted to his brother, who died in 1552 after having fallen into disgrace because of his vehement opposition to the design of King Erik XIV, who had adopted some Calvinistic thinking, to take to himself power in the Church. Laurentius then applied himself to consolidating the work begun by his brother.

These labors produced a proposal of an ecclesiastical Ordinance presented in 1561 to Erik XIV, which he then rejected. Petri reworked it, and, with the encouragement of the new king John III (sympathetic to Catholicism because of his Catholic wife, the Polish princess

---

times to the Father, sometimes to the Son, and sometimes to the Holy Spirit. This affirmation is followed by a quotation from *Epistolam ad ephesios* of Bucer.

[101] ". . . Und derhalben hat im gefallen sein **regiment, hüt und weide** gegen uns, die wir noch in diser welt sind, zü üben mit und durch den dienst seines worts, den er durch seine diener und werckzeuge auch eusserlich und befindt-licht geprauchet . . .," *Von der waren . . ., MBDS* 7, 107.25–108.2, and again on 110f.; see also *De ordinatione . . ., MBSA* 237, 16ff., and *De vi et usu . . ., MBSA* 590.24–31.

Catherine Jagellon), in 1571 he published the Ordinance such as we know it.[102]

1. RELATIONSHIP TO THE FORMULARY OF LUTHER

Petri borrowed only a few elements from Luther for his rite of ordination: the litany, the prayer after the ordination (in part), the missioning, the imposition of hands and the Lord's Prayer, and, in part, the structure. These elements most probably reached him via the KO of Mecklenburg of 1522.[103] We know that Petri insisted on the necessity for episcopal ordination, contrary to Luther: for Petri the rite of this ordination acquires a different status. We can then affirm that the formulary of Petri has some connections with that of Luther, but it also keeps some distance from the ideas of the Reformation, for Petri tried to maintain a certain continuity in the practice of the Church even while he maintained the primacy of the Word in all things.[104]

2. ORDINATION OF A PRIEST [*294–*311]

a. *Structure of the Formulary*

The structure is simple, and reproduces more or less that established by the formulary of Luther (cf. Table I.3, vol. IV). The rite comes at the end of a process of election, inquiry, interrogation, and

---

[102] For the bibliographical details on Laurentius Petri and on the history of the early Reformation in Sweden, see L.-M. DEWAILLY, "Petri (Olaus et Laurentius)," *Catholicisme*, fasc. 49 (1986) cols. 93–95; id., "Laurentius Petri et la Kyrkoordning de 1571," *Istina* 30, 3 (1985) 228–245 (+ bibliography); T. VAN HAAG, "Die apostolische Sukzession in Schweden," *Kyrkohistorisk Årsskrift* 44, 1 (1944) 4–168; E. E. YELVERTON, *An Archbishop of the Reformation. Laurentius Petri Nericius, Archbishop of Uppsala 1531–1573. A Study of His Liturgical Projects* (London: Epworth Press, 1958); M. PARVIO, "The Post-Reformation Developments of Episcopacy in Sweden, Finland, and the Baltic States," in I. ASHEIM and V. R. GOLD (eds.), *Episcopacy . . .*, 125–137; and for the relationship of the *Kyrkoordning* to later Swedish liturgies, see E. RODHE, *Svenskt gudstjänstliv. Historisk Belyning av den Svenska Kyrkohandboken* (Uppsala: Ulmquist & Wiksells, 1923) esp. ch. 16.

[103] Cf. SEHLING V, 193 for the text of the KO, and also E. E. YELVERTON, *An Archbishop . . .*, 88; and L.-M. DEWAILLY, "Laurentius Petri . . .," 236f.

[104] Cf. *Then Swenska Kyrkeordningen*, ed. E. Färnström (Stockholm: Svenska Kyrans Diakonistyrelses Bokförlag, 1932) 138–142 (= *L'Ordonnance ecclésiastique suédoise de 1571*, trans. by L.-M. DEWAILLY, *Istina* 30, 3 [1985] 297–301, hereafter *TSK* followed by chapter and page number and, in parentheses, the page number of Dewailly's translation).

prayer, in which all the elements of the Church were involved: the faithful, the civil authorities, and the clergy. We note that the bishop plays a more important role; it is he who has the last word in the election, since he interrogates, tests, and approves the persons presented as possible ordinands. The participation of the laity is assured by the presence of delegates from the parishes who suggest certain individuals for the office, and take part in the examination of their life and doctrine. Finally, the elect are presented to the king for ratification. The bishop confirms that essentially three aptitudes have been met: the proper age, sufficient knowledge of Scripture, and becoming conduct. If he thinks that an individual is not the right one for the office, he can suggest others. In all this the emphasis is on "recourse to God through prayer."[105] The ordination proper is to take place on a feast day, when all the people can participate.

Next the *Ordinarius* (the meaning will be clarified further on: the one who maintains order, i.e., the bishop) reminds the assembly of the importance of the act that is about to take place; he recalls also that these men have been found acceptable, and that the grace and help of God are necessary for a minister to acquit himself worthily of this office. Significantly, he then turns towards God in prayer by intoning the litany or by singing the hymn to the Holy Spirit; he continues with a prayer asking for the help of God and of his Spirit so that "his word may at all times dwell among us, grow and be fruitful; and that [his] servants may, as behooves them, speak the word with all freedom, so that [his] holy Christian Church may thereby grow better and serve [him] with constant faith, and remain steadfast in the knowledge of [him]."[*295] Then follows the presentation of the elect, in which we should note the insistence on the existence of a particular title (Church or diocese) for each person ordained: the ministry is rooted in a concrete context and is connected to a specific community, as in the early Church. This presentation is followed by three readings from the Bible that illustrate the aptitudes required of the ministers, and the principal task of the bishops—namely, governing and watching over the flock. The three readings speak of the "bishops," a fact that proves that in the Reformed spirit the biblical equivalence between presbyters and bishops is a matter of authority

[105] *TSK* 22, 139–141 (ed. Dewailly, 298ff.).

over several communities and in the larger towns.[106] These readings are followed by a short commentary on their meaning.

The commitment of the elect is formulated in five short questions bearing on their acceptance of the office, on their faithfulness to the Word of God, on their conduct, and on their desire to seek peace and to submit to legitimate authority. It has been suggested that these questions share a few points in common with certain questions of the ritual of Bucer.[107] This commitment is confirmed by the bishop with a declaration of transmission: "And I, by the powers entrusted to me in this matter by God through this assembly, I transmit to you the office of Priest, in the name of the Father, etc."[*307] This text presents some aspects of a legal declaration, but theologically it reveals another layer of meaning: firstly, the ordaining minister represents God to the community, and, secondly, he possesses the powers to do so, so that he may acquit himself well of his duties as the representative of the assembly in this matter, for it is the whole assembly which along with God has conferred these powers upon him. Thus we see the bishop acting as the minister of God as he answers the needs of his community, for he acts in the name of the Church by carrying out the will of God which was discerned by the entire process of election and ordination. This prayer is not found in its usual place (as in the tradition established at Württemberg) *after* the imposition of hands and the Our Father. Its purpose is to confer the office of priest upon the ordinand, and it has been suggested that it originates from the Latin prayer *"Accipe Spiritum sanctum."* It is clear that the Reformation was not as radical in Sweden as in other countries, and that Laurentius Petri, considering the formula of the pontifical as the essential element of ordination, transposed it to a position before the Our Father and suppressed the other elements of the Latin rite, such as the anointings and the conferral of the instruments of office. We recall that Petri was familiar with Luther's Reformed ritual through the ecclesiastical order of Mecklenburg, but this latter did not contain any prayer of transmission![108]

---

[106] *TSK* 25, 161f. (ed. Dewailly, 309f.).

[107] *277, *279, *280, *282, *283, and *284; the connection was made by E. E. YELVERTON, *An Archbishop . . .*, 89.

[108] Cf. E. RODHE, *Svenskt gudstjänstliv . . .*, 447–450.

Next, the imposition of hands was done during the Our Father, as from now on in Lutheran tradition; it ends with the collect.

Once this principal act has been accomplished, the missioning of the new ministers takes place with the traditional prayer taken from 1 Peter 5. A canticle to the Holy Spirit ends the ordination proper, and the celebration of the Swedish Mass begins.

b. *The Nucleus: the Imposition of Hands and the Prayer*

This part, which is traditional in any ordination, is found at the heart of the rite. One curious element was introduced in the rubrics for the imposition of hands: only the *Ordinarius,* or the other priests present, impose hands. We are at a loss as to why only the bishop would impose hands. The gesture is done with both hands, something new to Lutheran tradition, which normally prescribed "the hand." We should not read any particular meaning into this change. The deeply evangelical prayer is, of course, the Our Father, and from this point on it is traditional, and is followed by a second collect (that we shall examine more closely further on in our study).

c. *Prayer of Ordination*

Here is the text of the prayer that follows the Lord's Prayer:[109]

"O eternal and merciful God, dear heavenly Father, who by the mouth of your beloved Son our Lord Jesus Christ have said that the Harvest truly is plenteous, but the laborers are few, pray therefore that the Lord of the Harvest will send forth laborers into his Harvest. With these words you gave us to understand that we cannot receive honest and faithful Teachers otherwise than from your kindly hand. Therefore we pray you also with all our hearts that you will look graciously upon these your servants, whom we have chosen and preferred to this ministry and office of Priest, giving unto them the Holy Spirit, that they may faithfully and effectually perform your holy work, teach and reprove with all gentleness and wisdom; so that your holy Gospel may ever remain among us, pure and undefiled, and bring us the fruit of salvation, and everlasting life, through your Son Jesus Christ our Lord. Amen."[*309]

α) *Biblical Images Employed.* The central image is the same as in Luther's prayer, to which it is heavily indebted, but there are more

---

[109] The French translation is taken from Dewailly's edition, p. 306.

details given here on the various ministerial tasks. God, who is all-wise and all-generous, will provide the Church with the workers she needs. Petri takes pains to point out that the meaning of the quotation from Matthew 9 is to remind us that it is God himself who raises up workers for the vineyard. However, immediately after this text we read that the Church has collaborated in this effort by choosing the men who are presented. The ministry appears as a gift of God for the pastoral service of the Church.

β) *Qualities Requested for the Ordinand.* The congregation prays that the elect may have the grace to remain faithful, and the strength to persevere. It is the Spirit who confers these gifts to the new ministers to help them in the tasks of their office, that is, teaching and the governance of the community.

γ) *Gifts Received by the Ordinand.* As in the case of Luther's formulary, there is no light shed on this subject in this text. The grace received is not elaborated on in the collect, which says only that it is a divine favor.

3. ORDINATION OF A BISHOP [*312-*322]

a. *Structure of the Formulary*

Laurentius Petri clearly follows Luther's lead with his doctrine of the one sole ordained ministry and the identification of the office of bishop with that of priest.[110] In his ritual, for that matter, the ordination of a bishop does not contain its own prayer, but simply the directive that the prayer for the ordination of priests is to be used.[*322] On the other hand, he states, in connection with the institution of the office of bishop, that "this ordinance was very convenient and without doubt proceeded from God the Holy Spirit (who gives all good gifts) . . ."[111] This office is, then, more than an instance of human intervention, but he limits himself to saying this, without affirming in so many words the divine institution of this office.

His liturgical work contains a chapter on the election of the bishop[*312] which precedes the chapter on ordination. The election is carried out by a sort of electoral college, composed of several dele-

---

[110] *TSK*, 25, 161 (ed. Dewailly, 309); and E. E. YELVERTON, *An Archbishop . . .,* 83–85.

[111] *TSK* 25, 162 (ed. Dewailly, 310) (= E. E. YELVERTON, *An Archbishop . . .,* 81).

gates from among the clergy, and other persons "experienced in the matter" who cast one vote for the bishop. They swear an oath that they will elect "the one who before God they judge to be the most suited" for the office. Everything is based on the ancient rule that "the bishop is to be elected by his people," but the system is adapted to the historical and geographical exigencies and constraints of the country. The *electus* is then presented for confirmation to the authorities (here the king and his representatives replace the pope). Lastly, he is ordained by another bishop in the presence of the people, normally in the cathedral.[112]

The rite of ordination follows that of a priest (see Tables I.3 and I.4, vol. IV). The context is the same: it takes place on a Sunday or a feast day, which was traditional, before Mass. However, emphasis is laid on the fact that the elect will be presented by two priests from the diocese for which he has been ordained, another reminder of how important it was that the episcopal ministry be attached to a local Church, against the common abusive state of affairs at the end of the Middle Ages in respect to the absenteeism of the bishops. For Petri the bishop is a minister in and for the communities he serves.[113] The elect is presented in a context of prayer, as in the ritual of ordination for priests, and then follow the litany and the same collect as was used for the teachers or masters *(Lärarenar).*[*295]

The readings chosen for the ordination are two: 1 Timothy 3 (the same as for the ordination of priests), and Luke 12:42-48 which speaks of the faithfulness of the good steward. Immediately afterwards a brief commentary[*317] treats of the pastoral qualities required of the bishop: faithfulness, prudence, and discernment. Next the commitment of the elect is made through a first interrogation which asks him if he has understood what is expected of him, followed by the same questions[*300-*305] that were addressed to the priests. To prove that the witness he will bear is in conformity with that of the Church, he recites the Creed of Nicaea-Constantinople, which was not required of the priests.

[112] *TSK* 26, 168 (ed. Dewailly, 315f.) (= E. E. YELVERTON, *An Archbishop . . .,* 141).

[113] *TSK* 25, 162f. (ed. Dewailly, 310f.) and M. PARVIO, "The Post-Reformation . . .," 129.

The ordination ends with the expression of a kind of votive prayer[*320] that is not the same as that found in the ordination of priests, but is just as general: "May the Lord God strengthen you and comfort you always." After a *Responsorium* sung in Latin, the imposition of hands, the Lord's Prayer, and the collect follow. The ordination ends with the singing in Swedish of the *"Veni Creator Spiritus"* as the introit of the Mass. The ordinand is given the honor of receiving Communion before anyone else.

b. *The Nucleus: the Imposition of Hands and the Prayer*

These two elements are found here in their usual place, but the manner prescribed for their execution contains a singular innovation: Petri says that "The *Ordinator,* at the same time as the other Bishops or Priests who are available, puts his hands on the head of the *Ordinandus . . ."*[321] The inclusion of the priests as "co-consecrators" is unexpected, and there is no explanation given anywhere. Yelverton thinks he recognizes here the influence of Bucer's ritual, which does not distinguish clearly between the three orders.[114] This is a possible explanation, because only another bishop can properly officiate at the ordination of a bishop.[*312.2] This can be explained by the fact that, with a few exceptions, this rite is based on that of priests, emphasizing that it is a question of the one same ministry of preaching, which we see confirmed by the use of the same prayer of ordination and the lack of any distinguishing features in the formula of transmission.

c. *Prayer of Ordination*

What we have said above in our commentary on the prayer for the ordination of priests applies here, for nothing has been added.

4. RELATIONSHIP BETWEEN THE MINISTRY OF PRIEST AND THAT OF BISHOP

Throughout these rituals Petri has not emphasized the specific nature of the episcopacy, as he had in chapter 25 on the bishops. There he speaks of the evolution of the office, quoting the opinion of St. Jerome to provide an explanation for the origins of this division of the ministry into two. He never goes into any explanation of the differentiation of the two functions.[115] He has even given a divine origin

---

[114] E. E. YELVERTON, *An Archbishop . . .*, 91.

[115] *TSK* 25, 161 (ed. Dewailly, 309), including Dewailly's commentary in the note.

for this evolution, as we have seen above. The office of bishop, he states clearly, ". . . consists in this, to preach the word of God and to supervise those entrusted to his care, so that they also might preach correctly and conduct themselves as is proper . . ." He goes on to explain that the bishops have authority over the clergy in order to strengthen their powers of supervision regarding the preaching of the Word, the teaching (of catechism), the administration of the sacraments, confession, and the usual services in the parishes (for instance, visiting the faithful, providing comfort, etc.). A major part of their supervision consists in examining the life and behavior of the priests, and visiting the parishes to find out if there have been any omissions or excesses: persons, for instance, who never receive the Sacrament, or who live in sin, or practice black magic, etc. A bishop must judge all such cases and restore good order to the situation (including cases of marriages). As for the priests, their function is the same, but on the level of the parish.[116] The exercise of the bishop's office is also, one could say, collegial, as is shown by the fact that he is encouraged to take along with him one or two priests during his pastoral visits to the parishes, but under no circumstances is he to omit this principal responsibility. Lastly, it is part of the office of bishop to ordain priests, and to organize his diocese according to the examples of Paul and Titus.

It is evident from this somewhat cursory overview of the functions of the bishop that he does in reality assume greater and heavier responsibilities than does a priest. He even has different powers: the power to delegate in the diocese (which is linked to the power to ordain), to judge, and to demand that his judgment be respected by the curates in the parishes and by the faithful. There is even a sort of collegiality among bishops regarding the supervision of the conduct of the bishops, for they will be the "colleagues and brothers of the other bishops" who will judge any cases of abuse that may arise in the office of a bishop (the abuse of simony in particular).[117]

5. LATER INFLUENCE OF THE FORMULARY OF PETRI

This ritual influenced all the rites of ordination of the Swedish Church, including the last one (of 1989). After a few minor modifica-

[116] *TSK* 25, 162–164 (ed. Dewailly, 310–312).
[117] *TSK* 25, 167 (ed. Dewailly, 314f.).

tions in 1686 and again in 1811, the revision of the ritual in 1868 returned to Petri's model.[118] We do not see evidence of its influence outside of Sweden: the other Scandinavian countries seem to have turned rather to the ritual of the Lutheran Church of Denmark.

6. CONCLUSION: STRUCTURING OF THE CHURCH AND THE SUBSTANCE OF ORDAINED MINISTRY

a. *Structure of the Church*

The process of election and ordination in Petri's work is rooted in a theology conscious of the status of each member, and it engages all the elements of the community: faithful and clergy. With election we have seen the vocation of the ministers mediated through the examination of the candidates and the prayer; the members of the community bear witness to the faith and moral life of each person being considered for the ministry, and everything is done by "the Spirit and wisdom" of God. It is clear that it is God who calls to the ministry, but it is the Church who calls for reckoning: God is Master of the harvest, and it is he who calls and sends forth.[*295, *309/*322] It is through the ministry of the men chosen by the entire community that God's plan of salvation for the world is to progress, for the Christian assembly will be better equipped to serve the Lord.[*295]

We see that the ministry is received as a gift from God; it is not simply an act of delegation, but an important reality for the local community, indeed an essential reality, for these ministers are going to preside over the direction (governance) of this community.[119] This is another reason why the Church must take upon herself the responsibility of seeking out good stewards, but above all, praying that God will send them to her.

Once the new ministers are elected, they are installed in their office by the imposition of hands and the prayer of the entire community. Although the community can elect the candidates, it cannot ordain them in their office without the ministry of the bishop. This seems obvious from the terms *Ordinarius* and *Ordinator*. Unfortunately, the liturgical expression of this reality is not always clear, for Petri has

---

[118] Cf. E. RODHE, *Svenskt gudstjänstliv . . .*, 457–472 for a comparison between the rituals of 1571, 1686, 1811, 1868, and 1894.
[119] *TSK* 22, 139 (ed. Dewailly, 298).

given us, in fact, only one rite of ordination. We must wait for a later liturgical revision for a more clearly articulated version.

The pneumatological reality is expressed through the election and the "title" of the ordination. The rejection of all absolute ordinations, which were so prevalent at the end of the Middle Ages, is remarkable indeed. Each minister has a title of ministry—he belongs to a particular local community, or he is ordained the bishop of a real diocese. Lastly, we should note that the ordination takes place in a Eucharistic context, and always at a time when the people can (and must, as their responsibility dictates) be present. The community is called together by God to confer an office upon one of its members and to receive him as a gift of God.

b. *Substance of the Pastoral and Episcopal Ministries*

According to the liturgies we have examined, we can affirm that the dominant image is pastoral. It would be difficult to say much more, if we were to take only those liturgies into consideration. However, we have seen that in the other chapters of his ordinance Petri was much more thorough in his description of the substance of the two ordained ministries. Among the responsibilities of the office of priest we find preaching, the administration of the sacraments, teaching, supervision and discipline in the parish, confession, moral encouragement, comforting of the sick, and burial of the dead.

In the case of the bishop we find the same duties, and several others: the supervision and encouragement of the priests, visits to the parishes and to the clergy who serve them, the organization of the diocese and the ordination of a sufficient number of ministers for its needs, judgment in spiritual matters and discipline within the diocese, and, lastly, vigilance as to the purity of the faith against all forms of magic, etc.

As these enumerations show, ministerial work is pastoral, and the principles of the governance of the Church have great importance for the duties of the bishops. There also exists a collegial sense among the bishops, inasmuch as each bishop has supplementary prerogatives in the ministry of supervision. However, on the parish level, the priests collaborate fully in carrying out the pastoral mission and the responsibilities of the *episkopē*.

E. OVERALL CONCLUSIONS

This survey of a few liturgies of ordination produced by the Lutheran Reformation allows us to draw a few conclusions as to the structure and the meaning of the process of ordination, the structuring of the Church and of the ordained ministries as this structuring was understood from then on.

1. ELEMENTS USUALLY INCLUDED IN EACH FORMULARY

a. *The Election*

The election is the responsibility of the people concerned, or of a group of delegates (there are always representatives of the ministers and of the Christian people). Next, the election is submitted to the civil authorities for ratification. We see that the entire process puts the ordained Christian, God, and the local Church into a dynamic relationship. The religious status of the laity is respected, and the ministers are seen as part of the community, a fact which also reveals the communal aspect of the local Church, in which all Christians are active and responsible for their received faith. Of course, over time the process of election evolved, according to the requirements of each situation, as we saw in the different geographical and political arenas.

b. *The Ordination or the Liturgical Act Whereby the Elect Is Instituted/Installed in His Office*

This act includes the imposition of hands and the prayer, and it is presided by a minister charged with exercising this function of ordination or installation. At least for the formulary of Luther, ordination can be interpreted as a confirmation or an attestation of God's choice (at work already in the calling or vocation). The formularies of Bugenhagen and Bucer lend themselves more easily to an interpretation which sees something taking place because of the imposition of hands and the prayer: in Bugenhagen, following Luther, the consecration of the creature through the Word and the prayer; in Bucer, the communication of the Holy Spirit and the entrusting of the person of the ordinand to the protection of the power of God so that he may be able to fulfill the charge of his ministry.[120]

---

[120] Cf. *258, *264, and the KO of Hamburg of 1529 (SEHLING V, 502f.) for Bugenhagen; *De ordinatione . . .*, MBSA 249, 7–13 and 259, 20–23; *Von der waren . . .*, MBDS 7, 124.17f.; and *Ordenung der Kirchenübung . . .* (Cassel) of 1539, MBDS 7,

c. *The Sending Forth, or the Mission, to a Concrete Ministry, Most Often in a Parish or in a Wider Territory Such as a Diocese That Includes Several Reformed Communities*

We should note that the concept of "title," the significance of which we have already discussed, has been restored to all its original importance in these rites: the presentation of the elect to the community, the conception of the "ordination as first installation" (the tradition of Württemberg), or, in the case of a new installation, the rite of ordination in each new parish; and, above all, the end of the Church practice of absolute ordinations. Even though this element in the structuring is always present, the fact that the ordinand does not exercise his charge immediately after his ordination or installation in the liturgical celebration reflects the practice current at the end of the Middle Ages according to which the new bishop does not preside at the Eucharist that follows his ordination.

2. ACTORS INVOLVED IN THE PROCESS

a. *The Community Concerned*

The community plays an important role by bearing witness to the faith and the Christian life of the elect, by being the vehicle of God's call to the service of the community, and by praying in order to discern the will of God in the entire process so that the elect might receive the Spirit, enabling him to carry out his ministry. It is difficult to determine whether Luther truly perceived the minister as a delegate of the community: his language on this subject is ambiguous— we find in him both the theory of delegation and the theory of divine institution.[121] At the very least we can allow that, depending on the category of the reception and the tradition, the idea that God gives ministers to the Church is always present. This is clear in the act of

---

313.8f., 21–27, 35–37. See the commentaries of W. P. STEPHENS, *The Holy Spirit* . . ., 193f. and R. W. QUERE, "The Spirit . . .," 327–330.

[121] He certainly seems to be stating that it is God who appoints for the Church such and such a member, as the need arises (WA 9, 343.19f. *[genera et ordines Ecclesiae significat]*); cf. H. LIEBERG, *Amt und Ordination* . . ., 101ff.; and this seems true not only for the maintenance of good order, but also because it is God who sends ministers to his Church: cf. *An den christlichen Adel* . . ., WA 6, 408 (= *LW* 44, 128–130). This is also the opinion of P. MANNS, *Amt und Eucharistie* . . ., 128 and A. GREINER, "L'ecclésiologie . . .," 166.

the election of the ministers by the local community (the vertical dimension of reception). This perception was made progressively clearer as we examined the other rites. On the horizontal plane of the organization of the Church, we have seen that Luther (especially) found ways to articulate the relationship between local communities (such as the right of visitation and the synod). Nevertheless, the theological thought is insufficient to allow us to go beyond a kind of congregationalism. We are lacking a complete exposition of the theological basis on many topics: the singleness of the ministry, the legitimate authority in the Church, the ministry as the link between local congregations, the distinction between the unity of a congregation (vertical aspect) and the communion or union between congregations (horizontal plane). So we see that there was always the threat of a break between the community concerned and the other communities, a break provoked also by non-theological factors such as the various political factors at play or the reluctance of Rome to intervene in this critical situation other than in an authoritarian fashion, demanding obedience (thus making an ecumenical council impossible).[122]

b. *The Newly Ordained*

Here we find ourselves in a context more in harmony with the early Church, in which one did not become a minister from personal inclination, but through a call of God mediated by the community. The elect receives his ministry as a special gift also from God (through the community). His ordination does not place him in a position above his community, but rather he is fully integrated into his congregation, at the same time that he is its servant, charged with watching over the purity of the proclamation of the pure Word of God, and with the building up of the priestly people.

c. *The Holy Spirit*

God is certainly at the very center of the act of ordination, which is conceived of as a divine act. We have seen that the rituals that follow

---

[122] Cf. the convincing and highly nuanced observations on the non-theological factors in W. KASPER, "La 'Confessio Augustana' comme confession catholique et protestante," *Documentation catholique* 78 [8] no. 1784 (1980) 382. On the problem of the ministry of unity, read G. SIEGWALT, "Point de vue . . .," 129–135; and R. VOELTZEL, "Les ministères de direction dans les églises de la Réforme au XVIᵉ siècle," *Revue de Droit canonique* 23, 1–4 (1973) 127–145.

Luther's emphasize more and more the role of the Spirit (in particular, those of Bucer and Petri), and we can affirm that the role of the Spirit is more and more of primary importance. The inclusion of the liturgical action between two hymns to the Holy Spirit influences the climate of celebration in the work of all the Reformers we have studied. With the exception of the ritual of Bugenhagen, the Spirit is called upon to enable the elect to fulfill the ministry that is entrusted to him (cf. Tables II.3 and II.4, vol. IV).

d. *The Heads of the Neighboring Communities*

In the case of the installation of a bishop, the heads of the other Reformed communities play a role in conformity with the ancient canons. It is not possible to determine exactly the meaning of their participation. Are they there to ensure the legality of the act, or are they active participants in the "reception-tradition" that we have seen in the early Church? It would appear more likely that the first is the case. Their presence seems to have been interpreted as verification that the installation or ordination was carried out in due order. This would deprive their presence of its theological and ecclesiological content. It also affects the horizontal dimension of the reception-tradition, for the presence of the leaders of the neighboring Churches no longer is expressive of their intent to guarantee the manifestation of the true apostolic faith, and to welcome the newly ordained or newly installed as their colleague in shared responsibility for the faith and the discipline of the gospel. Their presence seems to have had more to do with the need to witness the installation itself. We may, indeed, have to concede some nuances in this interpretation in the case of the rite of Petri in Sweden, where the episcopacy seems to have more importance in the structure of the Church, and to be closer in some ways to the medieval episcopacy.

3. SUBSTANCE OF THE ORDAINED MINISTRY

With the priesthood of all the baptized having been restored to its original importance, ordained ministry is seen rather as a service of building up the body of the Church; it is described in pastoral terms: feeding and watching over the flock. The loving-kindness of God, Master of the harvest, is emphasized: the ministry finds in it its beginning and its end as a vehicle that God has chosen in order to keep alive the gift of the gospel in the midst of his people. Christ, the sole shepherd of the flock, and his minister carry on the plan of God, which is the free offering of the gift of salvation acquired through Christ's sacrifice. The category of the "common priesthood" of all the baptized[123] makes this gift available to all. The minister, ordained and installed publicly in the service of a concrete community, in a particular way represents Christ: the mouth of each minister is the mouth of Christ,[124] and when the people listen to the minister, they listen to God.[125] We know that Luther even taught that the administration of Holy Communion is the domain of the public ministry, as we read in the counsel given to J. Sutel in 1531.[126] Presiding at the sacraments is part of the function of feeding the flock, along with preaching the Word of God and celebrating the sacraments of salvation.

4. STRUCTURE OF THE ORDAINED MINISTRY

The structure of the ordained ministry is monolithic. The one ministry (of the Word and the sacraments) is divided into two functions: 1) the pastoral supervision of a community, which includes the preaching of the gospel and the administration of the sacraments (= the ministry of the Word); and 2) the supervision of several com-

---

[123] H. LIEBERG, *Amt und Ordination . . .*, 65–67. W. Brunotte identifies four points in Luther's teaching, which is sometimes ambiguous, on the "common priesthood": 1) Every Christian has the same spiritual dignity; 2) Every Christian is a collaborator and brother or sister of Christ, and therefore a priest who can approach God and his Word without fear; 3) Every Christian is a priest who can offer his or her personal sacrifice to God directly, without mediation; 4) Every Christian must, in accordance with the will of God, hear the gospel where and whenever he or she can: W. BRUNOTTE, *Das geistliche Amt . . .*, 138–140, 142, 153. Lieberg has criticized this position for its tendency to make too sharp a distinction between the office of pastor and the common priesthood.

[124] *Predigt am Sonntag Quasimodogeniti im Hause (Bruchstück) (12. April)*, 1534, no. 30, WA 37, 381.14.

[125] *Predigt am Sonntag Quasimodogeniti in Dessan gehalten (4. April)* [1540], no. 26, WA 49, 140.5–10.

[126] Luther advised him to wait for his ordination before celebrating Mass: ". . . *si vero serium fuerit, tum publice coram altari a reliquis ministris cum oratione et impositione manuum testimonium accipies et autoritatem coenae tractandae," Luther an Ioh. Sutel in Göttingen,* [Wittenberg] 1. März 1531, no. 1787, WA Br 6, 44.18–20. Cf. A. C. PIEPKORN, "The Sacred Ministry . . .," 105f., who believes he sees in CA 24, 34 (German version) (= BC 60) the implication that the sacrament of the altar will be celebrated by an ordained minister.

munities regarding the purity of the preaching, the teaching of doctrine, and the discipline of the ministers in their communities. According to the rites of installation/ordination, the two ministries are almost identical.

5. THE MEANING OF ORDINATION

Ordination is seen as a rite of the Church in which a person is called (elected) *by* the community; he is recommended *to* the community by those whose task it is to ordain; and he is confirmed in his function by *the imposition of hands and prayer.* All is accomplished under the guidance of God, so that the authority to preach and administer the sacraments may remain in good order *(auctoritatem praedicandi verbum et dandi sacramenta . . . ut maneat ordo).*[127] The setting of every ordination, as we have seen, is the celebration of Holy Communion, which takes place on Sunday, the day of the assembly of the Church, the day on which the Church is constituted for the honor of the holy name of God. One could say that ordination is conceived of as a process at once confessional, liturgical, and juridical. It is confessional, because ordination professes the faith of the community concerned in the continuity of the loving-kindness of God, who gives his Church workers for the harvest. It is liturgical, because it is the prayer of the whole congregation, and because its salient feature is that very ancient act of the imposition of hands seen as a blessing, a confirmation by God. And, lastly, it is juridical, because through his ordination the elect is installed in his function as minister of the Word and servant of the common priesthood of this community.

---

[127] *Predigt am 21. Sonntag . . .*, no. 55, WA 15, 721.3–5 and 13.

Chapter 2

Formularies Inspired by the Calvinist Reformation

In this chapter we will be discussing four sixteenth-century formularies of ordination from the Reformation that will have a broad influence down to our day on other ordination texts in the Churches that sprang from this tradition. These are: a) the first text which gives an ordination ceremony, the *Prädicantenordnung* of Zurich (1532);[*902–*912] b) the liturgy established by Jan Łaski for the Dutch refugees in London (1550) and in Frankfurt (1554);[*913–*938] c) "the form and the order for the election of ministers" drawn up by John Knox and included in the *Buke of Discipline* (1560);[*939–*959] and d) the formulary used for the Puritans who were exiled in Middleburgh (1586/1602).[*966–*975]

A. THE *ZÜRICHTER PRÄDICANTENORDNUNG*—1532

This text is interesting, for it presents, in the form of a liturgy of ordination, an early reaction on the part of the Reformed writers to the complexity of the ceremonies and rituals of ordination of the late Middle Ages. Its author is unknown, but it is one of the first rituals of ordination coming out of the Reformation. The complete title is *Von der Waal, Sendung und Handuflegen der Predicanten*.[1]

---

[1] Text published in RICHTER II, 169f.; and H. A. DANIEL (ed.), *Codex liturgicus ecclesiae universae in epitomen redactus*. T. 3, *Ecclesiae Reformatae atque Anglicanae* (Leipzig: T. O. Weigel, 1851) 231–234. This was the first Ordinance of the Reformed Church of Zurich (Zwinglian confession) that was authorized by the Synod, on October 22, 1532. For a discussion of this Ordinance see P. DE CLERCK, "L'ordination des pasteurs selon quelques liturgies de consécration réformées," in

1. ANALYSIS OF THE TEXT

This document describes the procedure followed by the Reformed Church of Zurich for the selection, examination, presentation, and ordination of a new preacher. In the preface[902] the Ordinance gives the reasons for the new redaction: the importance of and the necessity for the ministry in the Church, the abuses that must be rectified by this new rite, and the suppression of episcopal consecration and of the anointing and the mention of character. The imposition of hands, however, was retained, according to the command of the Lord and the practice of the apostles. Next, the practices that are found in Scripture are presented, according to the teaching of Paul (his Letters to Timothy, Titus, and the Romans).

a. *Examination*[903-907]

When the need for a new minister arises, the Dean announces to all the way in which it is suggested that a preacher be provided for a parish that lacks one. The process is not described in much detail. We are still at the very beginning of the elaboration of a process that will lead to the reform of Church ministry.

According to the text[904] a day is fixed for the examination. It will most probably take place in private, in the presence of two preachers of the Word, two councilors, and two readers of Holy Scripture. The examiners must be impartial, guided by care for the honor of God and the good of the Church. The material for the examination is described in detail: the *loci communes religionis,* the knowledge of the two Testaments, and the ability to explain the content of Scripture to the people.[907] Moreover, the personal conduct of the future ordained ministers must be carefully scrutinized.

b. *Presentation and Election*[908]

When the examination is completed, and a favorable opinion has been registered on the part of the civil authorities, if a particular person is held to be a possible candidate for the ministry, he is then presented and elected as a new preacher. In the presence of the Dean, the pastor of the neighboring parish, and most likely the faithful of the vacant parish (for Sunday worship will immediately follow), one of the councilors *(Radt)* or a representative of the civil authorities

---

Mélanges liturgiques offerts au R. P. Dom Bernard Botte (Louvain: Abbaye du Mont César, 1972) 79–81.

(Vogt) presents the man who is worthy of the call and declares that the election is now open. The election consists in asking the parishioners if they have any objections to the candidate. If there are no objections, the Dean preaches a sermon on the meaning of the ministry and on the attitude and the conduct of the Church towards her new pastor.

c. *Ordination*[*909–*912]

The ceremony of ordination is quite simple. After a sermon, the Dean addresses the elect with a short exhortation taken from Acts 20:28 and 1 Timothy 4:12; he then imposes hands on him while pronouncing a short epiclesis. Next he exhorts the faithful to pray for the grace their new pastor will need, and lastly a prayer is said (no text given); the pastor is then recommended to the faithful by the civil authority. Lastly, the document makes mention of the oath that the new pastor must swear at the next meeting of the Synod, if that has not already been done.

In this way a very simple office for installing a new pastor in his ministry ends. Do we have here a radical reaction against the abuses of the medieval Church which ordained men who lacked the necessary qualities for the service of the gospel and the flock of the Lord? This is the conclusion drawn by Paul De Clerck.[2]

2. FORMULA OR PRAYER OF ORDINATION

We present next the text of the short exhortation containing the epiclesis of ordination,[*910] which is recited by the Dean during the imposition of hands:

"Dear brother, we recommend to your care this loyal community with the words of Paul: Keep watch . . . over all the flock, of which the Holy Spirit has made you overseer (*Wächter* = episcopus) and shepherd to shepherd his people that he obtained with the blood of his own Son (. . . *das er mit sinem eignen Blut an sich erkoufft hat . . .)* [Acts 20:28]. Be for them a model through your word, your conduct, your charity, spirit, faith and purity [1 Tim 4:12]; **and may God grant you his Holy Spirit, so that you, as a faithful servant serves his master, may be able to serve, in the name of God.**"[3]

---

[2] P. DE CLERCK, "L'ordination . . .," 81.
[3] H. A. DANIEL (ed.), *Codex liturgicus . . .*, t. 3, 234.

P. De Clerck rightly notes that the first reference to Acts 20:28 is incorrect: it says that the Holy Spirit has acquired the Church through his blood, whereas the biblical text says this of Christ. Apart from this error, the first passage was a good choice to express the meaning of the ordained ministry, while the second is a moral exhortation.[4]

a. *Biblical Images Employed*

The principal image found in the epiclesis is that of the good and faithful steward (cf. Lk 12:14ff. and Lk 17:7ff.): he knows how to administer the affairs of his master, and he has only done his duty. We could compare this image to that of the shepherd and to the exhortation, both of which speak not only of the faithfulness of the servant, but also of his vigilance in his ministerial duties.

b. *Qualities Requested for the Ordinand*

This prayer is quite poor in content. The faithful pray only that the elect may receive the gift of "faithfulness" in order to accomplish what was described in the exhortation.

c. *Gifts Received by the Ordinand*

The epiclesis speaks only in very general terms of the gift of the Holy Spirit. This formula is not a consecration, and it does not contain any specific features.

3. CONCLUSION: STRUCTURING OF THE CHURCH AND THE SUBSTANCE OF ORDAINED MINISTRY

a. *Structure of the Church*

It is very difficult to see in this liturgical text a true model of the Reformed Church, due to the scantiness of the formulary itself. However, we can mention the following points without going into them in greater depth:

—There is a concern to ensure that the men chosen to be ministers possess the qualities necessary for proper vigilance in regard to the doctrine of the Church and for the preaching of the Word of God, so that in these men the community may find a model of Christian life;
—Despite the emphasis on the election and the examination of the elect, the congregation reserves only the right to voice objections;

[4]P. DE CLERCK, "L'ordination . . .," 81.

—There is a close connection between the Church and the civil authorities, with the latter participating several times in the process of admission to the ordained ministry;

—In the structure of the Church of Zurich, ordained ministry is important and necessary, as is shown by the preface and the choice of Sunday as the day of ordination, a day on which the entire community assembles;

—The close bond between the ordained ministry and the Church community is explicit, since the curate of the neighboring parish is to be present at the ordination, which is a matter that concerns not just the vacant parish, but the whole Church;

—At this stage in the development of the Reformed Church, at least in Zurich, there is no mention either of elders or of deacons. On the other hand, we find the Dean, the pastors, councilors (probably representatives of the civil authorities), and lectors. We do not know, either, whether the curate of the neighboring parish or other ministers of the Word who are present impose hands or not;

—Lastly, there is a brief mention of the existence of a Synod that is to receive the oath of fidelity from the new pastor; this is an institution that bespeaks the existence of a collegial structure.

b. *Substance of the Pastoral Ministry*

We find only a few generalities concerning the functions of the pastoral ministry in this formulary. The epiclesis asks the Holy Spirit to give the new minister the gift of faithfulness. However, with the exhortation, the formula adds the pastoral functions of feeding the flock (with preaching) and of supervising (the doctrine and the discipline of the Church); lastly, the minister is to serve as a model of Christian living for his people. Nothing is said about the administration of the sacraments, which does not mean that this function was not part of the ministry of the pastor in the Church of Zurich.

B. THE *FORMA AC RATIO* (1550)—JAN ŁASKI

With time, the thinking of the Reformers matured, and the rituals of the institution of ministers evolved. This was the case with the ritual elaborated by the Polish reformer Jan Łaski (1499–1560). Ordained a priest in 1521, he was influenced by the ideas of some of the great thinkers and reformers such as Erasmus, Bucer, Zwingli, and Melanchthon. His early tendency was towards a peaceful and syncretist Reform, which was first evident in Emden (1540–1549), and then in the foreign communities of London (1550–1553), then in Germany, and lastly in Poland from 1556 on.

1. DESCRIPTION OF THE RITE

The first part of the text describes the election/ordination of the elders (pastors or regents, with a superintendent at their head), and of the deacons. Since the vocabulary is still vague, Jan Łaski recognizes other scriptural names: the elders (*seniores*), the bishop (*episcopus*), the pastor (*pastor*), and the teacher (*doctor*). In a note on the subject of the ministry of the elder in the thought of Łaski, J.-J. von Allmen says that his ordinances acknowledge:

". . . the permanent character of the ministry of the elder, since they [the ordinances of 1550 and 1554] are the only ones to provide an ordination for the elders comparable to that of the pastors (whereas deacons are not ordained by the imposition of hands of the entire presbyterium, but by a single minister—in London—or they are not ordained at all because they change every year—in Frankfurt). We should note, however, that the discipline in London makes no theological distinction between the elders who administer the means of grace (the pastors) and those who see to discipline (the elders), between those whom later Presbyterianism calls 'teaching elders' and 'ruling elders.' This is doubtless the reason why the latter are consecrated as well as the former."[5]

The ritual divides the process into three parts: the election, the examination, and the ordination. The context is the usual worship service of Sunday, which is the Eucharist celebrated in the morning, and then the evening worship.[6]

a. *Election*[*913–*917 and *919–*923]

The election begins with the announcement that the community has need of a minister or ministers, and a day is set for the people to assemble to make the selection.[*913] The meeting consists of two parts, always in a context of prayer and preaching.

[5] J.-J. von ALLMEN, *Le saint ministère selon la conviction et la volonté des Réformés du XVIe siècle* (Neuchâtel: Delachaux et Niestlé, 1968) 184, n. 91.
[6] For a description of the ordination, see P. DE CLERCK, "L'ordination . . .," 82–85.

The first meeting takes place at nine o'clock, and consists of a psalm,[914] a sermon,[915, 917] an exhortation to the community,[919.1] a prayer,[919.2] and the celebration of worship.[920]

The second meeting is on the same day at two o'clock in the afternoon, and consists of a sermon,[921-922] other religious exercises accompanied by fasting and prayers,[922] and a commentary on the procedure of presenting the names of suitable persons, a procedure which will take place the following week.[922]

The content of the two sermons is quite revelatory of Łaski's conception of the ordained ministry. The first sermon was the longer one, delivered during the morning worship service. The following themes are suggested: 1) the importance of the election of a minister and the importance of prayer (communal as well as private) for the entire process, because the community receives the gift of its ministers through the goodness of God and not through any act of merely human wisdom; 2) the commentary on the substance of the ministry, that is, its institution by God for the building up of the Church,[915.1] its functions (*teaching* the pure doctrine of the Word, *administering* the sacraments and explaining their purpose and efficacy, *watching over* the community, *confounding* the enemy through the authority of the Word, *fulfilling* the tasks of their ministry as true servants of the community),[915.2] and the qualities required of the new minister (cf. 1 and 2 Tim, Titus);[915.3] and, lastly, 3) the attitude of the community[915.4] towards its ministers: welcoming them as they would Christ himself, and obeying them as ambassadors of the Lord.[7] As for the ministry of the superintendent, it is stated that his office was instituted by God, so that he might strengthen his brethren in the faith, and also ensure that all is done as it should be.[917.1] The functions of this office are: *watching* carefully over all the ministers of the Church, *convoking the entire ministerial body* to consider together the needs of the whole as well as to maintain unanimity among all, *using the services of other ministers* not only for the governance of the Church, but also to defend her against all adversaries, and *seeing to the observance of Church discipline* by all the members of the Church.[917.2] The qualities required of the elect are the same as in the case of the other ministers.[917.3] Lastly, the attitude of the entire community toward the superinten-

---

[7] See P. DE CLERCK, "L'ordination . . .," 82.

dent is considered (including the attitude of the other ministers): nothing should be done without his authority (regarding the governance of the community); his honor and authority in the Church must be upheld, elsewhere and everywhere; and, since the superintendent has responsibility for several Churches of foreigners, nothing can be enacted against him without the input of the ministers of the other Churches."[917.4]

The second sermon takes up the themes that there had not been time to discuss during the morning service. Also, the preacher exhorts the faithful to observe the fast, and to pray again that God may help the community in its choice."[921]

b. *The Assessment of the Results, and the Examination*

We see that the entire community has been actively involved in the process, for the ritual of Jan Łaski, unlike those of other Reformers, requires that each one reflect on the selection of the individual who may exercise the ministry among them, and hand in the names in writing *(in scripto)* to the ministers of the community during the following week *(tota . . . hebdomade illa Ecclesiae totius suffragia per Ministros ac Seniores privatim colliguntur")*."[922] At the end of eight days the elect are called to the meeting of the elders and the deans, if the ministers have not voiced any objections. During this meeting all the ministers present search their hearts.

But this is not the end of the involvement of the faithful, for, after the names of the elect have been announced at the end of the preaching on the following Sunday, the community is exhorted to reflect deeply during the coming week, in order to decide that these are the candidates that it truly wants for its new ministers."[923] Next, the ordination is set for the following Sunday.

One last remark concerning the election of the superintendent: since he has responsibility for all the Churches of foreigners, he also needs the consent of all of them to his election, as he will be exercising his ministry among them all. Once this has been obtained, public fasting and prayers are ordered in all the Churches, the vote is taken, and if no one candidate should have more votes than any other after all the assemblies have voted, then the ministers, elders, and deacons of all the Churches decide which one of the elect has the greatest aptitude for the office."[923.2]

This process is complex, but it allows each member of the community to play a role in the discernment of the will of God.

c. *Ordination*

The ordination itself *(inauguratio)* takes place during the normal Sunday worship.[8] However, no mention is made of the readings prescribed for the ordination or for the worship that follows. The ordination takes place as follows: after the sermon (both the morning and the evening sermons), the elect are presented by name before the community, and the other ministers and the elders of the community are asked if those who are about to be ordained have received the approval of the king."[924] An admonition is addressed to the elect,"[925] followed by the interrogation of the ordinands (four questions)."[926-"929] Next come the call to prayer"[930] and a communal prayer (to Christ),"[931-"932] then the Lord's Prayer followed by the imposition of hands by all the ministers and the elders"[933] while the presiding minister recites a brief prayer."[934] Then an admonition is addressed a) to the community (on its duties towards its minister),"[935] and b) to the ordinands (on their responsibilities)."[936-"938] Then the community sings a hymn, and the service ends with the missioning and the blessing. The ritual notes that for the inauguration of the superintendent all is done as prescribed, except that the new superintendent "will be confirmed by all, in all the Churches of the foreigners, as convenient" (". . . *Superintendens vero in omnibus Peregrinorum Ecclesiis per intervalla inauguratur, pro eo ac tempora ipsa id omnium commodissime permittunt"*).

Let us pause a moment over the four questions that are put to the elect. They tell us much about the commitment that the ordinands are making. First, the elect are asked if they acknowledge that it is the Spirit who is impelling them to accept the ministry for the glory of God alone and the growth of the Kingdom of Christ. The second question has to do with the grounding of the Church in Scripture, which contains all that is necessary for salvation, and with the fact that the head of the Church is Christ. Thirdly, the elect are asked if they will remain attached to Christ, the foundation of the Church, if

[8] For the order of worship and the celebration of Communion, see I. PAHL (ed.), *Coena . . .*, 433–460.

they will build the Church on Christ alone, if they will apply her discipline to themselves as well as to others. Lastly, they are asked if they promise to live a worthy life, if they will accept fraternal correction, and even if they will accept to lose their office if their behavior should so warrant.

Right after the admonition to the faithful we find the prayer pronounced by the ordaining minister. This is a prayer addressed to Christ on behalf of the elect. Normally the ordination prayers are addressed to God, but even the tradition of the early Church knows a few exceptions to this usage.[9]

2. PRAYER OF ORDINATION

We have seen that at this point in the structure of the ritual there is a prayer for the elect (ministers of the Word and superintendent) which ends with the Lord's Prayer followed by the imposition of hands and a prayer which, as we shall see, appears to be a prolongation of the epiclesis of the prayer over the elect. For this reason we shall consider all three elements as one ritual unit. Here is the text of the prayer of ordination:

"Lord God, Jesus Christ, Son of the living God,[10] you who have promised to be ever present to your Church until the end of time[11] in order to guide and govern it by your Holy Spirit, you so love your Church that you have not only poured out your innocent blood for it once and for all *[pro ea semel]*, but also, in your great favor you wish to raise up continually witnesses and teachers within your Church for the renewal and perfecting of the saints in your mystical body (which we are) *[sed huius quoque tanti tui beneficii testes ac Doctores in*

---

[9] Regarding the prayers addressed to Christ, cf. the comments of P.-M. GY, "Ancient Ordination Prayers," *Studia Liturgica* 13, 2–4 (1979) 82 (= *Ordination Rites*. Papers Read at the 1979 Congress of *Societas Liturgica,* eds. W. Vos & G. Wainwright [Rotterdam: Liturgical Ecumenical Center Trust, 1980]): "Sometimes, it (the prayer) is addressed to Christ himself; such is the case for the Hispanic prayer for a priest and, in the Barberini euchologion, certainly for the second prayer for a bishop, and probably, too, for the second prayer for a deacon. This goes along with the Byzantine tendency to address to Christ those prayers which are said in a low voice."

[10] Cf. Mt 16:16.

[11] Cf. Mt 28:20b.

illa perpetuo extare velis ad instaurationem sanctorum et consummationem absolvendam in mystico tuo (quod nos sumus) corpore].[12] And now we beseech you, O Lord, King, Teacher and our eternal High Priest *[Pontifex noster aeterne!]*, to fill with your Holy Spirit these men, our brethren (if several are elected to the ministry), elected in your holy name by us for the ministry of the Word so that the ministry of your divine Word and the salutary and efficacious testimony of your great kindnesses be maintained and preserved among us *[verbi tui divini ministerium beneficiorumque tuorum salutare atque efficax testimonium inter nos retineatur et conservetur].* O Lord, grant them the prudence necessary for breaking open [literally, "cutting open"] your Word *[prudentiam recte secandi verbum tuum].* Permit them to faithfully and attentively keep away from our community the wiles and tyranny of the Devil and the Antichrist, and to tear out and drive away absolutely everything that could still remain in us *[eiusque reliquias omnes, si quae adhunc inter nos haerent, prorsus extirpent ac propellant].* Give them, Lord, such a mouth and such wisdom that they may be able through the authority of your Word to silence all your enemies and drive away the wolves from your flock[13] in such a way that, thanks to their ministry, your people, instructed in true knowledge of you, may learn to praise you, to give you thanks and, in holy obedience to your will, to progress in the extension of your kingdom and in the eternal glory of your heavenly Father whom we humbly invoke in your Name (as you have taught us), saying: Our Father . . ."*931–*932

And during the imposition of hands, the ordinant prays thus:

"May God, our heavenly Father, who has called you to the ministry of his Word in this his Church, illumine *[illuminet]* you through his Holy Spirit, strengthen *[corroboret]* you with his powerful hand and guide and govern you *[regat et gubernet]* in your ministry, so that you may exercise it faithfully and fruitfully, for the increase of the kingdom of his only Son in his Church, through the preaching of his Gospel, through his same only Son Jesus Christ, our Lord and Redeemer. Amen."*934

---

[12] Cf. Eph 4:11 and 1 Cor 12:28.
[13] Cf. Titus 1:11, Lk 22:67-71, and 1 Tim 3:7.

a. *Biblical Images Employed*

In the prayer that precedes the imposition of hands, only one image stands out: that of Christ remaining with his Church and acting in her behalf, through the ministry of the pastors of the Church. The proximity of echoes of Luke 22:67-71 (Jesus before the Sanhedrin), Titus 1:11 (Titus must shut the mouth of the false teachers), and 1 Timothy 3:7 places the ministry of the newly ordained in the context of the Word of Jesus and his efficacious and continuous presence in the Church. Here we see an appropriate emphasis placed on the teaching function of the mission of Christ as the supreme Teacher, for it is through the power of his Word, his authority, and his wisdom that the enemies of the holy gospel are routed and vanquished.

b. *Qualities Requested for the Ordinand*

The qualities asked for are seen in the light of the function of teaching, which is emphasized in this prayer and this ritual. The prayer also asks for wisdom for him and "a mouth and the wisdom" to fulfill his primary ministerial charge of preaching the gospel, and, along with his preaching, the teaching of correct doctrine (cf. the references to Eph 4:11 and 1 Cor 12:28). This is the reason why the prayer asks that he be illumined by the Spirit, and receive the support and guidance of God.

c. *Gifts Received by the Ordinand*

Very simply, the gift received is that of the Holy Spirit (". . . we pray you humbly to fill these men with your Holy Spirit . . ."). The purpose of the gift is to preserve faithfully the service of the Word in the world, and to further the growth in the world of the Kingdom of God through the proclamation of the gospel.

3. LATER INFLUENCE OF THE FORMULARY OF JAN ŁASKI

We find Łaski's text in the Ordinances of M. Micron (1554)[14] and, in 1556, it was translated into French and published.[15] But this was not the full extent of its influence, for we see some degree of dependency on his ritual in the fourth edition of the rites of the election and ordi-

---

[14] Cf. SEHLING VII, 587f.

[15] French title: *La forme & maniere de tout le Ministere Ecclesiastique, obserué en l'Eglise des Estrangers, instituée a Londres en Angleterre, par le Roy Edouard VI de ce nom, Prince tres debonnaire du dict pays, lan 1550* (Emden: Giles Ctematius, 1556).

nation of ministers of the Puritans in Middleburgh (1602), and again
in the office composed by John Knox for the ordination of superintendents found in the *Book of Common Order* (1560). Through Knox's
work its influence spread into certain Presbyterian formulas right up
to the beginning of the 20th century.[16] This influence can be seen in
the structure of the office, the description of the office and the functions of the ministry, the examination of the elect, the prayer of ordination, and the prayer recited during the imposition of hands.[17]

4. CONCLUSION: STRUCTURING OF THE CHURCH
AND THE SUBSTANCE OF ORDAINED MINISTRY

a. *Structure of the Church*

In the formulary for the election and ordination of ministers in the
Church of the Dutch refugees in London, each person has his duty
and his responsibility in the process. At the beginning of the formulary we read that the Church is organized according to the model of
1 Corinthians 12:28. Two categories of ministers exist: the elders, who
are divided into those who "see to the Word and the teaching"
(bishops, pastors, and teachers or doctors) and those who govern (the
elders proper), and the deacons who see to the needs of the poor. The
Church has the right to choose her ministers.[18] It is precisely in the
process of the election of ministers that we perceive the organization
of the Church in the work of Jan Łaski. Each member has his role.
The superintendent supervises the process by convoking the assembly and seeing that the proper procedure is followed, the elders being
responsible only for the selection and examination of the elect. The
faithful put forth the names of persons whom they think possess the

---

[16] Cf. P. F. BRADSHAW, *The Anglican Ordinal . . .*, 51–56. For the precise influence on each office mentioned, see the technical notes at the end of each liturgy in
the fourth volume of the present work.

[17] This last and the prayer of ordination are very close to those of Bucer; cf.
*289–*291.

[18] Cf. H. A. DANIEL (ed.), *Codex liturgicus . . .*, t. 3, 262. On the subject of the
structure of the ministries, we should note that one of the elders is called to serve
as superintendent in the Dutch Church in London, but more so on the level of the
parish than on a regional level: cf. J.-J. von ALLMEN, *Le saint ministère . . .*, 221,
n. 48. Here we see a vision different from that of Bucer, who influenced Łaski:
compare M. BUCER, *Der Kürtzer . . .*, MBDS 6/3, 252–254.

qualities necessary for the office, and they also have the right to reject any of those proposed if they have good reason. The elect themselves are to accept this office with the awareness that they are subject to the judgment of God in the exercise of their ministry. And, lastly, the Holy Spirit inspires the hearts of all the members of the assembly and guides the entire process.[914] The whole community observes the ancient tradition of fasting and praying with sincerity during the entire process.

We see that responsibility for the choice of the new ministers is widely shared, including the preparation of the hearts and minds of all the faithful. The same is true of the duties of each member to the other. The admonition addressed to the faithful[915.4] speaks of the attitude of the community towards its ministers: all members of the community owe them obedience in their legitimate ministry, as ambassadors of the Lord, even as they would obey the Lord himself, for the ministers speak for the Lord; and, as for the ministers,[936] they must conduct themselves as would Christ, providing a model for their flock. This ritual links the election/ordination with the service of Holy Communion, a fact of capital importance for a clear understanding of the way in which the role of the new ministers[19] was understood in relation to the building up of the Church.[931]

b. *Substance of the Pastoral Ministry*

Several sections of the formulary treat of the substance of pastoral ministry. In particular, in the admonitions addressed both to the community and to the elect, we learn that ordained ministry is considered a gift of God for his Church,[914] and that the minister's pastoral tasks are: announcing the Word, administering the sacraments, and governing the community.[915.2.3, 936, 937] In the prayer of ordination attention is drawn to the purpose of the ministry: defending the gospel against the forces of deceit and false doctrine, and extending the Kingdom of Christ. The pastor is seen, therefore, as the first servant of the Word and the teacher of the correct and true Christian doctrine.[929] Even though Łaski does not make a clear distinction between the ministry of the superintendent and that of the minister, it is clear that the substance of the former is as pastoral as that of the ministers

---

[19] P. DE CLERCK, "L'ordination . . .," 86; and J.-J. von ALLMEN, *Le saint ministère . . .*, 136, n. 83.

of the local communities. He did, however, clearly articulate the principal responsibility of the superintendent particularly during electoral proceedings, for each community has the responsibility to pray, to fast, and to elect the superintendent and to support and advise him, and the other ministers are to do nothing without first consulting him. The Church will be built up through the various charisms received and according to the different responsibilities of each member. Everything that is done should respect good order and the freedom of each Christian. We might use Jan Łaski's own words, alluding to Ephesians 4:11f., to describe the ministers—the pastors in his Church are "charged with teaching . . . to build up the body of Christ."[20]

C. THE *BUKE OF DISCIPLINE* (1560)—JOHN KNOX

A third formulary of election and ordination, composed by John Knox (born in 1505 or 1513, died in 1572) for the Church of Scotland, is found in the first "Book of Discipline." This book is a revision of another work (the *Genevan Service Book*) written largely by Knox when he was in exile in Geneva between 1555 and 1559.[21] In the *Genevan Service Book* a "method of election" of ministers was prescribed, but no liturgical text was provided. When Knox returned home in 1559, he drew up a rite for the election of the superintendent whose function seems to have been considered a temporary expedient to help in organizing the Presbyterian system.[22] This rite served as a model for the ordination of other ministers, and it was used and published for the first time in 1560 in the first *Buke of Discipline*, a work which subsequently became the "guide book" for all ministers, the *Book of Common Order* of 1562.[23] The primary influence for the

[20] Cf. *915.
[21] Cf. W. D. MAXWELL, *The History of Worship in the Church of Scotland* (London: Oxford University Press, 1955) 43–87; and for the text of the *Genevan Service Book*, id., *John Knox's Genevan Service Book. The Liturgical Portions of the Genevan Service Book, Used by John Knox while a Minister of the English Congregation of Marian Exiles at Geneva, 1556–1559* (London: Faith Press, 1965) 165–169.
[22] J. L. AINSLIE, *The Doctrines of Ministerial Order in the Reformed Churches of the Sixteenth and Seventeenth Centuries* (Edinburgh: T & T Clark, 1940) 105–119.
[23] Cf. W. D. MAXWELL, *The History . . .*, 47ff. The text of the election of a superintendent in the *Buke of Discipline* is found in D. LAING (ed.), *The Works of John Knox* (N.Y.: AMS Press, Inc., 1966) 144–151.

structure and the contents of this formulary was that of Jan Łaski. Knox had met him when Łaski was the pastor of the English refugees in Frankfurt.

1. DESCRIPTION OF THE RITE

The first thing we notice is that the word "ordination" does not appear in Knox's formulary. He prefers to speak of election and of "benediction," instead of ordination.[*958] Next, the formulary is divided into two parts: a first part gives directions for the election of the ministers (pastors, elders, deacons), [*939–*941] and a second part gives the form and order for the election of the superintendent, a form that can serve in the election of all the other ministers.[*942–*959] Once the ministers have been chosen, the examination takes place, then the commitment of the faithful, the invitation to prayer, the prayer for the gift of the Holy Spirit, the Lord's Prayer, the fraternal handshake and the blessing, the admonition to the new minister, and the singing of Psalm 23.

a. *Election*[*941, *942]

There are, in fact, two texts treating of the election: the first deals with the election of the ministers, i.e., the pastors, and uses the text previously composed in the *Genevan Service Book*.[24] It is preceded by a description of the qualities required of the ministers in view of their responsibilities. The other, composed in 1560, on the election of the superintendent,[*942] represents an abridged version of the first.

The first text resembles that of Jan Łaski, but it is less specific and less detailed. The elements in the process of election are: the announcement of the need for new ministers, the gathering of the congregation by the ministers and the elders to ask the faithful for the names of those who might be able to meet the requirements, and the choice of two or three among the names proposed to be examined by the ministers and the elders (the examination bears on their doctrine and their knowledge of Scripture, on their aptitude for preaching [they must preach a sermon in private], and on their conduct and lack of any bad reputation). Lastly, after the examination, the ministers and the elders inform the congregation of the names of those

[24] See the text of the election of ministers in W. D. MAXWELL, *John Knox's . . .*, 165–168.

whom they consider the best choices for the ministry, and all engage in discussion of the matter over a period of a week, during which everyone fasts and prays to God that the election may be pleasing to him and of benefit to his Church; during this time also each member has the opportunity to find out about the life and conduct of the candidates. If any obstacle is found pertaining to any candidate, his name is removed from the list and another is proposed to take his place (no procedure for this is provided), but if there are no objections, then all proceed to the election (that is, the ordination).

In the second text,[942] we find an "official transcript" of the election of John Spottiswood as superintendent of the Churches of Lothian. It consists of basically the same elements as the one described above: a sermon on the necessity for ministers and superintendents, the crimes and vices that disqualify a person in office, the virtues required of the ministers, and the question of whether persons called to such an office have the right, with the consent of the Church, to refuse. After the sermon the presiding minister declares that the Lords of the Secret Council of the Churches of Lothian grant permission to elect Spottiswood; then he announces in a public declaration that the neighboring Churches (of Edinburgh, Linlithgow, Stirling, Tranent, Haddington, and Dunbar) and the persons of standing (earls, lords, barons, gentlemen) who have such a right or can lay claim to it have all been notified that they should be present on the day of election. After taking attendance and registering any absences, the minister asks three times if anyone knows of any crime or offense committed by Spottiswood that might disqualify him. Next the assembly is asked if they have anyone else to elect. Lastly, a sort of act of commitment by the faithful takes place, a commitment to accept the newly elect as superintendent, to honor and obey him, to comfort and assist him in his charge. The rite of ordination then begins with the examination of the elect.

The two texts (of the election of the ministers[941] and of the superintendent[942]) certainly bear a number of resemblances, allowing for differences relating to their different charges. However, we see that in the election of the superintendent the neighboring Churches play a role. This is in keeping with the tradition of the early Church, which provided for the participation of neighboring Churches in the election. The importance of the office of superintendent for the organization of the Churches is such that it demands the accord of all those concerned, even the civil authorities and persons of standing in society. Once more we see that election concerns all the members of the Church, and that it appears as a fundamental right of the faithful. In this we recognize the thinking of J. Łaski and M. Bucer. We should note that we do not have here a "democratic" process, but a system in which each member plays his role according to his position: the faithful put forth the names of possible candidates, but those who have responsibility for the governance of the community carry out the examination, sometimes in private and sometimes in public. It is clear that we have here communities whose relationships are all the more intimate that their numbers are small.

b. *Examination*[943–952] *and the Commitment of the People*[953]

The ritual examination consists of nine questions put to the elect. They are based on the four questions of Jan Łaski,[926–929] which are found in the rite of John Knox in an expanded form.[25] They are only mentioned here in order that we might take a look at the first question and first answer, which are from the pen of Knox. The elect is asked if he believes himself to be bound in conscience to support the faithful (whose commitment he has just received), who have need of his comfort and the fruit of his labors. His answer reveals the meaning of his vocation: ". . . I acknowledge myself bound to obey God calling by them."[943] His vocation, then, is mediated through the call (in this case, the election) of the people. This is the meaning of vocation that was current in the early Church.

After the last question, the elect makes a sort of personal statement in which he acknowledges his weaknesses and declares himself ready to accept fraternal corrections and even the loss of office in the Church that has called him.

After this, the presiding minister asks if the congregation requires anything else of its superintendent. If there is nothing more, the minister puts a series of questions (four in all) to the congregation. Are they ready to accept the ministry of a brother as the minister of Christ, and to accept the preaching, exhortations, corrections, and comforts

[25] For the correspondence between the ritual examinations of Knox and of Łaski, see the technical notes to texts nos. *943–*952 in the fourth volume of the present study.

that he will offer them in the discharge of his ministry? The people answer: "We will, as we shall answer to the Lord Jesus, who hath commanded His Ministers to be had in reverence, as His Ambassadors, and as men that carefully watch for the salvation of our souls.'"[*953]

c. *Blessing*

After the invitation to prayer,[*954] the prayer is addressed to Christ, asking for the gift of the Holy Spirit.[*955–*957] This is followed by the Lord's Prayer and the handshake of consent[26] (instead of the imposition of hands) which is given by all the ministers and elders who are present, before the blessing said by the presiding minister.[*958] A last exhortation to the elect closes the ceremony. As we see, the structure follows that of J. Łaski; the epiclesis alone reveals the influence of both Bucer and Łaski.

Before moving on to the study of the text of the prayer, two remarks are in order. We should note that Knox says simply, in the text on the

---

[26] The rubric is as follows: "The prayer ended, the rest of the Ministers and Elders of that Church, if any be present, in sign of their consent, shall take the elected by the hand . . ." This scenario of the ministers shaking hands might possibly call to mind a similar scenario, that of Paul, Barnabas, and the "pillars" of the Church of the circumcised, James, Cephas and John: "And when James and Cephas and John, who were acknowledged pillars, recognized the **grace that had been given to me**, **they gave** to Barnabas and me the **right hand of fellowship**, agreeing that **we should go** to the Gentiles and they to the circumcised" (*kai gnontes tēn **charin tēn dotheisan moi**, 'Iakōbos kai Kēphas kai 'Iōannēs, oi dokountes stuloi einai, **dexias edōkan** emoi kai Barnaba koinōnias, **hina hēmeis eis ta ethnē**, autoi de eis tēn peritomēn*" (Gal 2:9). It is recognized that this passage represents the reconciliation between the two factions of the circumcised and the pagans in the Church, but also the confirmation on the part of the "acknowledged leaders" (i.e., the apostles themselves; cf. Gal 2:2) of the gospel preached by Paul. This pericope (Gal 2:1-10), at the same time, refers to the fact that the apostolate of Paul to the uncircumcised was acknowledged to be on the same level as that of Peter to the circumcised ("On the contrary, when they saw that I had been entrusted with the gospel for the uncircumcised, just as Peter had been entrusted with the gospel for the circumcised . . ." [Gal 2:7]). Next, Paul acknowledges that the same power is at work in him and in Peter (v. 8), that it is grace (transmitted and above all, received, that is, acknowledged by the other apostles) that establishes him in the apostolate (v. 9a). Lastly, they shake hands, as a symbol of the communion (of their consent and acceptance) in the reality of the Church's mission represented by the ministry of Paul and Barnabas. We may perhaps interpret the "handshake of consent" in Knox in the same sense.

ministers (taken from the *Genevan Service Book*), that ". . . the minister exhorts at the election [= blessing or ordination], with the invocation of the name of God, *directing his prayer as God shall move his heart.* After the election, in the same manner, the minister gives thanks to God, asking for whatever he needs to fulfill his office . . ."[*941.6]

The second feature we should note is the rubric concerning the handshake of consent. It would appear that in this text the imposition of hands is lacking, the first time that this is so. Possibly it was the fear of a superstitious understanding of the imposition of hands that led Knox to suppress it "as if to detoxify [the Church] from the earlier superstitions, because the age of miracles is over, and that is no longer the way in which the Holy Spirit is communicated; but they [the Churches of Scotland] will nevertheless revert to this ritual gesture in their discipline of 1581."[27] In contrast with the practices of the medieval Church (ordinations conferred in private, absolute ordinations as the rule, lack of participation of the laity in the choice of their ministers, etc.), we have seen that the Churches of the Reformation view the act of ordination as an act of the entire Church: the election/ordination usually takes place on Sunday, always in the presence of the community or its representatives; the members of the congregation for which the minister is called all participate, etc. This being the case, the Church of Scotland explains that it is rather the action of God that creates the minister:

"It is neither the clipping of their crowns, the greasing of their fingers, nor the blowing of the dumb dogs called the Bishops, neither yet the laying on of their hands, that makes them true ministers of Christ Jesus. But the Spirit of God inwardly moving the hearts to seek Christ's glory and the profit of his Church, and thereafter the nomination of the people, the examination of the learned, and the

---

[27] J.-J. von ALLMEN, *Le saint ministère . . .*, 47, where he quotes pages 193 and 207 of the *Buke of Discipline.* For the corroboration of his interpretation, see G. DONALDSON, "Scottish Ordinations in the Restoration Period," *Scottish Historical Review* 33 (1954) 170; and P. F. BRADSHAW, "The Reformers and the Ordination Rites," *Studia Liturgica* 13, 2–4 (1979) 104–106 (= *Ordination Rites . . .*, eds. W. Vos & G. Wainwright). F. Schulz adds that there was also a political aspect to the decision to omit the imposition of hands in Scotland, and that the "handshake of association" also replaced the imposition of hands in the Low Countries; see F. SCHULZ, "Die Ordination . . .," 26. See also n. 26.

public admission (as before is said) makes men lawful Ministers of the word and sacraments."[28]

2. PRAYER OF BLESSING (OR OF ORDINATION)

Here is Knox's version of the prayer for the gift of the Holy Spirit:

"O Lord, to whom all power is given in heaven and in earth, Thou that art the Eternal Son of the Eternal Father, who hast not only so loved Thy Church that, for the redemption and purgation of the same, thou hast humbled thyself to the death of the cross, and thereupon hast shed Thy most innocent blood to prepare to Thyself a spouse without spot, but also, to retain this Thy most excellent benefit in recent memory, hast appointed in Thy Church Teachers, Pastors, and Apostles, to instruct, comfort, and admonish the same: look upon us mercifully, O Lord, Thou that only art King, Teacher, and High Priest to thy own flock: and send unto this our brother, who, in thy name, we have charged with the chief care of thy Church, within the bounds of L., such portion of thy Holy Spirit, as thereby he may rightly divide thy word, to the instruction of thy flock, and to the confutation of pernicious errors and damnable superstitions. Give unto him, good Lord, a mouth and wisdom, whereby the enemies of thy truth may be confounded, the wolves expelled and driven from Thy fold, Thy sheep may be fed in the wholesome pastures of Thy most holy word, the blind and ignorant may be illuminated with Thy true knowledge: finally, that, the dregs of superstition and idolatry which yet resteth within this realm being purged and removed, we may all not only have occasion to glorify Thee our only Lord and Saviour, but also daily to grow in godliness and obedience of thy most holy will, to the destruction of the body of sin, and to the restitution of that image to the which we were once created, and to the which, after our fall and defection, we are renewed by participation of Thy holy Spirit, whom, by true faith in thee, we do profess as the blessed of Thy Father, of whom the perpetual increase of thy graces we crave, as by Thee our Lord, King, and only Bishop we are taught to pray, 'Our Father,' etc."[955-957]

". . . The chief Minister shall give the benediction as followeth:

"God, the Father of our Lord Jesus Christ, who hath commanded His Gospel to be preached to the comfort of His elect, and hath called

---

[28] Quoted by P. F. BRADSHAW, "An Act of God . . .," 23.

thee to the office of a watchman over His people, multiply His graces with thee, illuminate thee with His Holy Spirit, comfort and strengthen thee in all virtue, govern and guide thy ministry to the praise of His holy name, to the propagation of Christ's kingdom, to the comfort of His Church, and, finally, to the plain discharge and assurance of thy own conscience, in the day of the Lord Jesus, to whom, with the Father, and with the Holy Ghost, be all honour, praise, and glory, now and ever: So be it."[*958]

a. *Biblical Images Employed*

Since this prayer largely repeats what we have seen previously, we shall refer to what was said when we examined the prayer in the ritual of M. Bucer (I, D, 1, c) and in that of J. Łaski (II, B, 2). Knox follows Bucer in the first part of his prayer (*955 = *289), except that Bucer addresses it to the Father, while Knox (along with J. Łaski) addresses it to Christ, and Knox restricts the list of ministries taken from Ephesians 4 to "doctors, pastors, and apostles," while Bucer gives "apostles, prophets, evangelists, doctors, and pastors." It is true that in the Church of Scotland, in the time of Knox, only three offices were instituted, the offices of pastor or minister, of elder, and of deacon. Knox noted, after his exposition on the office of deacon, that there existed a fourth office, that of teacher, but he did not think it opportune to institute it at that time.[29] Knox's epiclesis contains the ideas of Bucer and of Łaski.

Knox follows the formulary of J. Łaski for the use of the Lord's Prayer and the blessing[*958] which is an amplification of that of Łaski,[*934] which in turn is an amplification of Bucer's.[*291] In the rubric for the blessing, the ordaining minister in Knox, the "chief minister," corresponds to Bucer's *"primarius ordinator."*

Knox adds two details to the prayer for the elect: he names the Church in which the new minister is to serve ("of your Church in the territory of N."), and he joins the classic functions of the ministry of Christ who is the only King, Doctor, and High Priest, to those of the pastorate of the elect.[30]

[29] For the text of John Knox, see G. W. SPROTT (ed.), *The Book of Common Order of the Church of Scotland. Commonly Known as John Knox's Liturgy,* 2nd ed. [1st ed. 1886] (Edinburgh: William Blackwood & Sons, 1901) 16ff.

[30] P. De Clerck has criticized Jan Łaski's prayer because it does not make the pastoral ministry a participation in the ministry of Christ; see P. DE CLERCK,

b. *Qualities Requested for the Ordinand*

Rather than repeat what we have just said above, we shall give a simple enumeration: wisdom, effectual preaching, and exemplary conduct.

c. *Gifts Received by the Ordinand*

The gifts received are: the multiplication of the graces of God, the illumination of the Spirit, the comfort and consolation of the virtues, the guidance and help of God to enable the new minister to fulfill his ministry.

3. LATER INFLUENCE OF THE FORMULARY
OF THE *BUKE OF DISCIPLINE*

We find the text of the first *Buke of Discipline* in the *Book of Common Order*,[31] the second *Buke of Discipline*,[32] and, lastly, in the Ordinal of 1620 which was a compromise between the Anglicans and the Puritans of Scotland when James VI had the office of the episcopacy introduced in 1610. It included two rites: one for the consecration of a bishop, and the other for the ordination of a minister. The rite for the ordination of a minister uses the rite of Knox for the election of a superintendent and a few elements from the Anglican rite for the ordination of priests. The rite for the consecration of a bishop contains almost nothing from the formulary of Knox, but rather it was composed of elements from the Anglican rite. This Ordinal, which was revised in 1636 with the intention of imposing the Anglican rites, never received the authorization of the Parliament in Scotland; it had been definitively rejected in 1639 when the Presbyterian system was established.[33]

"L'ordination . . .," 86. It is true that the author did not study the rite of ordination in the original Latin, but in the German translation, which is not always absolutely faithful.

[31] G. W. SPROTT (ed.), *The Book . . .*, 13–30.

[32] This book was published between 1578 and 1580, and contains the imposition of hands as a usual element of ordination in Scotland; see J. L. AINSLIE, *The Doctrines . . .*, 176.

[33] The text of this ordinal has been published by G. W. SPROTT (ed.), *Scottish Liturgies of the Reign of James VI* (Edinburgh: William Blackwood & Sons, 1901) 111–129, 159–165. For the history of this episode, see P. F. BRADSHAW, *The Anglican Ordinal . . .*, 57–60; and G. DONALDSON, "Scottish . . .," 169–175.

4. CONCLUSION: STRUCTURING OF THE CHURCH
AND THE SUBSTANCE OF ORDAINED MINISTRY

a. *Structure of the Church*

We have said above in our discussion of the structure of the Reformed Church of Knox that each member plays his proper role in the election and institution of the ministers. There are three categories of ministers: the pastors, the elders, and the deacons. However, we have seen that Knox was not hostile to a sort of ecclesiastical inspectorate, whence his acceptance of the office of superintendent. Lastly, even though the imposition of hands is not kept in its usual form, we see that the collegial dimension of the ministerial structure is expressed by the close proximity between the gesture of the "handshake of consent" and the passage from Galatians which relates the reception of the ministry of Paul and Barnabas, expressed by the gesture of giving the right hand to the one received, and then the sending forth on mission.

The fraternal relationships existing between all the diverse components of the Church are visible from the very first meeting in the process of the election of the ministers, and are confirmed again in the declaration of the elect that he is ready to accept fraternal correction, and even the loss of office, if he does not prove faithful to his commitment. Vocation itself is seen as mediated through the call of the congregation, in the sense that vocation is the result of a process of discernment of the will of God for the particular Church. The elect is not seen as a delegate of the community, but as a minister of Christ,[953] set before the community to continue the ministry of Christ.[956] This is all in keeping with what we have seen in the work of Bucer and of Łaski. The organization of the Church is seen in the tradition of Ephesians 4 which Bucer had referred to for the diversity of the gifts of the lordship of Christ over the Church. These ministries, therefore, make the Church able to accomplish her task in the world. They take nothing away from the value of the membership of the other Christians in the Church, but they contribute to the building up of the Church of Christ and to the glorification of God.[959]

b. *Substance of the Pastoral Ministry*

Knox established a single rite for the election of ministers in the Church of Scotland, the rite of election of a superintendent, which could serve as a model for the other ministries. The function of a superintendent seems to have been considered as a provisional accommodation, accepted for the task of organizing the Presbyterian system. In fact, these superintendents have no power of ordination inherent in their office, but they receive their commission from the General Assembly of the Church. The fact that the same rite of election is used for both superintendent and minister shows Knox's intent.[34] J.-J. von Allmen correctly characterized the type of ministry established in the Reformed Churches to replace the diocesan episcopacy at the time of the Reformation: "Theologically speaking, the pastoral ministry was understood not as what the Churches of the 'Catholic' type called the priestly ministry, but as an episcopal ministry . . ."[35] And, "If we were to look for the sources in the Reformation of the abandonment of the diocesan episcopacy, it would be less the Reformers than those who, before them and for centuries, had made the unfortunate identification between bishops and priests, which the Reformers simply inherited."[36] For Knox, then, the ministry received by all the ordained ministers is the episcopacy (that is, the functions of the *episkopē*, including proclaiming the Word, administering the sacraments and the keys). This seems to be the reason why Knox used the same rite for the election of superintendent and minister.

Here, too, we find ourselves squarely in the tradition of Bucer and Łaski. The substance of the pastoral ministries includes the proclamation of the gospel, the administration of the sacraments, and the exercise of authority in the community."[940]

D. THE FORMULARY OF MIDDLEBURGH (1586/1602)

Any study of the ordination formularies of the Churches of the Reformation of the sixteenth century must take into account the rite that

---

[34] *942–*959. J. L. AINSLIE, *The Doctrines* . . ., 105–119; and J.-J. von ALLMEN, *Le saint ministère* . . ., 229f.

[35] J.-J. von ALLMEN, *Le saint ministère* . . ., 50.

[36] J.-J. von ALLMEN, *Le saint ministère* . . ., 229. In note 91 he comments: "One cannot be too overjoyed that the Fathers of Vatican II, treating of the Church, and more particularly of the ministry essential to the Church, should have spoken not of priesthood, but of the episcopate, and given the latter its specific nature as usual ministry of apostolic succession (*Constitutio dogmatica de ecclesia "Lumen Gentium,"* cap. III)."

resulted from the critical reactions of the Puritans to the *Book of Common Prayer (BCP)*. In his study of the Anglican Ordinal,[37] P. F. Bradshaw presents a summary of the criticisms originating in this wing of the Reform movement that appeared towards 1564, when certain members of the Anglican Church rebelled against the "Catholic" elements contained in the Ordinal of 1552, restored to usage when Elizabeth came to the throne in 1558. During the Puritans' exile at first in Frankfurt and then in Geneva, at the time of the persecutions of Queen Mary, they came into contact with the Reformed Churches that had drawn their inspiration from Calvin and Zwingli. They adopted the ministerial structure of these Churches, and, when they returned home to England, they opposed certain customs such as the liturgical ornaments of Catholic origin, the system of election with the approbation of the ministers, the absence of elders from the structure of the Church, the distinction between bishops and priests, etc. They were again persecuted around 1583, and a number of them emigrated first to Holland, and then to North America. Several attempts at revising the Ordinal of the *BCP* have come down to us. The basis of the proposed text was generally Knox's, the *Genevan Service Book*, to which were added some modifications in 1586 and again in 1602. However, the formulary for the election and the ordination of ministers drew little inspiration from the version of John Knox, and much more from the formulary of Jan Łaski, as we shall see.

1. DESCRIPTION OF THE RITE

We sense the influence of Bucer in the rite of J. Łaski, which is the primary source of the formularies of Middleburgh. The latter, however, presents only the rite of ordination of a single elected minister, while that of Łaski concerns the ordination of several ministers at a time. Moreover, in the Middleburgh ritual the imposition of hands takes place *after* the interrogation of the elect, and not before, as in Łaski. This imposition of the hands is accompanied by the blessing which from now on is a fixed feature with the Reformers. A long admonition then follows, with a prayer of thanksgiving to God, which concludes with the Our Father.

---

[37] P. F. BRADSHAW, *The Anglican Ordinal . . .*, 35–70.

a. *Election*

In the third edition, published in 1586,[38] we see a change in the method of election. After having prayed and fasted, the congregation (the faithful, the elders, and "certain pastors chosen by the next Conference to it") chooses one person only. This person is then presented to the assembly of the elders and the pastors, who then test his abilities in preaching and teaching, etc., and examine him. There is yet another change from the rite of Łaski: after the examination of the candidate's doctrine and conduct, and after his reception by the assembly of the elders and the pastors, twenty days are spent in studying his candidacy, during which he must preach to the congregation. At the end of this period, if there are no objections to the candidate, all proceed to the ordination by the imposition of hands by the elders and the ministers chosen for that purpose; one of the ministers recites the prescribed prayer. This is the end of the third edition of the formulary.

b. *Presentation and Examination*[*966–*972]

The presentation and examination are based on those of Jan Łaski. After a short declaration announcing that the person presented is the one chosen by the congregation and that no one has arisen in opposition,[39] the presentation[*966–*971] describes the office and its functions. We read of the divine institution of the ministry;[40] the foundation and the model of the ministry which are Jesus Christ and his ministry;[*966] Christ's will that his ministry ever remain in his Church for the salvation of men;[*971] the four functions of the ministry, namely, feeding, guiding, defending, and governing;[*966] the preaching of the Word of God[*967] (the making of public prayers in behalf of the whole Church);[*968] the administration of the sacraments;[*969] and discipline and supervision.[*970] All these are the means by which the pastor will accomplish his ministry.

Next comes the examination. We find here in a shortened form the four questions found in Łaski. First,[*972.1] the ordinand is asked if he

---

[38] *A booke of the Forme of common prayers, administration of the Sacraments, etc. agreable to God's worde, and the use of the reformed Churches* (1586), edition of P. HALL (ed.), *Reliquiae Liturgicae* (Bath: Binns & Goodwin, 1847) t. 1, 71–75. This edition does not contain the complete rites, which are found only in the fourth edition, published in 1602 (ed. Hall, t. 1, 77–96).

[39] Cf. *915.

[40] Eph 4:11f.

believes in his heart that he is legally called to this ministry by the Church of God and therefore by God himself. Secondly, does he believe that the Old and New Testaments are the Word of God and the perfect doctrine of salvation?"[972.2] Lastly, does he promise to exercise his ministry in all faithfulness and with good conduct, and does he promise to submit to the censure of the Church if he should so deserve?"[972.3]

c. *Ordination*

The classic form for the imposition of hands and the prayer is found here. We note a variation between the two versions of the formulary. The version of 1586 invited the ministers and the elders to impose hands, while that of 1602 says: "Next the minister who has asked him these questions, or another (when there are several), impose their hands on his head while saying . . ." (In a note in the margin we read that this is not done when confirming someone who had already been ordained; in such a case one simply offers him the handshake.) The prayer that accompanies the imposition of hands[973] corresponds to that of Łaski said after the Lord's Prayer. After the imposition of hands an admonition[974] is addressed to the ordinand, and then to the congregation. The celebration ends with a prayer of thanksgiving[975] for the ordinand, followed by the Lord's Prayer.

2. PRAYER OF ORDINATION

The prayer of ordination is composed, here as elsewhere, of two formulas. Let us examine first the two short formulas (the first from 1586 and the second from 1602) pronounced during the imposition of hands, ending with the prayer of thanksgiving of the formulary of 1602. Here are the texts:

Text of 1586:

"According to this lawful calling, agreeable to the word of God, whereby thou art chosen Pastor in the name of God, stand thou charged with the pastoral charge of this people, over which the Holy Ghost hath made thee overseer (Acts 20:28), to govern this flock of God, which he hath purchased with his blood."[965]

Formulary of 1602:

"God, our heavenly Father, who hath called you to this holy calling, illuminate you by his Spirit, strengthen you by his hand, and so direct you in your ministry, that you may walk in the same orderly, faith-

fully, and fruitfully, to the praise of his holy name, and the furthering and increasing of the kingdom of his Son Jesus Christ. Amen . . ."[*973]
. . .

"O merciful Father, we thank thee that it hath pleased thee, out of mankind that is corrupted, to gather thee a Church unto life everlasting by the ministry of man; and that so mercifully thou hast provided the Church here of a faithful and trusty Minister. We beseech thee, Heavenly Father, to make him by thy Spirit more and more fit for the service whereunto thou hast called him; giving him wisdom to understand thy holy Scripture, and utterance to open his mouth boldly, and publish the mystery of the Gospel. Endue him with wisdom and courage to rule aright, and maintain in Christian peace, the people committed unto him: and that thy Church, under his administration and good ensample, may increase in multitude and true godliness. Grant him a good heart in all troubles and crosses that may meet him in his charge; that, being strengthened by the comfort of thy Spirit, and continuing constantly unto the end, he, with all thy true servants, may be received into the joys of thee, his Lord God. Likewise shew mercy to this people, that they may behave themselves reverently towards this their pastor, acknowledging him to be sent unto them from thee, receiving his doctrine with all respect and honour, and submitting themselves unto his exhortations; that they, by his word, believing in Christ, may be made partakers of life everlasting. Hear us, O Father, through thy well-beloved Son; who hath taught us to pray: Our Father, etc."[*975]

a. *Biblical Images Employed*

The text of 1586 is more declaratory than apologetic, a little like the Lutheran formulas of transmission. It uses the same images as the prayer of the formulary of Zurich,[*910] which stems from Zwingli. This time we find Acts 20 quoted in its context. However, the formula of Middleburgh places more emphasis on the pastoral imagery.

The blessing of the formulary of 1602 reproduces Łaski's almost word for word. There is no need to repeat our analysis here. Suffice it to say that the minister appears here as the faithful steward of God, and that the congregation prays that the Lord bestow his favor upon him.

Lastly, the ordination ends with a prayer for the ordinand, for "no one is by nature inclined to these things [= the ministerial duties]."[*974.3]

The community prays, therefore, that the new minister might receive the gifts necessary for the exercise of his ministry. The image of God is that of a kind Father whose largesse includes the salvation of humanity, the gathering in of the Church, and the gift of the ministry. The image of the elect is that of a servant, prudent, faithful, and courageous.

b. *Qualities Requested for the Ordinand*

Among the qualities requested for the ordinand we find faithfulness, courage, and above all, constancy in the face of difficulties. All these personal qualities affect the new minister's service of the Church, his ability to feed the flock, to defend and govern it by preaching the Word of God, by administering the sacraments and by maintaining discipline and the good order of the Church of God."[966–*970]

c. *Gifts Received by the Ordinand*

By far the most important gift the ordinand receives is the gift of the Holy Spirit, which allows him to become "more and more fit for the service whereunto [God has] called him.'"[*975] A number of particular gifts are associated with the Holy Spirit:[*973] illumination, wisdom, that consolation which gives strength, and perseverance. It is through these gifts that the minister finds himself equipped to fulfill the responsibilities of his ministry.

3. LATER INFLUENCE OF THE MIDDLEBURGH FORMULARY

Certain elements of the formulary of Middleburgh are found again in the liturgies of ordination of the Reformed Church in America: they reached those shores with the establishment of the first Dutch Churches in America. But when we speak of the influence of the formulary of Middleburgh, we really mean that of Bucer and Łaski.

4. CONCLUSION: STRUCTURING OF THE CHURCH AND THE SUBSTANCE OF ORDAINED MINISTRY

a. *Structure of the Church*

The community of Puritans exiled in Middleburgh simplified the procedure of the election and ordination of ministers such as it had been provided by Łaski and even by Knox. However, certain elements were kept: the participation of the community (but to a lesser degree), the central role of the elders and the ministers of the community, the emphasis on the importance of prayer and fasting in this context, the participation of the "neighboring Conference," and the necessity of desiring and seeking its collaboration. All these elements show the meaning of the solidarity of all in the life and mission of the Church. The texts emphasize again and again the mutual respect that must be shown by all: by the ministers, because they have received responsibility for the flock for which Christ himself gave his life; by the faithful, too, for it is God himself who speaks through their ministers. It is God who calls men [at that time there was no possibility of women being called] through the discernment of the faithful, the ministers, and the elders of the community. And it is God, too, who sustains them in the exercise of their ministry through the gifts of his Spirit and above all with the power of his right hand, a sign of the blessing that the ministers receive so that they may faithfully render their service to the community. The structure of this Church, then, is a structure of collaboration: each member plays his role in the extension of the Kingdom of Christ.

b. *Substance of the Pastoral Ministry*

The formulary is categorical regarding the substance of the ministry of the Word: it is pastoral. The minister is to feed the flock, guide, defend, and govern all those who are entrusted to his care. The means available to him are above all the Word of God, preached and taught as the staff with which the flock is guided and governed; next, the sacraments as seals of the grace of Christ; and then prayer and discipline, which includes the ministry of the keys. These elements are found both in the instruction addressed to the whole community during the election, and in the prayers of ordination themselves.

According to this formulary, those who are ordained to the service of the community will receive all that they need for their ministry: the illumination of the Spirit, the power of the blessing of God, and his help in the accomplishment of their charge. Along with their flock, they will build up the Church and spread the Kingdom of Christ.

E. OVERALL CONCLUSIONS

The first formularies of the end of the sixteenth century inspired by the Reformed Reformation do not present a uniform conception of the institution of the ministries. In general, these Churches recognized four offices: those of pastor, doctor, elder, and deacon. But the way in which they were chosen and installed in their office was not the same everywhere.[41] However, certain features remain constant in the procedures which were developed over time in the Churches of the Reformation.

1. ELEMENTS USUALLY FOUND IN EACH FORMULARY

a. *Election*

This component, of prime importance in each one of the rituals we have studied, is never omitted. In some instances it represents the preponderant part of the formulary. The way in which the ministers were chosen varied greatly, from the highly complex formulary of J. Łaski to the simpler form of the Middleburgh formulary. Despite this diversity in the modes of election, however, it is clear that these Churches were in agreement in not recognizing the legitimacy of the "Congregationalist" procedure (election by the people alone), nor the election by the ministers alone, imposed upon the people without the input of their opinion regarding the person proposed.[42] The Reformers wanted both to guarantee that the voice of the faithful be heard and that the good order of the Church be maintained.

The election is important, also, because ministers are elected only when there is need for them (all the rites studied require in the admonition spoken at the beginning of the election that the minister declare in his sermon the need for new ministers). In this way the practice of absolute ordinations—ordinations without a concrete pastoral charge—is rejected by the Reformed Churches. Elsewhere we have seen that one of the criticisms the Puritans had of the Anglican Church was that the latter still kept the medieval system of choosing

---

[41] Cf. J.-J. von ALLMEN, *Le saint ministère* . . ., 43–51; id., "Ministry and Ordination According to Reformed Theology," *Scottish Journal of Theology* 25, 1 (1972) 75–82; R. STAUFFER, "L'ecclésiologie de Jean Calvin," *Positions luthériennes* 25, 3 (1977) 144–150; and G. CRESPY, *Les ministères de la réforme et la réforme des ministères* (Geneva: Labor et Fides, 1968) esp. 37–69.

[42] The extra-liturgical sources are given in J.-J. von ALLMEN, *Le saint ministère* . . ., 46f. We have seen that this is so through the liturgical witnesses presented: see the election in each formulary: *903, *913–*914, *941–*942, *966.

ministers.[43] For the Puritans, as for all the Reformers, the ministry is exercised concretely in the duties of preaching the Word and administering the sacraments, and in the exercise of the keys or seeing to the discipline in the community. These are the responsibilities mentioned in all the formularies we have examined. The specific Church in which they are to be carried out is mentioned at the same time.

These elections included a rigorous examination of the conduct and knowledge of Scripture of each person proposed for the ministry. We are reminded of the prescriptions of 1 Timothy 3:2-7 and Titus 1:7-9: the person chosen must be capable and worthy of the office.[*904-*907]

Other practices appear in the process of election in the Reformed Churches. Prayers and fasts are required of the entire Church which is preparing for an election. We may ask ourselves the reason for this. The answer can be found in the formularies: their purpose was to purify the hearts of those who are asking for the gift of the Spirit of counsel so that they might clearly discern the will of God and thereby choose the person most suited for such an important task in the Church. The ministry is not considered an honor, but a charge.[44]

b. *Ordination*

The word "ordination" is generally used, but, at least for Knox, the term "election" means ordination. This ceremony was considered necessary for admission to the ministry, and it included the imposition of hands (in most cases), and the prayers.[45] We have seen the reasons for the occasional omission of the imposition, or, more exactly, its replacement with another gesture, the "handshake of consent."[*958]

As for the meaning given this gesture, J.-J. von Allmen has identified four possible interpretations. The most frequently encountered interpretation is that the imposition is a sort of epiclesis, the ordinand

---

[43] Cf. the evidence of the documents quoted by P. F. BRADSHAW, *The Anglican Ordinal . . .*, 37–54, especially the debate between John Whitgift (Anglican) and Thomas Cartwright (Puritan) on the method of election and the examination, pp. 40–43.

[44] J. CALVIN, IC (1560) IV.5.10 (OC 4, 658f.) (ET: J. T. McNEILL [ed.], *Calvin: Institutes of the Christian Religion*, trans. and indexed by F. L. Battles [Philadelphia: Westminster, 1960] 2, 1094 [hereafter cited McNEILL, followed by the volume no. and then page no.]).

[45] For the sources taken from the ecclesiastical Ordinances or the Reformed Confessions of Faith, see J.-J. von ALLMEN, *Le saint ministère . . .*, 47f.

being "exposed, if you will, to the action of the Spirit; he (the ordaining minister) puts the ordinand before God so that God might fill him with his Spirit." Another interpretation "sees in the imposition of hands a consecration, a dedication to the service of God." Another, more juridical, way of looking at it "sees in the ordination a legitimation" of the ministry. Lastly, "to explain the imposition of hands, one may speak of a transmission of the pastoral ministry instituted by Christ."[46]

A comment is in order regarding the use of the term "consecration." In the *Second Helvetic Confession* we read the following explanation of sacramental consecration: "To sanctify or consecrate anything to God is to dedicate it to holy uses; that is, to take it from the common and ordinary use, and to appoint it to a holy use . . ."[47] It has been pointed out that, at the beginning of the Reform movement, Calvin had recognized the "sacramental nature" of the imposition of hands, because by this gesture "they (the apostles) recommended to God the one upon whom they were asking that the grace of the Holy Spirit be conferred: and he besought God that it [this grace] be distributed by their ministry for those times."[48] Lastly, the act of imposition of hands or of association to the ministry is not repeated when a previously ordained minister changes congregations: this was strictly forbidden.[*973]

---

[46] J.-J. von ALLMEN, *Le saint ministère . . .*, 48f.

[47] *Confessio et expositio simplex orthodoxae fidei* (1566), cap. XIX (ed. W. NIESEL, *Bekenntnisschriften und Kirchenordnungen der nach Gottes Wort reformierten Kirche* [Zurich: Verlag A. G. Zollikon, n. d. (1938)], hereafter *BKRK*, 260.29–33) (= "The Second Helvetic Confession" [COCHRANE 279]).

[48] J. CALVIN, IC (1541), XVI (OC 4, 1118 in the notes). It is appropriate to adduce two more texts of Calvin on this point, but from the IC of 1560:

1) ". . . For in it [office of presbyter] there is a ceremony, first taken from Scripture, then one that Paul testifies not to be empty or superfluous, but a faithful token of spiritual grace [1 Tim 4:14]. However, I have not put it as number three among the sacraments because it is not ordinary or common with all believers, but is a special rite for a particular office. Yet, since this honor is given to the Christian ministry, there is no reason why the papist priests should be proud. For Christ commanded that stewards of his gospel and sacraments be ordained, not that sacrificers be installed. He gave a command to preach the gospel [Matt 28:19; Mark 16:15] and feed the flock [John 21:15], not to sacrifice victims. He promised the grace of the Holy Spirit, not to enable them to make atonement for sins, but

Throughout all these formularies we have seen that the rite used to establish a person who has received the exterior call (through election) in his holy ministry by an official ceremony of the Church consists generally in the imposition of hands and the prayer. This last is a prayer for the gift of the Spirit to the elect, and at the same time for the Church, that she might receive this minister as the minister of Christ or of God.

c. *Missioning*

Every minister has a concrete charge in the Reformed Church. The minister of the Word is sent to serve a particular congregation, for which he was ordained. His service includes preaching the Word, administering the sacraments, leading in prayer, and exercising discipline. The Reformed formularies do not give another rite for the installation in a given congregation, for the rite of ordination is at once a rite of election, of ordination, and of installation.

2. ACTORS INVOLVED IN THE PROCESS

a. *The Congregation Concerned*

The congregation is active in the choice of its ministers. During the process of election it bears witness to the personal qualities of the minister, to the capabilities of the elect, to his conduct; and, having witnessed the examination concerning his faith that takes place before the congregation, it vouches for his faith. The community also receives the new minister, and promises to sustain him and to accept his preaching and his teaching as coming from the mouth of God.

---

duly to engage in and maintain the government of the church [cf. Matt 28:20] . . ." [Note that the original text cites Acts 1:8 in place of Mt 28:20.] IC (1560) IV.19.28 (OC 4, 1110f.) (= McNEILL 2, 1476).

2) ". . . There remains the laying on of hands. As I concede that it is a sacrament in true and lawful ordinations, so I deny that it has place in this farce, where they neither obey Christ's command nor consider the end to which the promise should lead us. If they do not wish the sign to be denied them, they must apply it to the reality, to which it was appointed." IC (1560) IV.19.31 (OC 4, 1118f.) (= McNEILL 2, 1479). Cf. the commentary of A. GANOCZY, *Calvin . . .*, 318–327 and 415f., and the thesis of L. SCHUMMER, *Le ministère pastoral dans l'Institution chrétienne de Calvin à la lumière du troisième sacrement* (Wiesbaden: Franz Steiner Verlag, 1965).

b. *The Newly Ordained*

He submits to a rigorous examination intended to confirm that he does in fact possess all that Scripture demands of him for the service of the Church. J.-J. von Allmen has noted that, although the early Reformed Churches condemned "ignorant ministers," they also showed in the *Second Helvetic Confession* "a certain mildness towards ministers without erudition, provided that they possess good conduct. This would be a safeguard against a certain intellectualization of the pastoral ministry which is worthy of note, all the more so that it breaks ranks with an undeniable tendency of the Reformed tradition."[49]

As with the Lutherans, vocation for the Reformers is conferred by the call of the Church, acting in obedience to the will of God in electing a given person. Vocation is not the fruit of a purely human initiative, but is in itself a gift of the Spirit. The newly ordained has only to receive his vocation in all humility. But we find in the thought of the Reformers another dimension of vocation, found, for example, in the writings of Calvin and in the first question put to the elect. Calvin says that there is also a secret vocation that "is the good witness of our heart that we receive the proffered office not with ambition or avarice, not with any other selfish desire, but with a sincere fear of God and desire to build up the church."[50]

The clearest liturgical expression is found in J. Łaski: "Do you feel in your heart the inward inspiration of the Holy Spirit impelling you to receive within this Church this ministry which is given into your charge, namely, that in this charge you will seek neither personal profit, nor your own glory, but only the glory of God alone and the increase of the kingdom of Christ in his Church through the preaching of his Gospel, in your ministry? I desire to hear this now from you, before God who sees and knows all things, and before his entire church, for the building up of the Church and the approval of your ministry within the Church."

The elect respond: "We do so feel it and we pray God that he may perfect what he has begun in us, for the love of Jesus Christ, to the

---

[49] *Confessio et expositio . . .*, cap. XVIII (*BKRK* 255.18ff.) (= COCHRANE 271); and J.-J. von ALLMEN, *Le saint ministère . . .*, 46, n. 29.
[50] J. CALVIN, IC (1560), IV.3.11 (OC 4, 626) (= McNEILL 2, 1062f.).

glory of his holy Name.'"*⁹²⁶ Knox has posed the same question, but it is more nuanced;*⁹⁴⁴ it is found also in the formulary of Middleburgh.*⁹⁷² Already in Bucer this conception was taking form, as we can see in the first question of the *Ratio ordinandi*.*²⁷⁷ But his doctrine of vocation is not as clearly expressed as is Calvin's. Nonetheless, it is through the formulary of Bucer that the Anglican rites of ordination inherited this conception of vocation (as both internal and external).

We should state at the outset that we can find in Calvin a germ of the modern distinction between internal and external vocation, a distinction which is certainly not part of patristic tradition (in the case of the bishop, he was often ordained against his will). It was not part of liturgical tradition either, as we saw in the first part of this study. Only three realities counted in the early Church: the task to fulfill, the faith and aptitudes of the elect, and the call of the Church. A. Ganoczy has shown that Calvin's intention was to acknowledge at one and the same time "a divine element, interior and invisible, and a human element, exterior and visible; a doctrine which presents striking analogies with that of the Church, which is both invisible and visible."[51]

c. *The Holy Spirit*

The presence of the Spirit is everywhere in the entire process of election/ordination. The Spirit inspires hearts—the heart of the elect by giving him the "necessary arms" for the fulfillment of his vocation,[52] and the hearts of the faithful, allowing them to perceive the

---

[51] A. GANOCZY, *Calvin . . .*, 304. Calvin tried to combat three conceptions he judged incompatible with the gospel: the papist conception, in which the official Church, apart from the community of the baptized, was the only intermediary of the call of God; the conception of certain evangelicals, according to which vocation is reduced to the royal priesthood alone, and the minister is a delegate of the community; and, lastly, the conception of the "spirituals" in which supreme disorder rules because vocation has been based on private revelations in which the individual is directly called by the Spirit, with no person or persons as intermediaries.

[52] J. CALVIN, IC (1560), IV.3.11 (OC 4, 626) (= McNEILL 2, 1062f.). Cf. also IC (1560), IV.3.16 (OC 4, 631) (= McNEILL 2, 1067) where Calvin links the imposition of hands to the action of the Holy Spirit: ". . . However, they [the Apostles] used it [the laying on of hands] also with those upon whom they conferred the visible graces of the Spirit [Acts 19:6]. . . . Moreover, it will be no empty sign if it

grace already given to the candidate so that they can elect the right person to the ministry. During the imposition of hands and the prayer, the elect receives the action of the Holy Spirit who illumines him, strengthens him with the virtues, and comforts him. The community prays that God may give the elect the gifts of the Holy Spirit that he will need in the ministry that is to be entrusted to him.

d. *The Neighboring Communities*

The formularies we have studied show that other communities are involved in a local election. As associates of the elders of the congregation concerned, ministers from other communities have been informed of the election by a public declaration, at the same time as the civil authorities. We see that the election of a new minister is not exclusively the affair of a local congregation, but of the entire Church of the region."[942]

3. SUBSTANCE OF THE ORDAINED MINISTRY

The substance here is the same as in the other formularies that we have studied. It consists of the preaching of the Word, the administration of the sacraments, and the exercise of discipline. We may see in it a pastoral ministry of *episkopē*. This ministry receives the help of two types of elders: those who teach, and those who govern. They are assisted also by the deacons, who are charged with sharing the worldly goods of the community with the poor.

As for the organization of these ministries within the Reformed Churches, we have seen that the situation is not the same in all geographical areas, neither in regard to the type of ministry, nor for the ordinances that govern their installation.

4. PERMANENCE IN THE SUPERINTENDENCY IS NOT EVIDENT IN THE TEXTS WE HAVE EXAMINED

This is so for several reasons: we see a real vagueness in the distribution of tasks between the ministries, because of the fact that the Reformers made little distinction between the role of the bishop and

---

is restored to its own true origin. For if the Spirit of God establishes nothing without cause in the church, we should feel that this ceremony, since it has proceeded from him, is not useless, provided it be not turned to superstitious abuse. Finally, we must understand that the whole multitude did not lay hands upon its ministers, but pastors alone did so."

that of the priest, a fact that harks back to the interchangeability of the same terms in the New Testament, and their use in the early Church. One example from Calvin will suffice: ". . . indiscriminatingly calling those who rule the church 'bishops,' 'presbyters,' 'pastors,' and 'ministers,' I did so according to scriptural usage, which interchanges these terms."[53] There is, then, a change in the use of these different words for the ministries: the traditional couplet, "bishop/priest" (the two ministries having the same specific substance: teaching, administering the sacraments, governing the Church), becomes progressively replaced by "elder" or minister (of the Word and the sacraments)/preacher/pastor. Some pastors are elected to supervise several parishes in a given area, and these are called "superintendents." Secondly, in order to avoid the confusion between the Catholic episcopacy and the Reformed episcopacy, the choice was made to use the term of superintendent. Next, the following phenomenon occurred, described by von Allmen:

". . . arguing from the generally admitted fact that there was only a difference in grade between the bishop, titulary of the Church, and the priest, titulary of a parish, and that this difference was without real *theological* importance, since both, on their different levels, share in the ministry instituted by Christ so that, between the death of the apostles and his return, the Church might live and grow, it was seen as feasible to separate the episcopal ministry (in the *sociological* meaning of the term) from the structure of the Church, because one was certain to preserve, even to restore, the episcopal ministry (in the *theological* meaning of the term) by ordaining men as ministers of the Word, of the sacraments, and of the keys. In the 16th century, there-

---

[53] J. CALVIN, IC (1560), IV.3.8 (OC 4, 623) (= McNEILL 2, 1060f.). The same thing is said also of the use of these terms in the early Church in the *Forma ac ratio* of Jan Łaski; see the preface: A. KUYPER (ed.), *Joannis a Lasco. Opera tam edita quam inedita* (Amsterdam: Frederic Muller, 1866) t. 2, 48–50. We have also seen the great influence that the so-called "opinion of St. Jerome" on the origin of the difference between episcopate and presbyterate had on the Reformers, and how extensive were the debates during the Middle Ages concerning the question of the sacramentality of the episcopate; see L. OTT, *Le sacrement . . .*, 201–225; O. H. PESCH, "Luther und . . .," 113–139; and J.-J. von ALLMEN, "Le ministère des anciens. Essai sur le problème du presbytérat en ecclésiologie réformée," *Verbum Caro* 18, 71–72 (1964) 222–226.

fore, there took place an ultimate 'episcopalization' of the titularies of the parishes—'ultimate' in the sense that this process was not limited, as before, by the presence of bishops who were different from priests. It was this generalized 'episcopalization' of the titularies of the parishes which ended up costing us what was traditionally meant by the episcopacy. And all the more so that two other measures, in parallel fashion, were to attenuate the episcopal character of the titulary of the local Church: the rejection of a Congregationalist structure even where the local congregation was called 'Church' rather than 'parish of the Church,' and the fear of ordaining the elders, and thereby conferring upon them through this ordination a truly ministerial, clerical character. So the pastors have neither the independence of a bishop of the early Church, since they are subject to a Synod or to a group of pastors, nor do they have as auxiliaries men received into their own ministry who participate in it. Although they preside over a college of elders, they resemble much more closely a parish priest surrounded by a group of certain lay counselors than a bishop surrounded by his presbyters."[54]

This is the reason why the ministry of the superintendency seems to have disappeared. But in reality its permanence was preserved, in another form.

This explains, also, the reason why a regional ministry is sometimes charged with ordinations (Zurich, the *Dekans*), and why at other times they were the responsibility of a temporary ministry (the superintendent), as in Scotland. Among the refugees in London and Frankfurt the superintendency was more or less a fixed feature. It would seem that the task of conferring ordination was entrusted to the one who had the pastoral charge of a *primus inter pares*, exercising a ministry of unity, either in a given region, or in the supervision of the other ministers because of his seniority in the ministry.[55]

---

[54] J.-J. von ALLMEN, *Le saint ministère . . .*, 217f.

[55] For example, the dean of a district (formularies of Zurich and of Knox), the superintendent of a group of communities organized according to their nationality (formulary of Jan Łaski), the minister charged with the discipline of the ministers (*Confessio et expositio . . .*, cap. XVIII [*BKRK* 255.14] [= COCHRANE 271] and probably the formulary of Middleburgh). See the note of J.-J. von ALLMEN on the ambiguity of the French translation of the Latin word *senior* in the *Second Helvetic Confession: Le saint ministère . . .*, 130, n. 2.

Chapter 3

The First Ordinals of the Church of England

As on the Continent, the "Anglican" Reform of the former Catholic Church in England took place over time. The first Anglican liturgical books were not authorized until the reign of Edward VI (1547–1553), with the *Book of Common Prayer (BCP)* on June 9, 1549, revised more radically in 1552. This revision was soon to be replaced in turn in 1554 by Catholic books during the reign of Mary Tudor (1553–1558). After this Catholic interlude, the second edition of the *BCP* was reinstated in 1559 during the reign of Elizabeth I (1558–1603). Both these prayerbooks were largely from the pen of Thomas Cranmer (1489–1556), the Archbishop of Canterbury. With the exception of some minor revisions in 1559, 1604, and 1662, it is this second *BCP* (1552) which has remained in vigor down to our day.[1]

The first *BCP*, brought out at Pentecost in 1549, did not contain an Ordinal. The ritual for ordination appeared only in March 1550, with the title: *The forme and maner of makyng and consecratyng of Archebishoppes, Bishoppes, Priestes and Deacons*.[2] The Ordinal was attached as an

---

[1] For the history of Anglican liturgy and the BCP, see F. A. GASQUET and E. BISHOP, *Edward VI and the Book of Common Prayer. An Examination into Its Origin and Early History, with an Appendix of Unpublished Documents* (London: Sheed and Ward, 1928); F. PROCTER and W. H. FRERE, *A New History of the Book of Common Prayer with a Rationale of Its Offices* (London: Macmillan and Company, 1965); and G. J. CUMING, *A History of Anglican Liturgy* (London: Macmillan and Company, 1982).

[2] P. F. BRADSHAW, *The Anglican Ordinal . . .*, 18ff. For the main part, the work of Bradshaw (+ bibliography) is the most complete for this history of the evolution of the Anglican ordinal. One can also consult the commentary of W. K.

appendix to the first *BCP* of 1549. From 1552 on, in a form that was on occasion slightly modified, it has been an integral part of the *BCP* and its revisions. We shall first consider these works historically, and then we shall look at the ordination of priests and bishops in the Ordinals of 1550/1552[*1538A/B–*1604A/B] and in that of 1661 published in the *BCP* of 1662.[*1538C–*1604C]

A. THE ORDINALS OF 1550 AND 1552

1. AUTHOR OF THE ORDINAL OF 1550

On February 1, 1550, the King was authorized by an act of Parliament (the House of Lords) to name a commission composed of six prelates and six men ("learned in the law of God") to prepare "a form and manner of making and consecrating archbishops, bishops, priests, deacons, and other ministers of the Church" before April 1. This commission was named on the following day, but the names of the persons so chosen do not figure in the official record. We do know, however, that the text was ready for February 8, but was only published in the beginning of March.[3] To have completed such a vast project in so little time, is it not possible that the commission had inherited an early draft? P. F. Bradshaw has shown irrefutably that the Ordinal is the work of T. Cranmer, who used the draft of M. Bucer (the *Ratio ordinandi* of 1549), completed with certain elements taken from the pontifical, or with some original elements.[4]

2. STRUCTURE OF THE ORDINATIONS

We have seen that Bucer drew up only one ritual, but he foresaw the possibility of three rites for the three orders of presbyters. This is precisely what Cranmer did in his redaction for the project requested

---

FIRMINGER, "The Ordinal," in W.K.L. CLARKE and C. HARRIS (eds.), *Liturgy and Worship: A Companion to the Prayer Books of the Anglican Communion* (London: SPCK, 1964) 626–682.

[3] Facts established according to the official reports quoted by P. F. BRADSHAW, *The Anglican Ordinal . . .*, 18f.

[4] P. F. BRADSHAW, *The Anglican Ordinal . . .*, 20–36. Some Catholics have reached the same conclusion, in particular E. C. MESSENGER, *The Lutheran Origin . . .*, esp. ch. 2. But against the opinion that the Ordinal is, rather, an exclusively Lutheran composition, Bradshaw shows the originality of Cranmer and the difference between his theology and the theology of Bucer: see the study on the ideas proper to Cranmer in ch. 1 of his work.

by the government. Although the title gives the succession of rites in the descending order ([arch]bishop, priest, and deacon), they are treated in the reverse order.

Before proceeding to our study of the two ordinations, we must pause a moment at the preface that introduces the Ordinal. We see, first of all, that Cranmer takes much more care than did Bucer to ascribe the establishment of the three orders of ministers to their founding in apostolic times. No one can, on his own authority, accept responsibility for these orders unless one is *called, tested, examined, and recognized as possessing the qualities required for such a ministry.* This is not all. One must be installed in the ministry by *public prayers and the imposition of hands.* It is, then, absolutely necessary to ensure the continuity of these three orders: "And therefore, to the intent these orders should be continued, and reverently used, and estemed in this Churche of England, it is requisite, that no man (not beeyng at this present, Bisshoppe, Priest nor Deacon) shall execute any of theim, excepte he bee called, tried, examined, and admitted, accordying to the forme hereafter folowyng."[*1538A/B] Next come the age requirements for each order. The preface ends by emphasizing once more the necessity for the bishop to verify that each candidate possesses the required qualities. Lastly, the ordination takes place on a Sunday or a feast day, and "in the presence of the Church." This last requirement is found in the ordination for the deacon, but in the rubrics for the two other offices it is clear that it applies equally to them.

The preface enumerates the essential elements of the Ordinal as a whole. We shall now go into closer detail for the two offices which interest us: the ordination of priests, and that of bishops. In his preface, Cranmer uses the following terms: admitting a deacon or priest to office; consecrating a bishop. However, he uses the word "ordination" for the office of deacon and priest, yet mostly "consecration" for bishop. P. F. Bradshaw has shown that it is probable that Cranmer understood these terms in this way: "consecrating" for him means the anointings and other similar ceremonies; "admitting" or "appointing" means ordination by the imposition of hands and the prayer.[5] We see here a continuation of the practice of the late Middle Ages.

[5] P. F. BRADSHAW, *The Anglican Ordinal . . .*, 15.

a. *Priest*

Looking at Table I.6 (vol. IV), we are struck by two features: 1) the contrast between the ritual of the "Sarum" Pontifical and Cranmer's of 1550 (Cranmer greatly simplified the former by suppressing repetitions and secondary ceremonies, in particular the anointing, the investiture, and the second imposition of hands); and 2) the resemblance to the ritual of M. Bucer (in the entire liturgy of the Word, in the ordination, and in the conclusion of the worship). This being said, we must now determine clearly the ways in which Cranmer departed from Bucer's text, and the significance of these departures. This point is essential for a clear grasp of the meaning that ordination had for Cranmer.

We can divide the rite into four stages: the liturgy of the Word,[*1539A/B] the preliminaries,[*1540A/B–*1559A/B] the ordination,[*1560A/B–*1565A/B] and the Communion.[*1566A/B–*1569A/B] We shall pay particular attention to the preliminaries and to the ordination, noting also the three minor changes made in 1552.

α) *Liturgy of the Word.*[*1539A/B] The ordination of deacons and priests probably took place during the same celebration, following the medieval pontificals, for the office of the ordination of priests begins with the rubric: "When the exhortation is finished, they will sing the Introit of the office of Communion"; then the same three psalms (40, 132, or 135) are presented. The rubric pertaining to the exhortation is found at the beginning of the office of the ordination of deacons: "First, when the day set by the bishop has arrived, there will be an exhortation on the duty and the office of those who are to be appointed ministers, [saying] the necessity of the orders in the Church of Christ, and also, how the people must honor them [the ministers] in their vocation." This can be explained by the traditional place of the ordination of deacons before the gospel—the deacons are presented and examined at the very beginning of the celebration, while the ordination of priests comes right after the gospel. In keeping with the Lutheran model, Bucer places the office between the singing of the *Veni Sancte Spiritus* and the beginning of the celebration with the introit, which includes the three psalms mentioned above. These psalms of the introit will be suppressed in 1552.

Next Cranmer took from among the readings suggested by Bucer for the epistle a choice between Acts 20:17-35 (the presbyters of

114

Ephesus) and 1 Timothy 3 (the personal attributes of the heads of the communities). For the gospel, he takes the three first texts of Bucer: Matthew 28:18-20 (the universal mission of the disciples), John 10:1-16 (the Good Shepherd), and John 20:19-23 (the sending forth on mission, the gift of the Holy Spirit). The fourth text suggested by Bucer (John 21:15-19—"Feed my sheep") is kept for the consecration of a bishop. And, lastly, he suppresses Psalm 67.

This first part of the office is simple, and emphasizes both the functions of the ministers (in the exhortation) and the personal qualities required of them (in the readings from Scripture). Cranmer tried to preserve the specific nature of the episcopal charge by reserving the fourth text of the gospel particularly for this office.

β) *Preliminaries.*[*1540A/B–*1559A/B] The ceremony begins with the singing of the *Veni Creator*[*1603A/B] in English, followed by the presentation of the elect (by the archdeacon) and the admonition to the people (derived from the *Auxilante domino* from the pontifical and from the ritual of Bucer[6]). The address to the people bears on the suitability of the persons proposed for the office of priest, and the people are interrogated on this subject. They are asked if anyone knows of any obstacle (criminal or other) to their ordination. Of course, we have already said in the preface that these men have been "examined, tested, etc." and this is now only a ritual election, a sort of final opinion poll of the people. Most probably, the election did not concern the entire congregation, but only the members of the clergy.[7] It is here that Cranmer differs from Bucer. At the end of the presentation there is a very traditional element in the rites of ordination proper to the pontificals (in which it immediately precedes the ordination), namely, the litany and its collects.[*1596A/B–*1601A/B] This is the new English litany (not the litany of the saints), which is composed of petitions similar to those in the pontificals, but with others added that stem from Lutheran and Eastern traditions. One request in particular is made for the ordinand: "May it please thee to bless these men and to pour

---

[6] For the sources of the Ordinal, consult the notes at the bottom of the page of the texts presented in vol. 4 of the present study.

[7] We know this because one of the criticisms of the Puritans was that the Anglican Ordinal does not have a true election by the faithful, as was the practice among the Puritans in Frankfurt and Geneva; cf. P. F. BRADSHAW, *The Anglican Ordinal . . .*, 38ff. for the source documents.

down thy grace upon them, that they may properly exercise the office which is now entrusted to them, for the building up of thy Church and thy honor, thy praise and thy glory." The litany ends with this collect, which is the same for the three offices (except for its designation):

"Almighty God, dispenser of all good who through thy Holy Spirit has established divers orders of ministers in thy Church; look down in thy mercy upon your servants here called to the charge [of the priesthood]; and fill them so with the truth of thy teaching and arm them with such integrity of life that both in word and example they may serve you faithfully in this office; to the glory of thy name and the building up of thy Church; through the merits of our Savior Jesus Christ, who lives and reigns with thee and the Holy Spirit, for ever and ever. Amen."

We must first note that the litany is missing in Bucer, but not in the pontificals. We know that Cranmer believed that the institution of a man in the ministry took place "by public prayer and the imposition of hands." This order is respected here, for the public prayers precede the imposition of hands. The opinion of Bradshaw[8] that the prayer for the ordinands is not that which accompanies the imposition of hands, but the one that ends the litany, is probably correct, for—as we shall see further on—the prayer of the imposition of hands is changed from what it was in Bucer (the epiclesis is omitted), and it has become a prayer for the *congregation,* a fact which means that we do not find any prayer for the ordinand in Cranmer's rite. We will have occasion to return to this singular intent behind the litany and its collect. For now, we shall simply note that these two elements constitute a prayer that the ordinands may receive the grace of the Holy Spirit, that they may exercise the priesthood and build up the Church of God.

Next the elect swear an oath as to the supremacy of the king,[1604A/B] rejecting all authority, power, and jurisdiction of the bishop of Rome over the Church of England, and affirming the sovereignty of the king over this Church. The sole change made in 1552 affected the conclusion, where we read "through Jesus Christ," instead of "through the saints and the holy Gospel," because the Puritans re-

---

[8] P. F. BRADSHAW, *The Anglican Ordinal . . .,* 26–28.

called that man must not swear by creatures,[9] according to the tradition of the Old Testament. After they have sworn their oath the elect are interrogated, after a long exhortation [*1545A/B-*1548A/B] taken from Bucer.

The examination contains eight questions also taken from Bucer. Cranmer omits the last question of Bucer on stability. The questions have to do with vocation,[*1550A/B] the sufficiency and necessity of the Scriptures,[*1551A/B] the faithfulness of the elect as they take upon themselves the charge of dispensing the doctrine and of administering the sacraments,[*1552A/B] the repudiation of the doctrines that falsify the Word of God,[*1553A/B] their disposition towards prayer and the study of the Scriptures,[*1554A/B] their conduct and that of their families,[*1555A/B] their desire to maintain the peace among Christians,[*1556A/B] and their obedience to the ordinary and to the other authorities.[*1557A/B] This part of the ritual ends with the prayer, pronounced by the bishop, asking that God may give them all that is needed for them to accomplish what they have just promised.

Let us pause a moment to consider the first question put to the elect: "Do you think in your heart, that you be truly called, according to the will of our Lord Jesus Christ, and the order of this church of England, to the order and ministrie of priesthood?"[*1550A/B] We recognize here the double conception of vocation that we found in Calvin, an interior vocation, and an exterior vocation. Let us recall that, according to Calvin, through the secret vocation, the person must attest in conscience before God that it is not from personal ambition that he accepts the priesthood, but out of a true fear of God and zeal for the building up of the Church in which he is about to accept ministry. The interior vocation comes from God, and not from the person, or from the Church, but from the secret operation of the Holy Spirit. The public or exterior vocation is the *ritus vocatus* required for a person to be held a true minister. In this way, Calvin opposed three conceptions that were incompatible with the gospel: ". . . The conception . . . that vocation was a call to the priesthood, a call from God through the intermediary of the official Church, to the practical exclusion of the community; . . . that the minister had only the same

[9] Cf. the writings of John Hooper quoted by P. F. BRADSHAW, *The Anglican Ordinal . . .*, 37f.

vocation to the royal priesthood as all Christians, that his status as minister derived from a simple act of delegation on the part of the community; the third was that held by certain 'spirituals,' who said they were called directly and individually by private revelations that the Spirit had granted them."[10] The same question is put to those elected to the episcopacy and to the diaconate.

In all these questions we discern the disposition of the ordinands and we see that their charge of priesthood includes the preaching of the Word, the defense of doctrine and of the Church, the administration of the sacraments, and great steadiness in their conduct and in that of their families and of the other Christians of the community.

γ) *Ordination*.[*1559A/B–*1565A/B] This part is made up of the following: the invitation to prayer and the silent prayer,[*1559A/B] the prayer of ordination,[*1560A/B–*1561A/B] the imposition of hands by the bishop and the priests[*1562A/B] accompanied by a prayer of command,[*1563A/B] the bestowal of the Bible, the chalice, and bread accompanied by another prayer of command,[*1564A/B] and the profession of faith sung by the whole congregation.[*1565A/B]

Except for the bestowal of the instruments, Cranmer's rite followed that of Bucer; Cranmer, however, omitted the epiclesis of Bucer's prayer, and the prayer said during the imposition of hands was taken from the pontificals. We shall examine these formulas further on in our study.

As for the rest, we have the bestowal of the Bible and the chalice, which in 1552 will be emended to the bestowal of the Bible alone.[*1564B] The text that accompanies this gesture is modeled on that found in the pontifical: "Take thou aucthoritie to preache the word of god, and to minister the holy Sacramentes in thys [this = 1550] congregacion [where thou shall be so appointed = 1552]." We see that the prayer has been made quite general, and all reference to the sacrifice offered for the deceased has disappeared. This formula says clearly that the ordinand has a concrete ministry in a particular community. Lastly, the whole assembly proclaims together the *Credo*, a usual element in the Sunday celebration.

---

[10] A. GANOCZY, *Calvin . . .*, 303. For Calvin's texts, see J. CALVIN, IC (1560), IV.3.10f. (OC 4, 625f.) (= McNEILL 2, 1062f.).

δ) *Communion.*[*1565A/B–*1566A/B] After the ordination, the office continues from the offertory up to Holy Communion, which is presided over by the bishop/ordinant. The ordinands remain in the place where they were ordained. The celebration ends with a last prayer for the ordinands based on Psalm 132:9: "Most merciful Father, we beseech thee to send upon these thy servants thy heavenly blessing; that they may be clothed with righteousness, and that thy word spoken by their mouths may have such success, that it may never be spoken in vain . . ."

To conclude this survey, let us reiterate the following:

—The ordination takes place during the celebration of Holy Communion, normally on a day on which the people can be present (a Sunday or feast day);

—The election and the examination have been carried out well before the liturgical celebration, and it is the responsibility of the bishop to verify the suitability of the men chosen. However, the faithful have a last chance to raise objections, during the celebration of ordination itself;

—The bishop is the minister of the ordination, and along with the other priests he imposes hands upon the ordinands;

—The ordination is effected through public prayer and the imposition of hands. The faithful are active during the celebration, especially at the crucial point of the prayer (the litany, its collect, and the silent prayer for the elect);

—The ministry is intended for a concrete Church; we even get the impression that the ordination is celebrated in the community concerned. This ministry is defined as a ministry of preaching the Word and administering the sacraments, for the building up of the Church.

b. *Bishop*

Before moving on to an analysis of the prayers of ordination, we shall first take a look at the structural elements of episcopal consecration. Since this structure is fairly close to that of the ordination of priests, we shall consider the elements that are different from the ordination to the priesthood. As in the latter case, episcopal consecration is composed of four parts: the liturgy of the Word,[*1571A/B–*1572A/B] the preliminaries,[*1573A/B–*1587A/B] the consecration proper,[*1588A/B–*1592A/B] and Communion.[*1593A/B] α) *Liturgy of the Word.*[*1571A/B-*1572A/B] The office begins with the introit, as in that of the ordination of priests; this introit will be suppressed in 1552. Cranmer reduced the choice of readings to three: the epistle is taken from 1 Timothy 3:1-7 (the qualities required of a bishop), and a choice between John 21:15-17 ("feed my sheep") and John 10:1-16 (the Good Shepherd). These are all excellent choices for the context of episcopal consecration. The epistle emphasizes the qualities necessary for the head of the community, while one of the gospel texts speaks of the pastoral ministry of Peter, and the other of the ministry of Christ. Also, Cranmer suppressed the psalm that Bucer put between the epistle and the gospel. The liturgy of the Word concludes with the *Credo.* Bucer has no *Credo* in his draft, and the office in the pontifical does not mention it either. It is curious that Cranmer gives no indication of a sermon on the tasks and the office of bishop. The usage of the "Sarum" placed the consecration of a bishop between the gradual and the gospel; Cranmer, following the example of Bucer, put the consecration after the gospel. In this way he puts into parallel position the rites for priests and bishops, while the ordination of deacons is placed before the gospel, as it is in the pontificals.

β) *Preliminaries.*[*1573A/B-*1587A/B] The ordinand (vested with the short-sleeved surplice and the cope) is presented by two assistant bishops who are also vested with the cope, but with their crozier in hand. The revision of 1552 will leave out any reference to vestments. One of them addresses the consecrator while presenting the elect as a "godly and well learned man." There is no interrogation of the people, and no election, in the Ordinal, nor is there in the pontifical. In the latter case, we know that the rite of election is usually carried out before the Mass of consecration.[11] Next the order of the king is read (parallel to the *mandatum apostolicum*), followed by the oath of fealty to royal supremacy. Then the elect reads the oath of obedience due the archbishop.

The solemnity of the ceremony is heightened by an invitatory [*1575A/B] to the litany based on Luke 6:12, Acts 13:3, Acts 13:2, and a text that goes back to the Gelasian Sacramentary (I, 90). The litany is chanted

---

[11] For the "Sarum" usage, see W. MASKELL, *Monumenta Ritualia Ecclesiae Anglicanae,* reprint [1st ed. 1882] (Westmead, Farnborough, Hampshire: Gregg International Publishers, Ltd., 1970) t. II, 255–267 (hereafter MASKELL II, followed by the page number).

as in the ordination of priests. It ends with the same collect, except for the designation of the office (". . . called to the work and the ministry of the episcopacy . . ."). Next comes an address to the elect, followed by his examination (seven questions). The text of the address is inspired by the pontifical and by 1 Timothy 5:22.[12] We see that Cranmer drew most heavily on the pontifical as his model. Even in the questions that follow he reworked some of Bucer's, adding material from the pontifical to describe the office of bishop in more detail than that of priest. The invitatory concludes: "Before I admit you to this Administration I will examine you in certein Articles to the end that the congregation present may have a tryal, and bear witness, how you be minded to behave yourself in the church of God."[*1578A/B]

Questions 1, 2, 4, and 6: 1)[*1579A/B] on vocation, 2)[*1580A/B] on the necessity of the Scriptures, 4)[*1582A/B] on the rejection of false doctrine, and 6)[*1584A/B] on the will to maintain the peace between Christians, correspond to questions 1, 2, 4, and 7 of the examination of priests. Questions 3, 5, and 7: 3)[*1581A/B] on the study of the Scriptures and the need to seek in prayer a true understanding of their meaning in order to teach them and be able to exhort with sound doctrine, 5)[*1583A/B] on the episcopal virtues of Titus 2:12, 7, 8, and 7)[*1586A/B] on the care of the poor and of pilgrims, are closer to the present-day questions in the pontifical. The nature of the pastoral superintendency was made more explicit by the changes from the office for the ordination of priests. It is made even more explicit in the formula of the *traditio instrumentorum,* further on in the celebration. Obviously, the aspect of preaching, teaching, and administering the sacraments is also present, for these are common to both offices. This second part of the ritual ends with the archbishop expressing a wish for the new bishop, as in the rite of ordination of priests.

---

[12] We recognize certain phrases taken from the PRG and even from the earlier *SEA,* for example: *"Antiquorum sanctorum Patrum institutio docet . . . manus nemini cito imposueris . . . quomodo oportet episcopo conversare in Ecclesia Dei";* cf. F. E. BRIGHTMAN, *The English Rite Being a Synopsis of the Sources of the Book of Common Prayer with an Introduction and an Appendix,* reprint [2nd ed. revised, 1921] (Westmead, Farnborough, Hampshire: Gregg International Publishers, Ltd., 1970) t. II, 1006, 1008 (hereafter *The English Rite* II, followed by the page number); and MASKELL II, 259–261.

γ) *Consecration.*[*1589A/B–*1592A/B] As we saw in the rite for priests, the consecration of the bishop begins with the singing of the hymn "Divine Spirit, God of Peace." Next follows the prayer of consecration said by the archbishop and introduced by the greeting "The Lord be with you," which will be changed in 1552 to "Lord, hear our prayer . . ." The prayer of consecration is made up of the beginning of Bucer's prayer as far as the epiclesis, and the Gallican interpolation *Sint speciosi.* Such a prayer is truly a prayer for the elect. We shall be taking a closer look at it at the end of this section.

With the prayer, and in accordance with the usage of the pontificals, all the bishops present impose their hands while the archbishop pronounces the prayer "Take the Holy Spirit . . ." drawn from 1 Timothy 1:6f. Next the Bible is held at the base of the neck of the ordinand (a gesture taken from the pontifical), with a formula drawn from the text of 1 Timothy 4:13, 15f. which begins ". . . Give attention to the public reading of Scripture, to exhorting, to teaching . . . Pay close attention to yourself and to your teaching . . ." He who is to be a confessor of the faith, as Paul reminds Timothy (see the prayer of the imposition of hands[*1590A/B]), must also, in his ministry, meditate on what is found in the Bible so as to draw from it sound doctrine and the exhortations that the community needs. Lastly, the pastoral staff is bestowed, with a prayer taken from the prophet Ezekiel (Ezek 34:3, 4, 16) and 1 Peter 5:4 which strongly emphasizes the pastoral role of the bishop in the community. This text is found in the PRG.[13] In 1552 the imposition of the Bible becomes a simple *traditio,* and the bestowal of the pastoral staff is suppressed, but its accompanying prayer is kept and joined with that of the bestowal of the Bible. This is the end of the consecration proper.

δ) *Communion.*[*1593A/B] As in the ordination of priests, Holy Communion follows, and the newly ordained receives Communion from the hand of the archbishop. After the collect and before the blessing, the following prayer is added:

"Moste merciful father, we beseche thee to sende doune upon this thy Servaunt, thy heavenly blessyng, and so endue hym with thy holy spirite, that he preachyng thy woorde [2 Tim 4:2], maie not

---

[13] Cf. PRG LXIII, 41 (Vogel-Elze I, 222), and for the text that Cranmer most likely was familiar with, MASKELL II, 289).

onely bee earnest to reprove, beseche, and rebuke with all pacience and Doctryne, but also maie be to suche as beleve, an wholsome example, in woorde, in conversacion, in love, in faith, in chastitie, & puritie [1 Tim 4:12], that faithfully fulfillyng his course at the latter day, he may receive the croune of righteousness, laied up by the lorde [2 Tim 4:7f.], the righteous judge, who liveth and reigneth, one God with the father and holy Ghoste, world without end. Amen."[14]

This prayer is a good summary of episcopal office. The bishop is a preacher of the Word, an administrator of discipline, and a model of Christian conduct. In classic New Testament terminology, he exercises a prophetic and pastoral ministry. It is evident that Cranmer simplified the medieval rites by giving primary importance to the public prayer and the imposition of hands. Most of the secondary rites are suppressed, and, with them, the priestly aspect. Cranmer still remains a prisoner, however, of certain medieval concepts, such as the necessity for an imperative prayer [take ye . . .] for each order, and the separation of the gesture of the imposition of hands from the prayer. Let us now turn to the main prayers of ordination.

3. PRAYERS OF ORDINATION (OR CONSECRATION)

a. *Priest*

Except for the omission of the introductory dialogue and a few changes in spelling made in 1552, the prayers do not change from one edition to the next. Here is the text of 1550:

"The Lorde be with you.
Answere: And with thy spirit.
Let us praie.
Almightie God, and heavenly father, whiche of thy infinite love and goodnes towardes us, hast geven to us thy only, and most dere beloved sonne Iesus Christ to bee our redemer and auctour of everlastyng lyfe: who after he had made perfecte oure redempcion by his deathe, and was ascended into heaven, sent abrode into the world his Apostles, Prophetes, Evangelistes, Doctours, and Pastors, by whose laboure and ministery he gathered together a greate flocke in all the partes of the world, to set forth the eternal praise of thy holy name.

[14] The text derives from the office of enthronement of a bishop in the "Sarum" rite (MASKELL II, 306).

123

For these so greate benefites of thy eternall goodnes, and for that thou hast vouchesaufed to call these thy servauntes here present to the same office and ministery of the salvation of mankynde, we rendre unto the moste hartie thankes, we worship and praise the, and we humbly beseche the by the same thy sonne, to graunte unto all us whiche either here or els where cal upon thy name, that we maie shew oure selves thankefull to the for these and all other thy benefites, and that we maie daily encrease and go forwardes in the knowlege and fayth of the, and thy sonne, by the holy spirite. So that as well by these thy ministers, as by theim to whom thei shal be appoincted ministers thy holy name maie bee alwaies glorified and thy blessed kingdome enlarged: thorough the same thy sonne our Lorde Iesus Christe whiche liveth and reigneth with the in the unitie of the same holy Spirite worlde withoute ende. Amen."*1560A/B–*1561A/B

In order for the reader to grasp more easily the points of convergence and divergence between the prayers of Cranmer and Bucer,*289–*290 both texts will be found in parallel columns in the appendix [in vol. IV]. We note two omissions: the suppression of Bucer's epiclesis, and the suppression of another passage on the regeneration of the assembled people and on the Christians of the day, who are the object of the same benefits. As a result, the original prayer of Bucer, which was a prayer for the elect, is transformed into a prayer of thanksgiving which barely mentions the ordinands.

As we compare these two prayers, we see that both begin by giving thanks for the love of God, and above all for the gift of the Son of God, come as Redeemer and Savior. Next follows an anamnesis of this redemption accomplished by Christ. Bucer's anamnesis continues the action of Christ down to our time, but Cranmer's is cut short at this point. In Cranmer there is a prayer of thanksgiving for the call gone out to the elect, while in Bucer these elect are "offered [by God] to us so that they may be ordained for this purpose," that is, for the same ministry of human salvation as that of the apostles, the prophets, etc. Cranmer suppresses Bucer's epiclesis after the anamnesis. This epiclesis, it is true, does not seem to pertain very closely to an ordination (the gift of the Spirit is asked for the elect), but it connects the Christological aspect of the ministry to the action of the Spirit (". . . that they might fulfill faithfully their ministry . . ."). The two prayers are the same at the end, asking for the progress of the community in the knowledge of God, the glorification of his name, and the spread of the Kingdom of Christ.

According to the thesis of Bradshaw that we saw above, Cranmer made a strong connection between the litany, with its special petition and its collect, and the imposition of hands, both essential elements of each rite that he established. This fact explains why he changed the prayer of Bucer and his prayer pronounced during the imposition of hands. In Bucer, this prayer[291] is of the benediction/missioning type; but for Cranmer it is the ancient prayer *"Accipe Spiritum Sanctum . . ."* of the "Sarum" usage. This formula speaks of the power of the keys, of the Word, and of the sacraments. In our consideration of the prayer that accompanies the imposition of hands we will also compare it to the petition of the litany and the collect, the text of which we saw above.

α) *Biblical Images Employed.* According to the collect, which is addressed to God, "the dispenser of all good . . . who has established divers orders of ministers in the Church," we find again an image of the minister as steward or servant, with the image of the steward of the treasure of God and the image of a God of good order who watches over all things. We recall that this collect is used for all three orders, which are therefore all seen as part of the category of service or *diakonia.*

A second image derives from the prayer which is modeled on that of Bucer: thanks to the ministries given by Christ to the world, the Church is gathered together and built up for the praise of the name of God. We can see in this text an image presenting the priests as builders of the Church, a very ancient image that we saw with an eschatological meaning in the *Apostolic Tradition.*

β) *Qualities Requested for the Ordinand.* These are mostly qualities of Christian living that are asked for: integrity of life, and Christian conduct that will give a good example to the flock. As from now on in the tradition of the Reformation, each candidate is examined as to the morality of his life, his teaching and his knowledge of Scripture.

γ) *Gifts Received by the Ordinand.* The special petition said during the litany asks for the blessing of God, but also for his grace for the building up of the Church to the honor, praise, and glory of God. The collect which ends the litany asks for the truth to fulfill the charge of the priesthood. The prayer said at the imposition of hands asks humbly "by the same thy blessed son, to grant unto all, which either here, or elsewhere call upon thy holy Name, that we may continue to shew our selves thankful unto thee for these, and all other thy benefits; and that we may daily increase and go forwards in the knowledge and faith of thee . . ." The prayer said during the imposition of hands, on the other hand, transmits the gift of the Holy Spirit in view of the exercise of the keys, of the ministry of the Word and the sacraments.

b. *Bishop*

We recall that the petition of the litany and the collect which ends it are identical for the ordination of priests and bishops. The only thing that changes is the designation of the office. What was said above on this subject, then, applies here as well. As for the prayer said before the imposition of hands, it also has its origins in the prayer of Bucer, but with some important changes. At the beginning of the prayer, Cranmer followed Bucer quite faithfully, but Cranmer suppresses the second part after the quotation from the Letter to the Ephesians (Eph 4:8-12). In order to bring out the specific nature of the episcopacy, he here inserted the Gallican interpolation *Sint speciosi,* scriptural in style, which transforms it into a true prayer for the ordinand. The prayer said during the imposition of hands is scriptural also (2 Tim 1:6f.); it is of the command form, imitating the tradition of the later pontificals. Here is Cranmer's text of the prayer of consecration:

"The Lorde be with you.
Answere: And with thy spirite.
Let us praie.
Almightie God and most mercifull father, whiche of thy infinite goodnesse, has geven to us thy onely and moste dere beloved sonne Iesus Christ, to be our redemer and aucthour of everlastying life, who after that he had made perfecte our redempcion by his death, and was assended into heaven, powred doune his giftes abundauntly upon men, makyng some Apostles, some Prophetes, some Evangelistes, some Pastors and Doctors, to the edifiying and makyng perfecte of his congregacion: Graunt wee beseche thee, to this thy servant, suche grace that he maie be evermore ready to sprede abrode thy Gospell, and glad tidynges of reconcilement to God, and

to use the aucthoritie geven unto him not to destroy, but to save, not to hurt, but to helpe, so that he as a faithfull and a wise servaunt, gevyng to thy famely meate in due season, maie at the last daie, be received into joye, through Iesu Christ our Lorde, who with thee and the holy ghost, liveth and reigneth one God, worlde without ende. Amen."'*1589A/B

α) *Biblical Images Employed.* These are identical to those commented on above. The paraphrase from Ephesians is an even clearer expression of the apostolic text. With the use of the Gallican text, the image of the bishop as the successor to the apostles, the prophets, etc., is sharpened. He appears as a faithful servant and a prudent steward of the house of God, the Church, which he is to build up.

β) *Qualities Requested for the Ordinand.* These are identical to those found in the ordination of priests; there is no distinction made here.

γ) *Gifts Received by the Ordinand.* These gifts do not differ from those received by priests. Nevertheless, the request is more specific in the case of the bishop, in that it mentions the results hoped for, that he might be more prepared to preach the gospel and reconciliation, and to use his authority for the building up, and not the destruction, of the Church. In the formula "Take the Holy Ghost . . ." we find the affirmation that, through the imposition of hands, the ordinand possesses the grace of God, which is power, love, and prudence.

4. RELATIONSHIP BETWEEN THE PRIESTHOOD AND THE EPISCOPACY

We saw at the outset that Cranmer largely took the only rite proposed by Bucer and that he broke it up to make three liturgical offices for the three degrees of the ministry. Even with this division, Cranmer continues to see equality between the office of the priesthood and that of the episcopacy; in this he believed he was returning to the teaching of the Fathers, such as Ambrose, Augustine, Basil, Chrysostom, and Jerome,[15] and that he was making no innovations. We can see that he thought this as we study the rites. Except for a few details in the questions put to the elected bishop, there is scarcely any distinction between the charges of priest and bishop. Both exer-

---

[15] Cf. his work "Common place Book" (430–436) quoted by P. F. BRADSHAW, *The Anglican Ordinal . . .,* 16.

cise a ministry of the Word and of administration of the sacraments for the building up of the Church. We did see, however, that the pastoral aspect of the bishop was slightly more emphasized than that of the priest.[16] The admonition[*1578A/B] which introduces the examination of the bishop shows that he is ordained to the governance of the Church (as made clear by the scriptural quotation).

5. LATER INFLUENCE OF THE ORDINALS

These Ordinals have had a direct influence down to our day. The revision made in 1661 was based on the Ordinals of 1550/1552, and the changes made had little to do with their content. Many Churches of the Anglican Communion use the Ordinal, or have used it.[17] Moreover, John Wesley used the Ordinal of 1661 for his rites of ordination; all rites that stem from Wesley's show, therefore, the influence of the Anglican Ordinal. Lastly, the Ordinal also influenced the rites of the Church of South India, through the participation of the Anglican Churches in this Union. The spirituality of the Ordinal of the *BCP* has had, then, a long history, continuing right down to our day.

6. CONCLUSION: STRUCTURING OF THE CHURCH AND THE SUBSTANCE OF ORDAINED MINISTRY

a. *Structure of the Church*

What sort of structuring of the Church do we find in our study of the Anglican Ordinal? The actors are the same in all the rites, but can the same be said for the relationships between them?

From information gathered from the preface we know that the ministers were elected, but we do not know the procedure followed. In the succession of rituals that were published very few traces of the procedure followed were left, no more than we find in the medieval pontificals. However that may be, we know that the people still have one last chance to present objections during the office of ordination

---

[16] Cf. *1586A/B, a question taken from the "Sarum" usage and that was always part of the episcopal ministry.

[17] The Churches that still use the Ordinal of 1661 are, e.g.: The Church of England, The Church of Ireland, The Spanish Reformed Episcopal Church, The Lusitanian Church. For still other Churches of the Anglican Communion that use it, see C. BUCHANAN (ed.), *Modern Anglican Ordination Rites* (Bramcote, Nottingham: Grove Books Ltd., 1987) passim.

(at least for priests). This possibility, however, seems to have been limited to a simple ritual question to which no response was expected.

As in the tradition of the early Church and that of the English Churches, ordination takes place on a Sunday or a major feast day, when the whole Church gathers. The people play a major role in the prayer that Cranmer considers essential. Since the litany was such an important prayer in the Church it necessarily involved the active participation of the faithful, as did the silent prayer just before the imposition of hands. The people are present also at the ordinand's commitment made during the examination. The bishop is to verify the suitability of each ordinand, obviously before this solemn moment. Moreover, the preface contains the requirements of age and other qualifications. We note, lastly, that the nature and intensity of the participation of the people in the Anglican rituals are less emphasized than in the other Reformed rituals, a fact that will be severely criticized by the Puritans.

Even though the Ordinal does not say that the minister at the ordination is the bishop, he is the presumed celebrant. We will see later that, in response to the criticism of the Puritans, the preface and even the rite of consecration will be modified to preclude the possibility of any other celebrant at an ordination.

At the ordination of a priest, the other priests appear as a college during the imposition of hands, but they do not appear as such anywhere else in the *BCP*. We cannot affirm that there existed a college of priests, for each priest was ordained for a particular congregation.

The tradition was kept in the consecration of a bishop with the participation of several bishops and at least three for the imposition of hands. Can we infer from this a collegial conception of the episcopacy? According to other documents presented by Bradshaw we know too that the bishops had the custom of assembling in synod to discuss pastoral and doctrinal problems. The role of the bishop in the structure of the Church will become clearer with the revision of the Ordinal in 1661.

Lastly, the role of the Spirit, so present in Bucer's office, is greatly reduced in the Ordinal for the ordination of priests. We see the Spirit more active in the ritual for the consecration of a bishop. In the prayers pronounced during the imposition of hands the Spirit is strongly involved in the transmission of the office and the authority of the bishop. During the admonition that takes place before the examination of priests[1547A/B] we also see the role of the Holy Spirit: the priest must pray to the Spirit for the capacity to assume such a dignity and such a heavy responsibility towards the community that he is to serve. In the same admonition[1546A/B] the Church is described as "the spouse and body of Christ," won at the price of his Blood, and this reality demands that the priest devote all his care and energy to his service. The quotation from Ephesians 4 in the prayer reveals also the Christological dimension of the ministry in the Church.

In the model of the Church which is revealed in these rituals, each person plays his proper role, but we must add that the rituals do not express clearly enough the nature of the relationships between those involved. The Church continues to be built up by Christ acting through his ministers, notably the priests and the bishops that he sends to her service. Nevertheless, the solidarity between the different members of the Church is hardly perceptible.

b. *Substance of the Ministries of Priest and Bishop*

Cranmer makes no distinction between the offices of priest and bishop; in this he believed he was returning to the practice of the early Church followed by the apostles and the Fathers of the Church. We have seen, however, that there is slightly more emphasis put on the pastoral ministry of the bishop. Priests are described in the following terms:[1545A/B] they are messengers, watchmen, shepherds, and stewards of the Lord. Their tasks are to teach, to exhort, to feed the flock, to support the family of the Lord, to seek the lost sheep of the flock of Christ,[1545A/B] and to administer doctrine, the sacraments, and discipline.[1552A/B]

There is no such series of terms applied directly to the bishop, but we do find certain designations applied to him, such as apostle and disciple.[1575A/B] Among his functions (aside from those that he holds in common with the priests) the text emphasizes preaching and teaching (in the questions [2–4] of the examination and in the readings from Scripture, the litany, the prayer of consecration, etc.), the pastoral aspect of ministry, the governance of the Church (in the readings, the introduction to the examination, the questions [6–7], etc.), as well as his exemplary life, which is to serve as a model for others.

The two ministries are intended for the service of a concrete Church: there are no absolute ordinations at this time. Even if the activity of the laity is not emphasized as much as in other Protestant rituals, several references are made to the congregation or the Church in which the ordinand is to exercise his ministry.

We should note that Cranmer expressly wanted to suppress the image of the ministers as offering sacrifice; he expanded Bucer's office only with texts from the pontifical, mostly based on the New Testament, which make no mention of sacrifice. Almost all the secondary rituals added during the late Middle Ages are gotten rid of, in particular all anointings and vestings. On the other hand, he kept the bestowal of the chalice and the Bible in the case of priests, and of the Bible and the pastoral staff in the case of the bishop, while making sure the formulas of transmission have a biblical meaning. In this way the meaning of the ministry of both priest and bishop becomes explicitly evangelical, based on the New Testament.

Lastly, both ministries studied have as their purpose the building up of the Church (the spouse and body of Christ), the assembly of a people reborn to the praise and glory of God, the Father, the Son, and the Holy Spirit. The priests and the bishop in this Church watch over doctrine and the discipline and worthiness of the Christian life of the community, by preaching the gospel, by exhorting all to right conduct, and by administering the sacraments of salvation.

B. THE ORDINAL OF 1661

To understand this definitive version of the Ordinal in its historical context we must have some knowledge of the political and theological tensions that existed within the Anglican Church between 1550 and 1661, as well as the Catholic criticisms issued during the same period.[18] The revision of the Ordinal was part of the general revision of the *BCP*, which itself was the object of a struggle between those who wanted to move closer to the Reformation on the Continent—a more presbyterian or evangelical structure (referred to as "Low

---

[18] Our guides for this period are: P. F. BRADSHAW, *The Anglican Ordinal . . .*, 37–86; G. J. CUMING (ed.), *The Durham Book; Being a First Draft of the Revision of the Book of Common Prayer in 1661* (London: Alcuin Club, 1975), esp. the introduction; and E. P. ECHLIN, *The Story of Anglican Ministry* (Slough: St. Paul Publications, 1974).

Church")—and those who, on the contrary, wanted to return to principles closer to the *BCP* of 1549, and therefore to a more episcopal or conservative structure (referred to as "High Church"). This last group had adherents of considerable stature, such as John Overall (1560–1619), Lancelot Andrewes (1555–1626, bishop of Winchester), William Laud (1573–1645), Matthew Wren (1586–1667), and John Cosin (1594–1672).

The Puritans reacted almost immediately to the *BCP* of 1549, and their opposition continued throughout this entire period, in England (from 1550 to 1602) and in Scotland (from 1560 to 1638). After the restoration of a Protestant monarchy and the *BCP* in 1559, a new wave of opposition began in England. This time, the Puritans called for a system of election and examination closer to that which they had known in exile on the Continent among Calvinists and the Reformed Churches. It was not so much that they were objecting to the men proposed, but rather that they wanted to be able to elect them according to the practice of the early Church. Moreover, they wanted to suppress the remaining papal customs such as certain liturgical vestments, certain postures assumed during the liturgy, etc. Other objections had to do with the absence of a body of elders (lay), and with the distinction between priest and bishop, for, according to their way of thinking, the New Testament postulates equality among all the ministers.[19] The Puritans also wanted the ordinations to be preceded by the traditional preparation of prayers and fasting; they demanded that the idea that ordination confers grace be abandoned, that Roman priests not be treated as true ministers of the gospel, and that the use of the word "priest" be given up. All in all, four attempts at revising the *BCP* and the Ordinal were required. In 1581 they presented a certain number of criticisms to the Queen, but without success. In 1584 a petition of sixteen articles was presented to the House of Lords. In 1586 their position had hardened, and they presented a complete revision of the book to Parliament with a proposal for legislation that would replace the *BCP* with another incorporating this new Puritan revision. It is this last book that we find in use among the Puritans

---

[19] See the "Puritan Manifestoes," quoted by P. F. BRADSHAW, *The Anglican Ordinal . . .*, 42f., who concludes that one can scarcely find a single author in the Elizabethan period who explicitly denied that priests could ordain.

exiled in Middleburgh. At length the final revision was finished in 1602; we find it in the formulary of Middleburgh already examined.[20]

The situation was different in Scotland, for there the Anglican Ordinal had never been adopted: the ritual introduced in 1560 by John Knox was in use, and it had been modeled upon the liturgical redaction of J. Łaski. It contained no office for the ordination or consecration of a bishop, nor any imposition of hands, for that matter. The second *Book of Discipline* (1580) turned out to be acceptable to the Puritans: it added the imposition of hands performed by the other ministers, and the fasting and prayers which were to accompany the entire rite. Under pressure from James VI, the rituals of ordination were made uniform, and in 1610 the episcopal rites were introduced. A compromise was worked out between the Anglican Ordinal and the Reformed form, and this resulted in the Scottish Ordinal of 1620.[21] This was revised in 1636, but temporarily rejected in 1638 by the General Assembly of the Church of Scotland when the episcopacy was discarded and Presbyterianism established.[22]

During the reign of James I in England, in 1604, the *BCP* was revised as the result of the Hampton Court Conference. This revision did not change the Ordinal, but we find some concessions in the Canons published later in the same year: the examination of the candidates is carried out by the bishop in the presence of other

[20] For all the details of this period, see P. F. BRADSHAW, *The Anglican Ordinal . . .*, 39–54. The two Puritans associated with these criticisms are Thomas Cartwright and William Fulke. There is a critical edition of all the demands of the Puritans in W. H. FRERE and C. E. DOUGLAS, *LXXII Puritan Manifestoes. A Study of the Origin of the Puritan Revolt with a Reprint of the Admonition to the Parliament and Kindered Documents, 1572* (London/N.Y.: SPCK/E. S. Gorham, 1907). In the opposing camp, the Angicans who defended a "High Church" concept of the ministry are John Whitgift, Matthew Sutcliffe, John Bridges (or Welles), Thomas Bilson, Thomas Cooper, and Richard Hooker, known for his important work, *Of the Laws of Ecclesiastical Polity* (1597). For the bibliographical material relative to each of the above, see Bradshaw.

[21] The text consists of two rituals, the ordination of bishops and that of minister. The diaconate persisted, but ceased to be a step along the way to ministerial ordination. This Ordinal is composed of the Anglican office for priests (but uses the word "ministers") and the order of Knox for superintendents. The text is found in G. W. SPROTT (ed.), *Scottish Liturgies . . .*, 111–129, 159–165. Cf. G. DONALDSON, "Scottish . . .," 169–175.

[22] P. F. BRADSHAW, *The Anglican Ordinal . . .*, 59f.

members of the clergy of the cathedral, and of at least three persons who impose hands. The ordination takes place in the cathedral, always on the Sunday following Ember Days. No one can be ordained deacon and priest on the same day, and no one can be ordained without a title. For the Puritans this was not nearly enough, given the Catholic understanding of the episcopacy developed by William Laud, which called for the power of ordination for the bishop, and held as null and void any ordination performed otherwise. The Presbyterian party rebelled, and rejected all compromise. The conflict between the Puritans and the partisans of Laud grew so fierce that in 1641 a committee charged with studying all innovations in the Church presented a proposal for reform to the House of Lords. The Puritans rejected any compromise that included the episcopacy. The bishops were expelled from Parliament, and were arrested wherever they fled. This brought Charles I to grant a concession in 1644 which required that the bishops never ordain except in concert with the presbyters (the dean and the chapter). This concession, too, was rejected, and in 1648 the episcopacy was abolished and the Westminster Assembly (composed of Puritan theologians nominated by Parliament) was charged with elaborating a new system of Church government, and a new Ordinal.

This group proposed a text entitled "A Directory for the Public Worship of God," which was nothing other than the Reformed model for worship. This still did not settle the question, because when the Independents (the most radical branch of the Puritans) took control of the Assembly, total confusion ensued. Finally, after the fall of the Commonwealth in 1660, Charles II was restored to the throne and both the bishops and the clergy returned. None of the subsequent attempts at finding a middle way was acceptable to the bishops or the Puritans. The king refused to concede the necessity for the approval of the presbyters for the ordination of a candidate. What was more, the bishops insisted that all those who had been ordained without a bishop presiding be reordained. In 1661, at Savoy, a conference finally was convened to revise the BCP.

Several men contributed to the revision of the BCP. When the king announced his decision to appoint a commission to revise it, Matthew Wren (bishop of Ely) prepared a manuscript, the *Advices*, which used annotations he had made on the BCP while in prison; he added the scriptural sources for the texts, and corrected typographical errors, the Latin expressions, and archaisms of language. J. Cosin (bishop of Durham) produced a similar project, the *Particulars*, but he paid more attention to the rubrics, to the elimination of ambiguities and inconsistencies, and to the juridical impact of the text. It is likely that he used Wren's text for his revision. William Sancroft (Cosin's chaplain) compiled the version of the Ordinal that was in fact submitted to the Convocation of the bishops and clergy on May 8, 1661. When the work was done, the book of public prayers was adopted on December 20, 1661; the act of uniformity passed on May 8, 1662, and the *BCP* went into effect on August 24, 1662. It received the Seal only on December 25, 1662, and on that date all the cathedrals received it.[23]

We shall limit our study to the changes made in the Ordinal of the *BCP* of 1662, and to their theological importance. But first two remarks on the title and the preface of the Ordinal are necessary.

First of all, the new title is, "The Forme and Manner of Making, *Ordeining*, and Consecrating of Bishops, Priests and Deacons, *According to the Order of the Church of England*." The words in italics show what had been added to the preceding book. This is a change proposed by Wren, who wanted to be more precise in the use of the words; more than anything else, regarding the consecration, he wanted to reject two extreme positions which set in opposition, on the one hand, a purely ceremonial meaning that is found in the Church of Rome according to which the use of the word "consecration" has as its purpose "thereby to draw Episcopacy to a dependency wholly on the Pleasure, and Power of ye Papacy, " and, on the other hand, a meaning found in the "Aërian faction" (that is, the Puritans), according to which "the Episcopacy is not a distinct Order in ye Church of Christ, but onely a Degree, in nature no otherwise above Presbytery, than as Archiepiscopacy is above Episcopacy . . ."[24] His intention is

---

[23] For the chronology of the book, see G. J. CUMING (ed.), *The Durham Book . . .,* xvi–xxvi.

[24] ". . . *thereby to draw Episcopacy to a dependency wholy on the Pleasure, and Power of ye Papacy, as but his Commissioners; . . . also by ye Aërien Faction . . ., that Episcopacy is not a distinct Order in ye Church of Christ, but onely a Degree, in nature no otherwise above Presbytery, than as Archiepiscopacy is above Episcopacy . . .,*" quoted by P. F. BRADSHAW, *The Anglican Ordinal . . .,* 87f.

clear: the episcopacy is an order distinct from the presbyterate, and it is independent of any higher ecclesiastical power.

The changes in the preface also merit commentary: they are intended to exclude any Puritan interpretation of ordination by suppressing the phrase ". . . no man *by his own private aucthoritie* might presume to execute any of them [ministerial charges], except he were first . . ."[*1538C] Through this omission, ordination by the congregation or by any other minister than the bishop is made inconceivable, and this is made clear further along in the text: ". . . and also by publique prayer with imposition of hands, were approved and admitted there-unto *by lawfull authority . . . no man shall be accounted or taken to be a lawfull Bishop, Priest, or Deacon in the Church of England, or* sufferred to *execute any of the said Functions,* except he be called, tryed, examined, and admitted *thereunto,* according to the Form hereafter following, *or hath had formerly Episcopall Consecration or Ordination."* The words in italics were added in 1661. Here we have episcopal ordination as a condition sine qua non for admission to the ministry in the Church of England.[25] We will see further on that other changes to the Ordinal will reinforce this interpretation.

Other modifications in the preface bring the ordination more into conformity with the canons of the Church according to which the deacon should be at least twenty-three years old, and a Sunday other than those which follow Ember Days or a feast day would be allowed, exceptionally, in cases of emergencies, to be the day on which the ordination would be conferred.

1. STRUCTURE OF ORDINATION AND CONSECRATION

a. *Priest*

In the structure of the office, three major changes are found: the presentation, the litany, and the collect are found at the beginning of the office (which begins with morning prayer) right after the sermon or exhortation, and before the readings, which are modified. Next,

---

[25] P. F. BRADSHAW, *The Anglican Ordinal . . .,* 97; and also E. P. ECHLIN, *The Story . . .,* 140, where he states that ". . . the changes in the Ordinal in 1662 were meant to counter the spectrum of non-conformist opinions which reduced episcopacy and blurred the distinctions within the hierarchy . . . what was signified was that bishops, priests and deacons were distinct orders and that bishops succeeded the apostles in government, discipline and the power to ordain."

the hymn to the Holy Spirit is sung after the invitation to silent prayer just before the prayer of ordination. Lastly, two special collects were added before the conclusion of Holy Communion.

The text for the presentation is identical to that of 1552. The only change is the restoration of a rubric pertaining to the investiture: "each of them being properly vested." The beginning of the office was doubtlessly reworked so that the ordination of priests had the same structure as that of deacons, and so that both could easily be celebrated on the same occasion.[26] The most important change is found in the choice of readings, for now each office has its own readings. For priests, a new epistle is provided, Ephesians 4:7-13 (on the different gifts of grace in the ministry),[27] while the ritual keeps John 10 (the Good Shepherd) for the gospel, adding Matthew 9:36-38 (on the workers for the harvest). The other pericopes were transferred to the consecration of a bishop (Acts, 1 Tim 3, Mt 28, and Jn 20). Bradshaw thinks, with good reason, that these changes were made in order to dispute the opinion of the Puritans, who held that priests and bishops constitute one and the same order; for one of the epistles previously prescribed for the ordination of priests, 1 Timothy 3, describes the qualities of bishops, while Acts 20 describes the Church of Ephesus governed by elders (presbyters). This last text has been cited to show that the Church of England wants her priests to do the same thing, with the bishop presiding.[28]

A few changes, both linguistic (for instance, the word "congregation" is replaced each time with "Church") and stylistic, were made to the exhortation to the ordinands; these changes do not require commentary. The omission of the word "pastors"[*1545C] in the list of charges entrusted to the priests was contested by the Puritans, who maintained that priests and bishops are equal in the governing of the Church. The same omission was made in the petition of the litany for the ministers ("all the bishops, *priests,* and *deacons*"[*1598C]). Along with the other modifications made in the ordinations, this change confirms the tendency to maintain a clear distinction between the two orders, and to reserve the function of overall governance primarily to the

---

[26] Cf. *The English Rite* I, ccxxiii.

[27] The third reading of Bucer.

[28] P. F. BRADSHAW, *The Anglican Ordinal . . .,* 91.

bishops. This will become even clearer when we examine the changes made in the office of the consecration of bishops.

Two remarks are in order regarding the examination: 1) in the first question we read that the priesthood is not only a ministry, but also an "order";[*1550C] and 2) the third question says it is "this Church" which has received the doctrine and the sacraments, and not only the Kingdom, as was said in the text of 1552.

The relocation of the hymn to the Holy Spirit to a position in the ceremony just before the prayer of ordination helps establish a certain parallelism with the other rites, but it also calls attention to the action of the Spirit in the conferral of ordination.[29]

As for the prayer itself, the changes do not merit particular comment: they mainly serve to clarify or to polish the style of the text.

Because of the questions raised by certain Puritans and Catholics at the time, the revision of 1661 added the following sentence to the prayers pronounced during the imposition of hands: "Receive the Holy Ghost, *for the Office, and work of a Priest, in the Church of God, now committed unto thee by the imposition of our hands.*"[*1563C] There is no longer any doubt as to which order is meant. The bestowal of the Bible then follows, as was customary, with its usual prayer, which more or less repeats what had just been said: it grants the ordinand jurisdiction over a particular flock. In 1661 the word "thereunto" was added at the end of the formula "where thou shall be *lawfully* appointed . . ."[*1564C]

Lastly, at the conclusion of Holy Communion two collects were added: the first[*1567C] is taken from the office of Communion[30] and is a sort of act of thanksgiving; while the second[*1568C] is the usual blessing which ends the Communion service.[31] The formulary ends with a rubric[*1569C] which describes the way in which deacons and priests are

[29] Bradshaw distances himself from Brightman, who gives a purely logical reason for this change. Bradshaw bases himself on the writings of Cosin himself to emphasize that there was a more theological reason that could explain this change: the necessary association of the role of the Spirit in the gesture of the imposition of hands; cf. P. F. BRADSHAW, *The Anglican Ordinal . . .*, 90.

[30] From the "Sarum" usage for the Saturday of the Ember Days in Lent, prayer 5; cf. *The English Rite* II, 712.

[31] This was a fairly common benediction in the pontificals; it is composed of two biblical quotations: Phil 4:7 and 2 Pet 1:2; cf. *The English Rite* II, 710.

to be ordained in one ceremony. Certain readings are prescribed for this office: Ephesians 4 and Matthew 9 (from the office of priests), or Luke 12 (from the office of deacons).

b. *Bishop*

As for the ordination of priests, little was changed here. Nevertheless, those changes that were made had considerable theological importance. First of all, we note the new title of the office: "The Forme of *Ordination* or Consecrating of an Archbishop or Bishop *Which is Always to be Performed upon some Sunday, or Holy-Day.*" A new collect is placed after the morning prayers, before the readings, which also were changed. There is no change before the examination, which is found in its usual place, but a new question has been added to it. Between the examination and the singing of the hymn to the Holy Spirit the new bishop is clothed with the rest of the bishop's vestments. Two special collects are added to the end of the Communion service.

The change in the title (which we also see in the presentation of the ordinand[*1573C]) is significant, for it puts an end to the discussion as to whether the office was a simple ceremony or a true ordination. The fact that this ordination takes place on the usual day of the assembly of the Church, or at least on a major feast day, is also significant. The collect[*1570C] which was chosen (taken from the Feast of St. Peter) brings out the link between the apostles, the ordination of the bishop, and the charge entrusted to the bishops who are pastors of the Church: the tasks of preaching the Word and exercising the discipline that the Word prescribes.

We have already looked at the significance of the changes made in the liturgy of the Word for the ordination of priests. It has the same importance here in the case of the bishop. For the epistle, the reading from 1 Timothy 3 (on the attributes of a bishop) was kept, but a reading was added from Acts 20:17-35 (the bishops are established by the Holy Spirit as shepherds of the flock). For the gospel, the reading from John 21 was kept, but the pericopes from Matthew 28 and John 20 from the rite of priests were transferred to that of bishops. By so doing the revisers clearly emphasized the difference between the two orders, while presenting the bishops as successors of the apostles.[32]

[32] Cf. P. F. BRADSHAW, *The Anglican Ordinal . . .*, 91.

A phrase specifying the functions of the bishop was added to the collect which concludes the litany:[*1577C] ". . . the edifying and well governing of thy Church."

The new question added to the examination asks: "Will you be faithfull in ordaining, sending, or laying hands upon others?"[*1585C] Such a question underscores the fact that the function of ordaining belongs to the episcopacy, and not to the presbyterate.[33] The same versions of the hymn to the Holy Spirit are found after the examination, as elsewhere. There are no substantial changes to the prayer of ordination.

However, the rubric and the prayer said during the imposition of hands both show changes. The ordinand receives the imposition of hands upon the head, "kneeling before them [the bishops]." The prayer reads as follows: "Receive the holy Ghost, *for the office and work of a Bishop in the Church of God, now committed unto thee by the Imposition of our hands, in the Name of the Father, and of the Son, and of the holy Ghost, Amen.* And remember that thou stir up the grace of God which is *given* thee, by *this* imposition of *our* hands . . ."[*1590C] Two objectives were attained in this prayer: it mentions from now on the office received; and the ambiguity created by the way in which the scriptural quotation (1 Tim 4) is used is hereafter cleared up by the addition of the phrase, "the grace of God which is given thee, by this imposition of our hands." This text demonstrates clearly the Church of England's teaching that the gift of grace is bestowed in ordination.

The service of Holy Communion ends with the same collects as the ritual of ordination of priests. The two prayers of ordination said just before the imposition of hands are not altered in respect to their content: the changes made in the rituals served to modify the relationship between the priesthood and the episcopacy.

2. RELATIONSHIP BETWEEN THE PRIESTHOOD AND THE EPISCOPACY

The desire to emphasize the distinction between the two orders of the Anglican hierarchy, priests and bishops, was realized. From now

---

[33] Another interpretation, though not very plausible, is the explanation advanced by G. J. Cuming, who thinks that, because of the lack of bishops towards the end of the Commonwealth, Lord Clarendon found it difficult to convince the remaining bishops of the urgency of filling their posts: the question would have been added to remind them of their charge. Cf. G. J. CUMING, *A History . . .*, 164.

on ordination is reserved to the episcopacy, and it is clearly understood as one of the primary responsibilities of the bishop's office. Another function that is stressed, although less so, is that of the governance of the Church, by likening the ministry of the bishop to that of the apostles. At the same time the pastoral and prophetic aspect of the ministry received more emphasis as well. But this did not mean that the priests did not help the bishop in his charge of governing the Church; it only excluded all possible interpretation along Presbyterian lines.

3. CONCLUSION: STRUCTURING OF THE CHURCH AND THE SUBSTANCE OF ORDAINED MINISTRY

a. *Structure of the Church*

The only truly essential change had to do with the relationship between the bishop and his priests. Nothing in regard to the laity has been changed; lay people still have their own role to play. Moreover, the Holy Spirit is seen as more intimately involved in the act of ordination, and it is clear that the grace of the Spirit is truly conferred in the rite. The bishop is charged with the governance of the Church, as is made abundantly clear; in this he is assisted by his priests.

b. *Substance of the Ordained Ministry*

Obviously, the most important change that emerges from the revisions of 1661 is the unequivocal affirmation that only the bishop can confer ordination. In this manner the Church of England declares that no ministry conferred by a minister other than the bishop will be acceptable.

C. OVERALL CONCLUSIONS

The process of revising the *BCP* involved not only the ecclesiastical reformers, but also the king and the English Parliament, which follows from the recognition by this same Parliament in 1534 that King Henry VIII was "the supreme head on earth of the Church of England." In 1559 Queen Elizabeth I even had this "Act of Supremacy" renewed, recognizing her as ". . . the only Supreme Governour of this Realm . . . as well in all spirituall or ecclesiasticall things, or causes, as temporall."[*1604C] Awareness of this conjunction of political and religious interests is important for a clear grasp of the negotiations accompanying the revision of the *BCP*. The revision of the

Ordinal is to be seen as part of the same process. From this state of affairs we can draw a first conclusion: the liturgical reform in the Church of England was not a matter of doctrine and religion alone. It has to be viewed also against the background of a permanent dialogue with political authority. We saw that certain movements within the Reformation threatened the principle of the monarchy and even resulted in its violent overthrow and the establishment of a Commonwealth and a presbyterian Church. Keeping this fact in mind, we can draw the following conclusions:

1. ELEMENTS USUALLY INCLUDED IN EACH FORMULARY

a. *Election*

Some of the most heated criticisms of the Ordinal coming from the Puritans concerned the manner of election. Representing a movement in the English Church that had been strongly influenced by the Reformed Calvinists, they wanted more participation of the faithful and less episcopal independence regarding the choice and examination of the men proposed for the ministry. They believed that the Ordinal merely copied the pontificals. But, in fact, not a single concession was made to the Puritans on this point. The three Ordinals repeat in their prefaces what the Anglican Church considered sufficient: ". . . no man might presume to execute any of them [ministerial charges] except he were first *called, tried, examined and known* to have such qualities as are requisite for the same . . ." But the manner of election is not described. The faithful have the right to reject a candidate, in the case of a crime in his background or some other grave obstacle: this is the ritual election. It is the bishop's responsibility, with the help of the ministers of other Churches, to make sure that the persons proposed are suitable for ordination.

Concerning election, the Anglican Ordinals follow in the tradition of the English pontificals. The right of the people to choose their own ministers is indirectly referred to, in keeping with the late model found in the Latin Church: it is a right of exclusion. The selection of ministers by the faithful played an important role in the Reform movement on the Continent, but this aspect of the reform of the Church does not seem to have been as important in the Church of England.

b. *Ordination*

We mean by this term the public prayers and the imposition of hands: progressively over time it came to be applied to the consecration of the bishop. The entire process of election/ordination was not necessarily included in this term alone. As we see in the preface, ordination is necessary for a person to assume official ministerial functions in the Church of England. It was more and more clearly articulated that ordination must include the imposition of hands by the bishop, departing firmly from the Puritan interpretation of this rite.

The two essential elements are the public prayer and the imposition of hands, which were the traditional heart of any ordination. Again in the preface it is made clear that by this gesture the Anglican Church wants to maintain the three orders (bishops, priests, and deacons) which are of apostolic origin.

The significance of the gesture and of the formula, "Take the holy Spirit . . .," were the object of much discussion among Puritan and Anglican theologians. The clearest interpretation was articulated by the bishop Whitgift to the Puritan Cartwright: the bishop acts as an instrument *(instrumentaliter)* when he pronounces the words of Christ, "to signify that God by our ministry and imposition of hands, as by the instruments, doth give his Holy Spirit to all such as are rightfully called to the ministry."[34].

Doubtless because of the criticisms of the Puritans, on the one hand, and of the Catholics, on the other, the redactors of the Ordinals produced an ever more precise formulation of the office that is being conferred. Still, the prayer that precedes the imposition of hands in the rite of ordination of priests is not truly a prayer for the elect, but rather a prayer for the congregation. If we except a special petition during the litany and its collect, we do not find any prayer that is said specifically for the ordinand. Moreover, the prayer of the litany is identical for the three orders, with only the designation of the office being different, and nothing at all being said as to the substance of the offices conferred. The revision of 1661 attempted to remedy this oversight by specifically mentioning the office in the prayer said during the imposition of hands. There is, on the other hand, a true prayer for the new bishop.

[34] P. F. BRADSHAW, *The Anglican Ordinal . . .*, 47.

The same problem was partially resolved in 1661 with the reworking of the Liturgy of the Word for each office. Here we find an intelligent choice of readings, making explicit the way in which the Church of England understood each office.

c. *Mission*

Every minister is ordained for a concrete charge, as is always said unequivocally in each rite. Moreover, with the clarification brought in 1661 through the new choice of readings, we see that the mission of the bishop is described as including the governance of the Church, the pastoral duties of his office, the exercise of the keys, the ordination of other ministers, and the preaching and teaching of the Scriptures. To these we could add the defense of the poor, and the maintenance of peace among believers. As for the priests, the readings indicate that their mission is the building up of the Body of Christ through the charism given them, and their tasks as servants of the Lord and good shepherds. They are also referred to as messengers, guardians, and stewards of the Lord, who teach, exhort, and pasture the family of the Lord with the Scriptures and the sacraments. Lastly, they owe obedience to their bishops.

2. ACTORS INVOLVED IN THE PROCESS

a. *The Local Church*

Even though the local Church is not actively involved in the process of election, it is so passively. The right the local congregation possesses means that it is to receive its ministers. The community is also actively involved in the prayer said for the ordinand in two places in the liturgy: in the prayer of the litany, and also in the silent prayer calling upon the Holy Spirit. In the first volume of this study we saw the latter in the ancient rite of the *Apostolic Tradition* for the ordination of a bishop. The vocation of these ministers, then, is mediated through the local community. In the case of the ordination of a bishop, even though the local community has chosen the one who is being ordained, this choice has been made with the help of the other bishops, the heads of other Churches.

The priests and the bishop profess the *Credo* along with the people whom they have been called to serve. The priests recite the creed immediately after their ordination, while the bishop does so just before his presentation to the people. All these practices are intended to be faithful to the ancient tradition, as we saw it throughout volume I of this study. We see throughout the entirety of the process of ordination that priest and bishop share the common grace of the baptized in the proclamation of faith that they both make as they assume the charge of their ministry.

b. *The Newly Ordained*

The newly ordained is called to this ministry, and he affirms in the ritual examination that he believes he has been called. We have seen that the Anglican rituals inherited a Calvinistic conception of vocation (the internal vocation) in which the secret vocation lies in the deep conviction that one is drawn to ministry in the Church and the service of God from strictly disinterested motives (not from personal ambition). Besides this internal vocation, there is the ecclesial element, an external call from the Church which recognizes the aptitudes and graces that God has given to the elect. The visible elements of vocation include faith and the required qualities, the need or the task to fulfill, and the call of the Church.

c. *The Holy Spirit*

We have seen that the 1661 revision of the Ordinal brought the hymn to the Holy Spirit closer to the imposition of hands, making it even clearer what the Church is actually doing at that point. Whitgift's response, mentioned above, shows that for the Anglican Church the ministry of the bishop is a ministry of the Spirit, for through the imposition of hands and the prayer to the Holy Spirit the gift of the Spirit is conferred upon the ordinand. This gift is considered necessary for the ministry, because it is God who, hearing the prayer of the community, gives his Spirit. So the role of the Spirit is very important in the process of ordination, as we see particularly clearly in the ordination of a bishop. The epiclesis is lacking in the ordination of priests, however. We recall that Cranmer suppressed it when he used the prayer of Bucer. This epiclesis was never restored to its original place. The imperative formula said during the imposition of hands could be considered a substitute for the epiclesis. In the revision of 1661 its meaning was made explicit: it is a gift of a precise office, and a help in the fulfillment of the functions of the ministry.

d. *The Neighboring Bishops*

We saw that the participation of all the bishops present during the imposition of hands was required. It is not clear what the significance of their role really was. This practice kept alive an old tradition which from then on will no longer be questioned. Whitgift's statement opens the door to a possible interpretation that would see in them the ministers of the gift of the Spirit. In any case, a bishop is never ordained without the participation of other bishops.

3. SUBSTANCE OF THE ORDAINED MINISTRY

In the beginning of the English Reformation the first Ordinal allowed of several interpretations. The Puritans took advantage of this situation by affirming the equality of all ministers. This in turn led to a series of successive revisions of the ritual precisely to exclude this equality, and to establish the necessity of ordination by a bishop as a sine qua non condition for every ordination. These revisions made it ever clearer that the episcopal ministry includes the governance of the Church, and therefore the task of ordaining her ministers, as well as the functions of watching over doctrine and discipline, the power of the keys, teaching, preaching, and the administration of the sacraments. The priests are associates of the episcopal ministry in all its tasks, except for ordination, which is reserved to the bishop alone. In both cases, ordained ministry is intended for the building up of the Body of Christ according to the plan of Christ himself. This ministry is described in pastoral terms.

4. PERMANENCE OF THE ORDAINED MINISTRY

There is no mention of any re-ordination after a change of parish. Ordained ministry is always described as permanent and concrete, linked to a precise community. The episcopacy also is a permanent ministry.

Chapter 4

First Formulary of the Methodist Church

A. THE *SUNDAY SERVICE* (1784)—JOHN WESLEY

1. AUTHOR: RELATIONSHIP WITH THE RITUALS OF THE CHURCH OF ENGLAND

This formulary was born both of necessity and of a "political" tension within the Church of England. For one thing, John Wesley had seen the pressing need in the American colonies for a ministry of supervision independent of England. By 1784 the Church of England had still not appointed a bishop for the colonies, in which the Church was part of the diocese of London. For another thing, Wesley and the "Methodists" found themselves in a state of "political" tension with the Anglican Church of England. John Wesley loved this Church: he never wanted to leave it or break away from it.[1] Yet it became more

---

[1] Originally Wesley never envisaged a ministry distinct from that of the Anglican Church; he always considered himself an "extraordinary minister" of the Church of England. He saw it as a sort of intra-parish ministry coming to the aid of the usual parish ministry, for the pastoral care of converts and for itinerant preaching. However, he always believed that his authority derived from the Church of England, through his ordination to the priesthood in 1728; cf. A. C. OUTLER (ed.), *John Wesley* (N.Y.: Oxford University Press, 1964) 21, n. 72: the ordination conferred a *"ius ubique praedicandi."* Elsewhere Wesley wrote: "Being ordained as a Fellow of a College, I was not limited to any particular cure, but have an immediate commission to preach the Word of God in any part of the Church of England"; see N. CURNOCK (ed.), *The Journal of the Rev. John Wesley, A.M. Sometime Fellow of Lincoln College, Oxford, England from original MSS, with Notes from Unpublished Diaries, Annotations, Maps, and Illustrations* (London: Epworth Press, 1938) t. II, 257. This manner of regarding his ministry can seem

and more difficult for him to stay, for the whole movement of spiritual awakening, represented by his Methodist "Societies," was a threat to the clerical establishment of the Church of England. With increasing frequency Methodists were refused Communion in the Anglican Churches. Despite this, out of love for the Anglican Church, Wesley opposed until his death in 1791 the separation of his Societies from the Church of England, and he even spoke out against the prayer meetings held at the same time as the worship services of the Anglican communities, because this was a sin against charity and a stumbling block for the non-believer.[2]

Similarly, his decision to bring his lay assistants into the ministry of those few Anglican priests who believed in his form of piety, and to organize into a conference the Societies who had such a lay leader at their head—a decision which Wesley made around 1744—did not help him in his dealings with the Anglican Church. For their evangelical activity did not limit itself to the parishes, but was extended far beyond them, while some of these leaders began to overstep the limits established by Wesley between expounding and preaching.[3] We should not underestimate this transgression, because it was clearly a threat to religious control and power.[4] Meanwhile, within his

---

somewhat strange, especially if we recall the question of the "ministry without concrete charge" that the Churches coming out of the Reformation contested, as did the early Church. In reality, Wesley was a sort of *"praedicator vagans,"* like the wandering prophets of Israel in a certain period. He had a saying: "I look upon all the world as my parish," and he would pronounce this when a certain James Harvey polemicized against Wesley's irregularities in the exercise of his ministry; see J. TELFORD (ed.), *The Letters of the Rev. John Wesley, A.M. Sometime Fellow of Lincoln College, Oxford* (London: Epworth Press, 1931) t. I, 284–287, here 286.

[2] See his sermons: Sermon LXXIV "On the Church" (1786), T. JACKSON (ed.), *The Works of the Rev. John Wesley, A.M. Sometime Fellow of Lincoln College, Oxford* (London: John Mason, 1856) t. VI, 392–401; Sermon LXXV "On Schism" (1786), T. JACKSON (ed.), *The Works . . .,* t .VI, 401–410 ; and Sermon CXV "On the Ministerial Office" (Cork, May 4, 1789), T. JACKSON (ed.), *The Works . . .,* t. VII, 273–281. For a thorough study of his relationship with the Church of England, see F. BAKER, *John Wesley and the Church of England* (London: Epworth Press, 1970).

[3] A. C. OUTLER, "The Ordinal," in W. F. DUNKLE and J. D. QUILLIAN (eds.), *Companion to the Book of Worship* (Nashville/N.Y.: Abingdon Press, 1970) 109.

[4] A. R. GEORGE, "Ordination," in R. DAVIES, A. R. GEORGE and G. RUPP (eds.), *A History of the Methodist Church in Great Britain* (London: Epworth Press, 1978) t. 2, 143–145.

Methodist Societies, voices arose clamoring for the right of their own ministers to celebrate Holy Communion in a regular fashion. When Wesley and his collaborators were deprived of their pulpits, they addressed immense crowds out in the open, with great success. A great evangelical awakening was abroad, but so also were ever-increasing tensions between the partisans of the Methodist Societies and the established Anglican Church.

To explain the actions that Wesley had recourse to in 1784, we must go to two works that he read around 1746. Both contributed to the formation of his ideas on the government of the Church and its ministerial structure. These were: *An Enquiry into the Constitution, Discipline, Unity and Worship of the Primitive Church, that Flourished within the first three Hundred Years after Christ*, by P. King;[5] and *Irenicum: A Weapon-Salve for the Churches' Wounds or the Divine right of Particular Forms of Church Government*, by E. Stillingfleet, bishop of Worcester.[6] Convinced by these authors that presbyters and bishops were equal in order, and as a priest of the Church of England and scriptural *episcopos* of the Methodist Societies,[7] he ordained two presbyters for

---

[5] London, 1691, reprinted in N.Y.: G. Lane & P. P. Sandford, 1841; cf. an entry in his journal for January 20, 1746: N. CURNOCK (ed.), *The Journal . . .*, t. III, 232. There he concludes that: "In spite of the vehement prejudice of my education, I was ready to believe that this was a fair and impartial draught; but, if so, it would follow that bishops and presbyters are (essentially) of one order, and that originally every Christian congregation was a church independent of all others!"

[6] London, 1661 (2nd ed.), reprinted in Philadelphia: M. Sorin, 1842; cf. the references of Wesley himself in his letters: J. TELFORD (ed.), *The Letters . . .*, t. III, 135f. (of July 16, 1755, to his brother Charles), 181f. (of July 3, 1756, to James Clark); IV, 150 (of April 10, 1761, to G. Downing, Earl of Dartmouth); VII, 21f. (of June 8, 1780, to his brother Charles). For the influence that these two books had on J. Wesley, see A. B. LAWSON, *John Wesley and the Christian Ministry. The Sources and Development of His Opinions and Practice* (London: SPCK, 1963) 47–70.

[7] J. TELFORD, (ed.), *The Letters . . .*, t. VII, 284 (to his brother Charles). The expression *"scriptural episkopos"* is used here by Wesley on August 19, 1785, and another reference exists in a letter dated from March 25, 1785, in which he presents himself as a "Christian bishop" ("I know myself to be as real a Christian bishop as the Archbishop of Canterbury"), J. TELFORD (ed.), *The Letters . . .*, t. VII, 262 (to Barnabas Thomas); and further, "When I said, 'I believe I am a scriptural bishop,' I spoke on Lord King's supposition that bishops and presbyters are essentially one order": J. TELFORD (ed.), *The Letters . . .*, t. VIII, 143 (of June 2, 1789, to the editor of the "Dublin Chronicle"). For an explanation of this term in

North America (Richard Whatcoat and Thomas Vasey, whom he had already ordained deacon the day before) on September 2, 1784, and ordained Thomas Coke superintendent for America; he also gave instructions for the ordination of Francis Asbury as superintendent of the Methodists in America.[8] For these ordinations he used the Ordinal of the *BCP* of 1662. When Coke left for America, he brought along three documents: a certificate, a letter from Wesley dated September 10, 1784 written to the brethren in North America, and the *Sunday Service of the Methodists in North America. With Other Occasional Services.*[9]

The certificate, which explained Wesley's actions by saying he was "called providentially in these times to set aside certain persons for the work of the ministry in America," declares: "I have this day set apart as a Superintendent, by the imposition of my hands and prayer, (being assisted by other ordained Ministers), Thomas Coke, Doctor of Civil Law, a Presbyter of the Church of England . . ."[10]

The letter[11] accompanying the Liturgy explains the motive for his actions (his belief that bishop and presbyter are equal in order, and therefore have an equal right to ordain). The letter also informs the receivers that Coke and Asbury had been named co-superintendents and were to organize the Societies of brethren in North America, and that Whatcoat and Vasey were also sent to serve as ministers in America, and that the enclosed Liturgy was for their use.

Lastly, the Liturgy was that of the *Sunday Service of the Methodists in North America. With Other Occasional Services.*[12] Among these "occa-

---

Wesley, see J. K. MATHEWS, *Set Apart to Serve. The Meaning and Role of Episcopacy in the Wesleyan Tradition* (Nashville, Tenn.: Abingdon Press, 1985) 13–37.

[8] N. CURNOCK (ed.), *The Journal . . .*, t. VII, 15–17 (of August 31, September 1 and 2, 1784).

[9] Cf. A. R. GEORGE, "Ordination," 146.

[10] Text of the certificate published in its entirety in J. A. VICKERS, *Thomas Coke: Apostle of Methodism* (London/Nashville, Tenn.: Epworth Press/Abingdon Press, 1969) 367. A. R. George believes that the "other ordained ministers" mentioned in the certificate must be the two presbyters Whatcoat and Vasey; cf. A. R. GEORGE, "Ordination," 146.

[11] For the text, see J. TELFORD (ed.), *The Letters . . .*, t. VII, 238f. (of September 10, 1784, to the brethren in North America).

[12] A facsimile edition of this Liturgy was published on the occasion of the bicentenary of the establishment of Methodism in the United States. In the preface of

sional" services we find the Ordinal for the American Methodists. Wesley himself stated that the model for his Liturgy was the *BCP*, for, he said, it had not been surpassed, and was "of a solid, scriptural, and rational Piety."[13] Commentators on the Ordinal have remarked that Wesley, when he took as his model the Ordinal of 1661, modified it very little, and those few changes were mostly stylistic, except for three: the term "superintendent" replaced "bishop"; he omitted any reference to canon law or sworn oaths; and he transformed the diaconate into a kind of itinerant ministry.[14] We should also note that Wesley did not reproduce the preface of the Ordinal of 1661 explaining the origin of the ordained ministry and the necessity for episcopal ordination. Nowhere does he give his reasons for so doing, but we can imagine that it was due to his opinions on the equality between bishop and presbyter, and to his rejection of the notion of episcopal succession deriving from apostolic succession. On this last point he is adamant: ". . . for the uninterrupted succession I know to be a fable, which no man ever did or can prove . . ."[15]

We shall limit ourselves to a look at the changes Wesley made in the Ordinal of 1661 from the viewpoint of their originality and their theological importance. An in-depth study of the Ordinal of the

---

this edition the editor describes the history of this book in North America, while presenting a study of its manuscript tradition: J. WESLEY, *The Sunday Service of the Methodists in North America,* introd. by James White (Nashville, Tenn.: United Methodist Publishing House, 1984) (hereafter, *Sunday Service*).

[13] "I believe there is no Liturgy in the world either in any ancient or modern language, which breathes more of a solid, scriptural, rational Piety, than the Common Prayer of the Church of England," J. WESLEY, *Sunday Service*, 1.

[14] A. C. OUTLER, "The Ordinal," 113. Some other important commentators of the Ordinal are: J. D. GRABNER, *A Commentary on the Rites of "An Ordinal, The United Methodist Church"* (Ann Arbor, Mich.: University Microfilms International, 1983) 1–40; N. B. HARMON, *The Rites and Ritual of Episcopal Methodism with Particular Reference to the Rituals of The Methodist Episcopal Church and The Methodist Episcopal Church, South, Respectively* (Nashville, Tenn./Dallas, Tex./ Richmond, Va./San Francisco, Calif.: Publishing House of the Methodist Episcopal Church, South, 1926) 324–408; see also the comments of P. F. BRADSHAW, *The Anglican Ordinal . . . .,* 111f. (comments made in the context of the revisions of the *BCP*) and A. R. GEORGE, "Ordination," 143–153 (comments made in the context of the history of Methodist ordinations).

[15] See J. TELFORD (ed.), *The Letters . . . .,* t. VII, 284 (of August 19, 1785, to his brother Charles) (the emphasis is Wesley's).

Sunday Service has been made by the principal redactor of the 1979 Ordinal of the United Methodist Church, J. D. Grabner.[16]

2. STRUCTURE OF THE ORDINATIONS OF THE *SUNDAY SERVICE*

A few alterations affecting all three ministries (superintendent, elder, and deacon) include modernizations of the language used in the *BCP* of 1662 (grammar, punctuation, and spelling). One curious fact: the spelling "Superintendant" [sic!] is found only in his Ordinal. In general, Wesley changed the text of the Ordinal of 1661 very little indeed. Alterations consistently made include: 1) the use of "elder" for priest/priesthood, "superintendent" for (arch)bishop, "ordain" for consecrate in the case of the superintendent; 2) the omission of any reference to canon law, or to the Church as a state institution (suppression of all oaths); 3) the suppression of the confession of faith in order to be in conformity with the structure of the Holy Communion service in the *Sunday Service*; and 4) the suppression of ceremonial references.[17] We shall discuss the other changes made in the ordination of elders and superintendent further on when we look at those rituals themselves.

a. *Elder*

The structure of the Ordinal of the *Sunday Service* is identical to that of the *BCP* of 1662, except for the following points: the suppression of the dialogue between the superintendent and the elder when the elect are presented;[*1541C] the omission of the pericope from Matthew 9:36ff. ("ask the master of the harvest . . ."); the text of the litany is not reproduced in the Ordinal of Wesley, and therefore the special petition for ordination is omitted, because the text of the litany as we find it elsewhere in the *Sunday Service*[18] does not contain this petition; the suppression of the second part of the third question on the tradition of the Church of England;[*1551C] the omission of the original version of the *Veni Creator Spiritus*;[*1603C] the omission of the phrase "If you forgive the sins of any, they are forgiven them" [Jn 20:22b-23] in the prayer said during the imposition of hands;[*1563C] the omission of the phrase

[16] J. D. GRABNER, *A Commentary* . . .
[17] Cf. J. D. GRABNER, *A Commentary* . . ., 4–25; and A. C. OUTLER, "The Ordinal," 113f.
[18] *Sunday Service*, 20–26.

". . . where thou shalt be lawfully appointed thereunto" from the prayer said at the bestowal of the Bible;"[1564C] and the alteration of the gospel[19] read for the ordination of deacons and elders together."[1569C]

The constant use of the term "elder" for priest is not explained anywhere in Wesley's writings. We know that he distinguished between the function of proclamation and teaching, called the "prophetic ministry," and the administration of the sacraments and the pastoral governance, called the "priestly" ministry; but more than this he does not say.[20] The ministry of his lay assistants belongs to the first, and the ministry of the elders to the second.

By suppressing the oath sworn to royal supremacy, Wesley joined the reading of the gospel of the Good Shepherd (Jn 10) directly to the address of the superintendent, which is Cranmer's adaptation of the homily on the Good Shepherd taken from Bucer. The scriptural interpretation of the office of elder is revealed in the liturgical reworking by Wesley. It would seem that this office should be understood as mainly pastoral, even priestly, in Wesley's meaning of the term, meaning the functions of pastoral governance and the administration of the sacraments. This having been said, we see right away that he suppressed the quotation from John on the forgiveness of sins found in the prayer pronounced during the imposition of hands. This fact seems to have the opposite effect to what we would expect: it works against a sacerdotal interpretation. We shall have other occasions to observe other persisting ambiguities of this sort.

One last change has to do with the originality of Wesley's conception of the ministry. By suppressing the last part of the formula of transmission of the Bible, he confirmed his preference for a ministry without a concrete charge ("the whole world is my parish"), for he removes from the Anglican formula the reference to a particular parish ("where thou shalt be lawfully appointed thereunto"). We can, perhaps, understand this change if we keep in mind the vast regions of American geography that the Methodist preachers had to cover at the end of the eighteenth century. This did not mean that the ministers were independent of all ecclesiastical authority. The territories

---

[19] Wesley does not offer any choice as in 1662 (Mt 9:36-38 or Lk 12:35-38), but he prescribes the reading of Jn 10:1-16, the usual gospel for the ordination of elders.

[20] Cf. Sermon CXV, called the "Korah," of May 4, 1789: T. JACKSON (ed.), *The Works . . .*, t. VII, 273–281.

were divided, in fact, into Church conferences or into missionary territories each of which had its principal ministers with governing power, as we see in the eighth question of the examination.

b. *Superintendent*

Wesley made few changes in the Ordinal of 1661, and the purpose of those he made was to bring the conception of the Anglican episcopacy more into line with his own conception of the superintendency. J. D. Grabner, following some observations of N. B. Harmon, notes that Wesley changed the Anglican Ordinal in order to make it fit his own idea that "'superintendent' was presumably nothing more than a New Testament 'bishop,' who was nothing more than a new Testament presbyter."[21] These changes were: the omission of the word "bishop" of the Anglican ritual, and the use of "superintendent," "elder," or "minister," depending on the context; the presentation of the elect by two elders who do the readings; the use of Acts 20:17ff. alone (Paul's farewell speech to the elders of Ephesus) for the epistle; the suppression of John 20:19ff. (the power to forgive sins) in the choice of readings for the gospel; the petition of the litany proper to the ordination of a bishop; the omission of the original version of the *Veni creator* during the imposition of hands performed by the elders present with the superintendent.

Certain of these modifications were necessary because of the unique situation in America, where the absence of a college of superintendents required the substitution of the elders for the bishop in the ceremony, at, for example, the presentation or the reading of the lessons from Scripture. The elimination of the two readings of the Anglican Ordinal (1 Tim 3:1ff. and Jn 20:19ff.) is completely in conformity with the ideas of Wesley, for the first reading contains a reference to the bishops, a word that he did not use at all, and the second confers the power to forgive sins. This last reading was also suppressed in the ordination of elders, in the prayer pronounced during the imposition of hands.

As for the rest, Wesley remained faithful by and large to the Anglican Ordinal while adapting it for his purpose: to provide a ministry for the Methodist Societies of North America. We can refer to the de-

[21] J. D. GRABNER, *A Commentary . . .*, 27; cf. N. B. HARMON, *The Rites . . .*, 399–401.

scription found above for the Anglican ordinations contained in the Ordinal of 1661, *mutatis mutandis.*

3. PRAYERS OF ORDINATION

We have seen that these prayers are identical to those of the *BCP* of 1662. Wesley had great esteem for this Anglican tradition, as we mentioned above, and he intended to continue in it. The heart of the ordination ceremony remained the prayer and the imposition of hands. We should note, however, that with the omission of the special petition of the litany Wesley suppressed what Bradshaw considers an essential part of the prayer of ordination of a presbyter. We find only a prayer said for the congregation, if we except the imperative formula pronounced during the imposition of hands. In their subsequent revisions, the American Episcopal Methodist Churches will remedy this situation in later times.[22]

4. RELATIONSHIP BETWEEN THE PRESBYTERATE AND THE SUPERINTENDENCY

Wesley was fairly clear on the relationship between presbyter and bishop: there is scarcely any difference of order between them. However, as the documents prepared and sent by Wesley to the American brethren show, there is a distinction in charge. Coke was set apart or ordained[23] as "a fit person to preside over the Flock of Christ,"[24] while

[22] Cf. J. D. GRABNER, *A Commentary . . .*, 49f. and 60; and N. B. HARMON, *The Rites . . .*, 365.

[23] Wesley did not use the word "ordain" on the certificate, but rather, "set apart." Nevertheless, he did use "ordain" in his private Journal and in his adaptation of the Ordinal; compare N. CURNOCK (ed.), *The Journal . . .*, t. VII, 15f., n. 2, and his private Journal published in T. E. BRIGDEN, "Wesley's Ordinations at Bristol, September 1st and 2nd, 1784," *Proceedings of the Wesley Historical Society* 7 [part 1] (1909) 9, n. 1. We also read in the Journal of Whatcoat: "September 1st, 1784, Rev. John Wesley, Thomas Coke, and James Creyton, Presbyters of the Church of England, formed a Presbytery, and *ordained* Richard Whatcoat and Thomas Vasey, Deacons. And on September 2nd, by the same hands, &c. Richard Whatcoat and Thomas Vasey were *ordained* Elders, and Thomas Coke, LL.D. was *ordained* Superintendent, for the Church of God, under our care in North America": W. PHOEBUS (ed.), *Memoirs of the Rev. Richard Whatcoat Late Bishop of the Methodist Episcopal Church* (N.Y.: Joseph Allen, 1828) 17f., our italics; see also A. R. GEORGE, "Ordination," 146.

[24] From the certificate of ordination of Coke: ". . . a fit person to preside over the Flock of Christ": N. CURNOCK (ed.), *The Journal . . .*, t. VII, facsimile facing p. 16.

Whatcoat and Vasey were ordained elders "to feed the flock of Christ, and to administer Baptism and the Lord's Supper . . ."[25]

To help us understand the specific nature of the office of superintendent, we must look to the first "Discipline" of the Episcopal Methodist Church established during the first Conference which took place December 24–31, 1784. During this Conference, Asbury, who would have refused the office of superintendent if it had not been the will of his brethren in the ministry, was elected and ordained superintendent of the new Church.[26] Four questions and answers are important here (this question-and-answer style was already used by Wesley in the Conferences in England):

"Q. 26. What is the Office of a Superintendent?

"A. To ordain Superintendents, Elders and Deacons; to preside as a Moderator in our Conferences; to fix the Appointments of the Preachers for the several Circuits; and in the Intervals of the Conference, to change, receive or suspend Preachers, as Necessity may require; and to receive Appeals from the Preachers and People, and decide them.

"N. B. No Person shall be ordained a Superintendent, Elder or Deacon, without the Consent of a Majority of the Conference and the Consent and Imposition of Hands of a Superintendent; except in the Instance provided for in the 29th Minute.

[25] Quotation taken from the certificate of ordination of Whatcoat: ". . . to feed the flock of Christ, and to administer Baptism and the Lord's Supper, according to the usage of the Church of England," W. PHOEBUS (ed.), Memoirs . . ., 18. In his letter "to the brethren in America," Wesley moreover distinguished between the two functions of "'feeding' and 'guiding' the poor sheep in the wilderness" ("If any one will point out a more rational way of feeding and guiding those poor sheep in the wilderness, I will gladly embrace it") when he justified his decision to ordain these men; cf. J. TELFORD (ed.), The Letters . . ., t .VII, 239.

[26] It is interesting to hear Asbury himself as to his sentiments just one month before the Christmas Conference; he writes: ". . . the preachers and people seem to be much pleased with the projected plan; I myself am led to think it is of the Lord. I am not tickled with the honour to be gained—I see danger in the way. My soul waits upon God. O that he may lead us in the way we should go! Part of my time is, and must necessarily be, taken up with the preparing for the conference": E. T. CLARK, J. M. POTTS, and J. S. PAYTON (eds.), The Journal and Letters of Francis Asbury (London/Nashville, Tenn.: Epworth Press/Abingdon Press, 1958) t .I, 472f. (of November 26, 1784). We perhaps see here the same sentiments and literary expression as in the ancients who did not seek the charge that was laid on them.

"Q. 27. To whom is the Superintendent amenable for his Conduct?
"A. To the Conference: who have Power to expel him for improper Conduct, if they see it necessary.
"Q. 28. If the Superintendent ceases from Travelling at large among the People, shall he still exercise his Office in any degree?
"A. If he ceases from Travelling without the Consent of the Conferences, he shall not thereafter exercise any ministerial Function whatsoever in our church.
"Q. 29. If by Death, Expulsion or otherwise there be no Superintendent remaining in our Church, what shall we do?
"A. The Conference shall elect a Superintendent, and the Elders of any three of them shall ordain him according to our Liturgy."[27]
From this quotation we get a good idea of the charge of the *episkopē* exercised by the superintendent: he presides, watches over, ordains and organizes, disciplines, visits, judges, and helps to keep his parishes connected with each other. We should note, however, that the superintendent remains responsible before the Conference of the Church which is composed of all the superintendents, elders, deacons and assistants (these are the lay preachers); it is a sort of yearly synod. It is clear here what Wesley meant by "ordaining to watch over the flock of Christ."

As for the elders, their role was expressed in the rite of ordination, and includes the daily pastoral administration of the congregations of faithful, feeding them with the sacrament of Baptism and the Communion of the Lord, and preaching the gospel, assisted by the lay preachers. We recall that at that time, in North America, the vast distances to cover required an itinerant ministry on the part of all ministers.[28]

5. LATER INFLUENCE OF THE ORDINAL
OF THE *SUNDAY SERVICE*

Even though the *Sunday Service* was quickly abandoned as the official liturgy of the Episcopal Methodist Church (in 1792),[29] the Ordinal

[27] J. J. TIGERT, *A Constitutional History of American Episcopal Methodism*, 6th ed. revised and expanded (Nashville, Tenn./Dallas, Tex./Richmond, Va.: Publishing House of the Methodist Episcopal Church, South, 1916) 548f.

[28] For example, even before the first Christmas Conference, we see Coke and Asbury traveling continually among the Methodist communities, to preach and celebrate the sacraments. Cf. the comments of Coke on this subject, quoted by J. K. MATHEWS, *Set Apart . . .*, 98.

[29] N. B. HARMON, *The Rites . . .*, 49.

remained in vigor, in a slightly altered form, until the revision of 1980.[30]

Methodism in England, Scotland, Wales, and Ireland also accepted the *Sunday Service* of Wesley, including the Ordinal, but without the ordinations of superintendents and deacons. Wesley himself ordained at least twenty-seven persons.[31] As the Methodist Societies did not immediately separate from the Anglican Church, and as Wesley met with opposition to his ordinations (even from his brother Charles), the Societies maintained a policy of great prudence as to the manner of ordaining. After Wesley's death, a controversy broke out between ordained preachers and non-ordained preachers concerning their status. The Conference of 1793 decided to suppress this distinction, for it was creating a problem in that only ordained ministers could celebrate the sacraments. In 1794 a proposal to provide British Methodism with bishops was rejected. A Plan of Pacification (in 1795) legislated on the question whether, with the consent of the Conference, Holy Communion could be administered by persons authorized by the Conference, that is, even by preachers who had not been ordained but were in full connection.

With the passage of time, the idea arose that those who were in full connection with the Conference without imposition of hands were truly ordained, through their acceptance (which took place by a vote by raised hand). After more than twenty years of debate, in 1836, the Wesleyan Conference finally adopted a motion requiring preachers to be ordained by the imposition of hands. The rite used was that of Wesley for the elders, called presbyters since 1789. In 1846 the three forms of ordination of the *Sunday Service* were replaced by a single office, the "Forme for the ordination of the candidates for the ministry in the Wesleyan-Methodist Connection." The main components of this rite, which was based on that of Wesley, are: an examination, a ritual election (because admission to the Conference took place the day before), the imposition of hands and the prayer, and other hymns and prayers ex tempore.[32] This form is the

[30] N. B. HARMON, *The Rites . . .*, 324–408; and for the revisions later than 1924, see J. D. GRABNER, *A Commentary . . .*, 92–157.

[31] Cf. A. R. GEORGE, "Ordination," 152f.

[32] This whole story is told in the related documents of A. R. GEORGE, "Ordination," 152–158.

basis of the rite of ordination of the Methodist Churches of the English tradition.

The two principal forms of Methodism today are those of the United Methodist Church (of episcopal type[33]), and of the British Methodist Church (non-episcopal type). The influence of the *Sunday Service* of Wesley is found all over the world, wherever one finds Methodist Churches or missions of either type.

6. CONCLUSION: STRUCTURING OF THE CHURCH AND THE SUBSTANCE OF ORDAINED MINISTRY

a. *Structure of the Church*

It is easy to discern Wesley's desire to adopt the Ordinal of the Anglican Church of 1661, but he did show his originality in his adaptation by the creation of a new ecclesiological dimension, the annual Conference. The structure of the Anglican Church in which the bishop plays a very important role has been "democratized," with the result that the Conference becomes the principal governing body in the Church. This organ, as we have seen, is composed of the three ordained ministries and the lay preachers who are the assistants of the ordained ministers.

If we analyze the structuring of the Church by applying the category of the actors and their roles, we arrive at the following analysis:

There is little mention of the role of the faithful in the entire process, as was true also of the Ordinal of 1661. Nevertheless, they are always active in the high points of the celebration, that is, during the prayer of the litany and at the moment of the silent prayer. They have always kept their right to reject their ministers at the time of the interrogation, in the case of some crime in their background, or some other grave obstacle. There is no mention of a process of election by suffrage or other direct system, because the election is enacted by the Conference when it admits a candidate to full connection. This is an election carried out by a ministerial body plus the lay preachers, who represent the faithful.

Aside from the prescription that the ordinations take place after the usual morning prayers on the day on which the whole Church

---

[33] The switch from "superintendent" to "bishop" took place in 1788 in the Minutes of the Conference of the Methodist Episcopal Church. On this subject, see J. K. MATHEWS, *Set Apart . . .,* 120–125.

gathers, nothing else is said about the Church concerned. In the ordination of a superintendent we see that other elders present the elect, do the reading of the biblical pericopes, and most importantly, impose hands. It is possible that Wesley did not require that other superintendents participate in this liturgy, for the simple reason that there were no other superintendents on American soil; and, after all, he considered the presbyters the equivalent, in order, of the superintendents.[34]

The role of the superintendent is an important one, for the ordination, according to the first discipline of the American Church, must be done by the imposition of hands; and it is only in the case of necessity (the absence of any other superintendent) that three elders, chosen by the Conference, can accede to the function reserved to the superintendent, that of conferring ordination. The higher power is then reserved to the collegial organ of the Conference.

As for the roles of the elect and of the Holy Spirit, they are the same as in the Anglican Ordinal.

b. *Substance of the Ministries of the Elders and the Superintendents*

We cannot speak of a stable ministry, for we have seen that the aphorism of Wesley, "the world is my parish," is taken seriously, especially on the American continent, where a state of necessity is the rule. From the start, Wesley[35] categorically forbade the lay preachers to celebrate the sacraments, and that remained the rule in America. All ordained ministers were obliged to be always on the road—the spreading of the gospel demanded it! The task of presiding at baptisms and Holy Communion was shared between superintendents and elders, as were preaching and the other functions mentioned in the rites of ordination.

---

[34] It bears repeating that this fact derives from his analysis of the New Testament, with the help of the two works of King and Stillingfleet; on this point, see the commentary of J. K. MATHEWS, *Set Apart . . .*, 20–37, and on the influence of King and Stillingfleet, 109–113.

[35] Cf. his sermon ("Korah" Sermon) on the ministerial office, preached in Cork in 1789: T. JACKSON (ed.), *The Works . . .*, t. VII, 273–281. The same interdiction is affirmed, as attested in the report of the Assembly of Philadelphia held July 14, 1773 and published by T. Rankin who was a sort of assistant to Wesley sent to America: "Minutes of Some Conversations Between the Preachers in Connection with the Reverend Mr. John Wesley (Philadelphia, July 1773)," in D. HITT and

However, certain tasks were reserved to the superintendent, as we saw above: watching over the flock, ordaining (in the sense of imposing hands and supervising organization), exercising discipline, visiting, linking the parishes together, and conferring judgment.

We can add to these conclusions that the usual elements, namely, election, ordination, and the mission are always present, but organized in a way that was original to Wesley. Election and ordination preserve just about the same meaning that they had in the Anglican Church. There were new elements in the mission. It is not easy to discern a concrete charge, because of the broadening of the mission by Wesley from within the Anglican Church. Methodism was a movement of spiritual awakening which knew no boundaries. Wesley saw the world as fertile ground for his ministry, and the ministry was conceived of primarily as an "itinerant ministry." The same will hold true in the Societies and later in the "Methodist Church." A great deal later, when the situation had stabilized and had in fact become "institutionalized," we will find a more stable parish ministry and a superintendency more limited to a particular geographical area.[36]

T. WARE (eds.), *Minutes of the Methodist Conferences, Annually held in America; from 1773 to 1813, Inclusive* (N.Y.: John C. Totten, 1813) t. 1, 5f.

[36] For the later evolution of the office of superintendent (called bishop already under Asbury), see J. K. MATHEWS, *Set Apart . . .*, 118–190; and G. F. MOEDE, *The Office of Bishop in Methodism. Its History and Development* (Zurich/Nashville, Tenn.: Publishing House of the Methodist Church/Abingdon Press, 1964).

Chapter 5

Theological Reflection

A. IMAGES MOST FREQUENTLY USED IN THE RITUALS

In the sixteenth century, with the new emphasis the Reformers placed on the priesthood of all the baptized, a new way of looking at the ministry emerged. We have seen that Luther did not accept the differences between Christian brethren that had crept into the thinking of the Church,[1] for all the faithful have received the grace of baptism and this grace enables them to give thanks to God, since all participate in the one priesthood of Christ. The priesthood from now on is seen as a global reality; it is no longer viewed as the privilege of a few, but as embracing the whole of the Church, made up of a priestly people. Within this reality, and in its service, is found the *"ministerium verbi et sacramentorum."* The concern of the Reformers was to get rid of what had been (mis)understood as a qualitative difference between Christians, and to reaffirm the primary dignity of all, acquired through baptism and the granting of salvation: this is the *"nulla differentia personarum"* of Luther.[2] He elaborates on the consequences of this position in his description of the relationship between the minister and his Christian brethren:

". . . We let our pastor say what Christ has ordained, *not for himself* as though it were for his person, but *he is the mouth for all of us* and we all speak the words with him from the heart and in faith, directed to the Lamb of God who is present for us and among us, and who

---

[1] *An den Christlichen Adel . . .*, WA 6, 408.26–28 (= *LW* 44, 129f. In the same line among the Reformed, see *Confessio et expositio . . .*, cap. XVIII (*BKRK* 255.22ff.) (= "The Second Helvetic Confession" = COCHRANE 271).

[2] *De abroganda . . .*, WA 8, 429.31 (= "The Misuse of the Mass," *LW* 36, 159).

according to his ordinance nourishes us with his body and blood"[3] (emphasis added).

A passage such as this one clearly expresses the ecclesiological impact of this restoration of the value and meaning of "baptismal priesthood," for the minister is once more seen as carrying out his role from within the activity of the entire Church, and not from a position above the community. He is *the voice* of the assembly, which (including the minister himself) is the actor in the offering of the Eucharist. In no wise can the minister act in isolation from the community of the Church; he can only participate in her actions.

This basic theological orientation is accompanied by a change in the terminology and images used. The study of the early rituals of ordination coming out of the Reformation shows that the priesthood (expressed in Old Testament metaphors) is no longer one of the most commonly used images. It was overwhelmingly superseded by the pastoral image of the shepherd or guardian of the flock. In every case, except in the ritual of Bugenhagen, this image of the shepherd is present in the prayers of ordination or in the admonitions addressed both to the ordinands and to the community. The second most commonly found image, and it is found almost everywhere, is that of the faithful steward or servant, or of the worker sent out into the harvest. In Bucer's ritual and in the Anglican and Methodist texts, two other images are commonly found: the care of souls, and the *diakonia* of the Kingdom of Christ. The Anglican texts of the prayer of ordination quite rightly stress the image of the steward.

In each ritual the ministerial charge of the ordinand is expressed in terms of these images: his ministry is a "service for" a concrete community (most often). Each ordinand is to represent in his community this figure of the shepherd or the steward. These images are based on the New Testament; they go back to Christ himself and to the apostles.

The specific nature of the ordained ministry in its relationship to the Christian community emerges clearly from these images. The

---

[3] "Und lassen unsern Pfarrher nicht für sich, als für seine personen, die ordnung Christi sprechen, Sondern er ist unser aller mund und wir alle sprechen sie mit jm von hertzen und mit auffgerichtem glauben zu dem Lam Gottes, das da für uns und bey uns ist und seiner ordnung nach uns speiset mit seinem leibe und blut," *Von der Winckelmesse und Pfaffen Weyhe* (1533), WA 38, 247.26–31 (= "The Private Mass and the Consecration of Priests," *LW* 38, 208f.).

minister is a Christian among other Christians; he is therefore also a priest through the priesthood conferred by baptism. However, he is charged with providing certain services in the name of the community, and even vis-à-vis the community (in the exercise of the power of the keys and of discipline, the minister is clearly acting from a stance facing the community). This global reality which is the baptismal priesthood has a major impact on the way Christian reality in its entirety is understood. To grasp this concept clearly we have to turn to the anthropological basis of the priesthood. The Lutheran jurist Hans Dombois has put forward a very interesting conception of the priesthood which departs from the classic Protestant understanding of the common priesthood of all Christians. Although Dombois expresses himself in general terms, it would seem that the earliest Reformed rituals of ordination support his analysis. He thinks that the priesthood is a highly important category in all human experience, and especially in Christian life. According to Dombois, a human being cannot exist for and in him- or herself alone: human existence is by nature relational.[4] In the deepest parts of his or her being, the human person cannot take any steps towards salvation without engaging others. This relationship is not one of service so much as one of metaphysics. Priesthood then has less to do with service than with the boundless mercy of God, who gives himself through the concrete and personal mediation of human relations.[5] In this context the functions of preaching and administering the sacraments assume their fullest meaning as means of communicating salvation. In all these human actions it is really Christ who is acting.[6]

All, then, are priests in the sense of the priesthood *coram Deo* and *coram hominibus,* but only a few are priests *in ecclesia pro fratribus.* If

[4] H. DOMBOIS, *Das Recht . . .,* 245.

[5] Ibid., 243.

[6] Ibid., 255. A. Ganoczy (a Catholic), without referring to the work of Dombois, attempted to develop a theory of communication that applies to the sacraments. In parallel fashion with Dombois, he uses a concept of sacrament in which the latter is one of a number of modalities of communication by representation. His theory rests also on an anthropology comparable to that of Dombois, and it has the advantage of articulating in a balanced fashion several aspects of the functioning of the symbolic act; see A. GANOCZY, *La doctrine catholique des sacrements,* trans. from the German *[Einführung in die katholische Sakramentenlehre]* by J. Burckel (Paris: Desclée, 1988) ch. 4.

all were to exercise all the modes of communication, all would find themselves acting in a sort of autonomy, which would destroy the interrelationships and human mediation which make up a person's individual and human identity. The danger is that the ordained ministries could thereby lose their substance, with "the Christian as an autonomous and sovereign subject, no longer needing the priestly service of his or her neighbor, or of the ministers."[7] We have seen, in the first volume of this study, this same phenomenon (of "autonomization") taking place as the priesthood was absorbed into the ministry of the priests, leading to an autonomous clergy, which ended in the religious disqualification of other Christians (reduced from then on to a passive state in the whole process of ordination), and to the split between the ordained ministers and the *ecclesia* (as seen in the ordinations without title, the current interpretations of the sacramental character of ordination, etc.).

However, the rituals which came out of the Reformation clearly restored to its original importance the interrelatedness of the particular ministries, characteristic of their pastoral charge. All the metaphors used express this: the shepherd/pastor/steward/envoy faces the flock to which he is sent, not only to guide it, but also to exhort it, correct it, and feed it, even while he is himself a member of the Christian community. The image of the faithful servant also contains the meaning of Christian charity, and of the ministerial *diakonia*.

The fact that these metaphors were applied to a particular ministry during a celebration of ordination or installation also shows that in the Church there is a ministry that is not identical to that of all the baptized. This specialized ministry is exercised publicly by "certain individuals" who are designated for this service by God and by the Church, but it is true that this designation does not have the same importance everywhere and is not expressed in the same way. We shall be elaborating further on these concepts.

B. THE ORDAINED MINISTER AS A PERSON AND THE QUALITIES THAT ARE REQUIRED

The rituals we have studied certainly have placed the ministers squarely in the center of their functions and in their relatedness to

---

[7] H. DOMBOIS, *Das Recht . . .*, 256f.

others, quoting faithfully Ephesians 4:11-12. The result is a balanced relationship between the person of the minister and the object of his ministry. The vocation of the minister "is given" by the Church through the election, seen as carrying out the will of God for this Church. The process of election (definitely in the Lutheran and Reformed rituals, less clearly in the Anglican and Methodist) entails the discernment of the will of God in the choice of minister and in the examination of his faith and his manner of living, as shown in his conduct. In certain cases the whole community is involved, but most often we see a delegation of the faithful and of the ministers directly concerned. In every case the faithful have kept the right to reject an individual as their minister if his faith does not conform to the biblical teaching of their Church, or if there is a serious crime in his background or some other major obstacle to his election.

The qualities required are the same as we find in the New Testament tradition of the pastoral epistles: a life of integrity and good conduct, constancy in faith, and the necessary aptitudes. As we have just seen, all these elements are expressly aimed at the service of the faithful in the community, as well as the building up of the Church. Recalling the Reformed, Lutheran, Anglican, and Methodist traditions for the prayer said during the imposition of hands, we see that the minister is given to the Church for the spreading of the Kingdom and the public proclamation of the gospel.[8]

During an ordination or installation, the chosen Christian enters into a ministry and therefore into a new relationship with his brothers and sisters. Through his ministry he represents the faith of this Church; he watches over its purity, he sees to it that it is correctly taught, and, in the case of a superintendent and or a bishop, this can involve several communities. He does not act as an individual, for his status is always linked to the pastoral charge entrusted to him. He has not been given an indelible character, but we see that there was no reordination in the case of a minister changing parishes; in one specific case (in Middleburgh), we even find a formal prohibition against a second imposition of hands when a pastor changes parishes.

[8] Cf. our Tables II.3–8 (in vol. IV).

167

C. FUNCTIONS OF THE ORDAINED MINISTERS

Without exaggerating their similarities, it can nevertheless be said that the ministerial functions described in the rituals we have studied very closely resemble each other.

In the rituals of the *Lutheran family* we mainly find the prophetic function (preaching) and the pastoral (the administration of the sacraments, the exercise of the power of the keys, and discipline). Other tasks are attributed to the one ministerial office, such as visiting the parishes, teaching, ordaining, watching over the doctrine and the conduct of the pastors, etc.[9] The fact that we are talking about *one unique* ministerial office should be emphasized, for we have seen that Luther admitted no distinction between Christians (in general) which would take away from the integrity of baptismal priesthood and create a split within the Christian fellowship. The only distinction admitted is that of the function or task in the apostolic *diakonia* (cf. *"diakonia tou logou,"* Acts 6:4).[10] There is no question, then, of the min-

[9] In the spirit of Luther, these tasks—everything that could be called Church government—constitute the "spiritual power" *[geistliche Gewalt]: "die hiest leren, das ist das Evangelium"* ("what is called teaching, that is, the gospel") or the pastoral office (cf. *Predigt zu Vorna am Sonntag Misericordias domini 4 mai 1522, no. 24,* WA 10/III, 122.20, and *CA* XIV: "Vom Kirchenregiment wird gelehrt, dass niemand in der Kirchen offentlich lehren oder predigen oder Sakrament reichen soll ohn ordentlichen Beruf" ["It is taught among us that nobody should publicly teach or preach or administer the sacraments in the church without a regular call," *BC* 36]). This power is an integral part of any pastoral ministry.

[10] The affirmation of the baptismal priesthood of all the faithful does not imply that the ordained ministry is seen as simply derived from this common priesthood, for ministry is a function exercised from a stance facing the other Christians as well as from within their midst. Ordained ministry is not understood as a delegation on the part of the community; its authority is the authority of Christ: "Christ, your Lord, and the Holy Spirit say and do everything in so far as he [the minister] adheres to correct doctrine and practice" (". . . sondern Christus, dein Herr, und der Heilige Geist redet und thuts alles, so fern er bleibt in der rechten weise zu leren und zu thun . . ."), *Von den Konziliis . . .,* WA 50, 634.29f. (= "On the Councils and the Church," *LW* 41, 156); see "To the Christian Nobility of the German Nation Concerning the Reform of the Christian Estate" (= *LW* 44, 127): ". . . all Christians are truly of the spiritual estate *(geystlichs stands),* and there is no difference among them except that of office. Paul says in I Corinthians 12 [12:12-13] that we are all one body, yet every member has its own work by which it serves the others. This is because we all have one baptism, one gospel, one faith, and are all Christians alike; for baptism, gospel, and faith alone make us

istry of the pastor being second in relationship to that of the bishop. Even if their tasks are different for reasons of ecclesial organization, both the pastor and the bishop exercise the plenitude of the ministry. Both share the indispensable task of "giving, dispensing, exercising the function of preaching, baptism, the Eucharist, the power of the keys."[11] Both exercise the pastoral ministry: guiding and building up the Church through the public proclamation of the Word, presiding at worship (especially at baptism and Holy Communion), and governing the Church (the power of the keys).

In the exercise of these functions, the ministry acquires an instrumental significance at the service of the salvation of humanity. Its nature and function are based on the *"mandatum Dei"*: God chooses, authorizes, and sends forth ministers in cooperation with the congregation.[12] This service is exercised in the power of the Spirit and following the example of the apostles and their collaborators.[13] Since the

---

spiritual and a Christian people" (WA 6, 407.13–19). Other examples: WA 6, 408.26–409.10 (= *LW* 44, 129f.); WA 6, 566.26–30 (= *LW* 36, 115f.); WA 7, 58.19–22 (= *LW* 31, 356). On his thesis that the distinction between cleric and lay is a pure invention, see WA 6, 407.10–12 (= *LW* 44, 127); WA 6, 408.22–25 (= *LW* 44, 129f.); WA 6, 410.11–19 (= *LW* 44, 131f.); WA 6, 563.27–564.5 (= *LW* 36, 112); WA 7, 58.12–19 (= *LW* 31, 356); WA 7, 58.23–27 (= *LW* 31, 357).

[11] In the fifth note on the constitution of the Church (that the Church has ministries entrusted to certain of its members), Luther enumerates the functions of the ordained ministers (whom he calls bishop, curate, preacher); see *Von den Konziliis . . .,* WA 50, 632.35–634.33 (= *LW* 41, 154ff.), quotation taken from p. 633.1–3 (= *LW* 41, 154).

[12] Cf., for example, WA 12, 191.16–27 (= *LW* 40, 37); and V. VAJTA, *Luther on Worship. An Interpretation,* American trans. of the German *[Die Theologie des Gottesdienstes bei Luther]* by U. S. Leupold (Philadelphia: Muhlenberg Press, 1958) 116.

[13] The biblical readings, the exhortation, and the prayer of ordination support this, in all the rituals studied: *241–*242 (Luther); *263 (Bugenhagen); *273, *274, *290 (Bucer); and *298, *316–*317 (Petri). Two representative Lutheran authors speak of the apostolic ministry in terms of instrumentality, in relationship to salvation; thus, for example: "Apostolic ministry is consequently a fact of God's salvation, added to the salvation accomplished in Christ. It is not added as an independent entity, separable from Christ, but as a service, as the 'ministry of reconciliation'": E. SCHLINK, "La succession apostolique," *Verbum Caro* 18, 69 (1964) 76 and 79–82 where he shows how the ministry of the shepherd is the continuation of the ministry of the apostles in that "the fundamental ministry begun by the apostles must be prolonged" (p. 79). The other author writes rather of the service given to the work of salvation by the individual ministry; see P. BRUNNER,

minister has been sent, he has an authentic mandate from God, and he enjoys a certain authority. This is the meaning of the spiritual gift that enables him to fulfill the tasks of his ministry. This responsibility demands total obedience to the Word of God and a constant revitalization of the gift received (cf. 2 Tim 1:6). We recall that, according to the Confession of Augsburg, the proclamation of the gospel, which includes the administration of the sacraments, can only be done by the one who is called to it, *"rite vocatus"* (*CA* XIV), and only the Church of God, obeying the command of her Lord, has the power to call persons suitable for each particular ministry, and to confer upon them this mandate through ordination.[14]

In the *Reformed family*, we find more or less the same situation, but articulated differently. The main function of the ordained ministers is pastoral, including the tasks of proclaiming the Word (Zurich, J. Łaski, Knox, Middleburgh), the administration of the sacraments (Łaski, Knox, Middleburgh), the discipline of the community including admonitions and exhortations and the exercise of authority (Zurich, Łaski, Knox, Middleburgh). In the case of a superintendent, the governing aspect is emphasized (Łaski, Knox). In two specific cases the purpose of the ordained ministry is expressed: it is to build up the Body of Christ (Łaski[915]) and to continue the action of Christ, for the minister is the "minister of Christ and his ambassador" (Knox[953]). The practice encountered in the rituals is also illustrated in the theology of Calvin and in the early confessions of faith of the Reformed Churches.[15]

"Salvation and the Office of the Ministry," *Lutheran Quarterly* 15, 2 (1963) 114ff., American trans. of the German ["Das Heil und das Amt, Elemente einer dogmatischen Lehre vom Predigt- und Hirtenamt," in id., *Pro Ecclesia, Gesammelte Aufsätze zur dogmatischen Theologie*] by P. D. Opsahl. We see that the minister does not act independently, but always within the framework of the *diakonia* of the minister with respect to the gift of salvation.

[14] "*Habet enim ecclesia mandatum de constituendis ministris, quod gratissimum esse nobis debet, quod scimus Deum approbare ministerium illud et adesse in ministerio*" ("The Church has the command to appoint ministers; to this we must subscribe wholeheartedly, for we know that God approves this ministry and is present in it"), P. MELANCHTHON, *Apologia confessionis Augustanae* XIII, 12 (*BSLK* 294 = *BC* 212).

[15] For example, in Book IV of his *Institutes of the Christian Religion* (3.6): ". . . it is not my present intention to set forth in detail the gifts of the good pastor, but

Lastly, in the *Anglican and Methodist families,* we find the same prophetic and pastoral functions which are exercised in the tasks of preaching the Word, defending the doctrine, teaching the faith, administering the sacraments, and exercising the power of the keys and discipline. These tasks are common to both the priests/elders and the bishops/superintendents. In the Anglican Church there will be added the task of governing. In the 1661 revision of the preface of the Ordinal, and in the examination of the candidate elected to the episcopacy, episcopal ordination is said to be necessary in such a way that from then on we can affirm that "ordaining" is a task linked to the pastoral function of the bishop. Even though Wesley considered the elder and the superintendent as equals, he reserved certain tasks to the latter: those of watching over the flock, ordaining, organizing, exercising discipline, visiting, judging, and keeping the different parishes in communication. However, we must keep in mind that in all this he was thinking of the situation of the Methodist Church in North America rather than that of the Church in Great Britain, which did not always have an office of personalized superintendency. We see that Methodism agrees largely with the point of view of the Lutheran and Reformed Churches: the ministerial, prophetic, and pastoral functions are included in the main tasks of preaching, administering the sacraments, and exercising the power of the keys.

---

only to indicate what those who call themselves pastors should profess. That is, they have been set over the church not to have a sinecure but, by the doctrine of Christ to instruct the people to true godliness, to administer the sacred mysteries and to keep and exercise upright discipline" (OC 4, 622) [= McNEILL 2, 1059]. On the function of the pastors in Calvin, see A. GANOCZY, *Calvin . . .,* 327–344. Calvin compared the office of pastors to that of the apostles: "Yet pastors (except that they each govern the several churches assigned to them) have the same charge as the apostles" (IC [1560] IV.3.5 = OC 4, 621 [= McNEILL 2, 1058]). The *Second Helvetic Confession* states that "the duties of the ministers are various; yet for the most part they are restricted to two, in which all the rest are comprehended: to the teaching of the Gospel of Christ, and to the proper administration of the sacraments. For it is the duty of the ministers to gather together an assembly for worship in which to expound God's Word and to apply the whole doctrine to the care and the use of the Church, so that what is taught may benefit the hearers and edify the faithful," *Confessio et expositio . . .,* cap. XVIII [*BKRK* 257.31–37 = COCHRANE 275). On the function of the pastors in Calvin, see A. GANOCZY, *Calvin . . .,* 327–344. On the functions of the ministers among the Reformed, see J.-J. von ALLMEN, *Le saint ministère . . .,* 78–104.

D. USE OF THE CATEGORY OF PRIESTHOOD

We have seen that the term "priest" (or its equivalent) is applied to ministers ordained in the liturgical traditions of the Churches that emerged from the Reformation, except for Luther himself and the Reformed and Methodist traditions. However, for these Churches that were born of the Reformation (as, for that matter, in the liturgical tradition of the Roman Church [see vol. I of this study, ch. 2, D]), ministers are ordained mainly in view of a pastoral (royal) charge whose purpose is to watch over the Church and to feed the flock, that is, to build up the Church. In the case of Bucer, the term used (in the ritual studied) for the ordinand is "presbyter." Elsewhere, as A. Ganoczy has remarked, Bucer designated the pastoral ministry "without explanation or reserve, by the term *'sacerdotium'* or *'verum sacerdotium.'*"[16]

For the Reformers, ordained ministry is henceforth thought of as part and parcel of service, of *diakonia*, and it consists in supporting the community and nourishing its faith with preaching and the sacraments. We could express the logic at work in this way: the minister is one faithful member of a priestly community who has been chosen for the pastoral service of all. The only priesthood in which anyone can share is that of Christ, received through baptism, which makes an individual a member of the priestly people.[17] The

---

[16] A. GANOCZY, *Calvin . . .,* 252f. Elsewhere Bucer does not hesitate to use the word "priests" (*"Prister"*) when listing the ministries of the Church; see *Der Kürtzer . . ., MBDS* 6/3, 252.28.

[17] For example, *An den christlichen Adel . . .,* WA 6, 407.9–415.6 (= *LW* 44:127–139). In his analysis of the conception of the doctrine of the priesthood in Calvin, A. GANOCZY thinks that the latter "found it more important to emphasize the unique priesthood of Christ than to analyze how it operates within the Christian community": *Calvin . . .,* 247. See, for example, two texts from the IC (1560), II.15.6: ". . . Christ plays the priestly role, not only to render the Father favorable and propitious toward us by an eternal law of reconciliation, but also to receive us as his companions in this great office [Rev. 1:6]. For we who are defiled in ourselves, yet are priests in him, offer ourselves and our all to God, and freely enter the heavenly sanctuary that the sacrifices of prayers and praise that we bring may be acceptable and sweet-smelling before God" (= OC 3, 571 = McNEILL 1, 502), and II.7.1: ". . . the law was not devoid of reference to Christ. For Moses proposed to them as the purpose of adoption, that they should be a priestly kingdom unto God [Ex. 19:6]. This they could not have attained if a greater and more excellent reconciliation than that procured by the blood of beasts had not intervened [cf. Heb. 9:12ff.]. Because of hereditary taint, all of Adam's children are born in

sacrifice offered in this perspective is "the sacrifice of praise of life."[18]

Even if the minister is called "priest," the substance of his ministry has nothing to do with sacrifice, as we see clearly in Calvin's response of 1544 to his own question, asking what mission and what spiritual gift are conferred by the rites of ordination: ". . . [I]n ordination the thing chiefly to be looked at is the end, and the office to which priests are destined, (1 Tim 4:14; 2 Tim 1:6). Priests ought, moreover, to be appointed according to the command of God, and the rule of Scripture, not to sacrifice, but to govern the Church, and feed the flock with the word of the Lord, and administer the sacraments. As to the power of absolution, the true doctrine is, that the ministry of reconciliation has been given to true pastors, in order that by their doctrine, *i.e.*, the preaching of the gospel, they may absolve men from their sins by bringing them back into favor with God."[19]

---

bondage to sin. What, then, is less fitting than for them to be elevated to royal dignity, and in this way to become partners in God's glory, unless such pre-eminent good come to them from some other quarter? Also, how could the right of priesthood thrive among them, abominable as they were to God in the filth of their vices, were they not consecrated in the sacred Head? For this reason, Peter neatly turns that saying of Moses', teaching that the fullness of grace that the Jews had tasted under the law has been shown forth in Christ: 'You are a chosen race,' he says, 'a royal priesthood' [1 Peter 2:9]. In inverting the words, he means that those to whom Christ has appeared through the gospel have obtained more than their fathers did. For all have been endowed with priestly and kingly honor, so that, trusting in their Mediator, they may freely dare to come forth into God's presence" (= OC 3, 397 = McNEILL 1, 349f.).

[18] G. SIEGWALT, "Sacerdoce ministériel et ministère pastoral d'après les livres symboliques luthériens," *Verbum Caro* 22, 85 (1968) 34f., states in his conclusions drawn from a study of the basic Lutheran texts and the biblical conception of the priesthood: ". . . the sacrifice of praise of life . . . is also propitiatory as we have said, in the unity of the propitiatory sacrifice of Christ, and following in his footsteps, but it is not to be reified, it is the living sacrifice of the Church and of each Christian." In his chapter "Sacerdoce et ministère," von Allmen points to the same reality, according to the *Second Helvetic Confession* and certain writings of Calvin and others; see J.-J. von ALLMEN, *Le saint ministère . . .*, 55–64.

[19] ". . . Quamquam in ordinatione finis potissimum spectandus est, atque officium cui destinantur sacerdotes (Act. 13, 3; 1 Tim. 4, 14; 2 Tim. 1, 6). Constitui porro ex Dei mandato et regula scripturae debent, non ad immolandum, sed ad regendam ecclesiam, pascendumque gregem verbo Domini, et sacramenta administranda. De absolvendi potestate sic habendum est, datum quidem ministerium

What we see described in these rituals is the function of the *episkopē:* governance, pastoral functions (preaching, sacraments), the power of the keys (reconcilation and absolution). The rituals of ordination that we have studied constitute the verification of this in practice.

Whereas the medieval Catholic Church continued to use Old Testament metaphors to describe the ordained ministry, the new Churches emerging from the Reformation opted for New Testament metaphors[20] and emphasized the aspects of service and *diakonia.* We saw, however, that this fact did not keep some of these Churches from using the word "priest" for the ordained minister. The implementation of the concept of the universal priesthood (of baptism) served, then, to reestablish the fraternal communion (the *koinōnia*) among Christians, but, as we have seen, it did not preclude the existence of particular ministries within this communion. In other words, the Reformers "wanted to bring out the equality of state *between* ministers and laity *more than* any equality of competence in specific tasks."[21]

---

reconciliationis veris pastoribus, ut sua doctrina, hoc est, evangelii praedicatione, homines reducendo, cum Deo in gratiam, a peccatis absolvant (2 Co 5, 20) . . .," J. CALVIN, *Articuli a facultate sacrae theologiae Parisiensi determinati super materiis fidei nostrae hodie controversis. Cum Antidoto,* Art. VIII, *Antidotum* (1544) (= OC 7, 19) (= "Articles agreed upon by the Faculty of Sacred Theology of Paris, with the Antidote," in *Tracts relating to the Reformation,* trans. from the original Latin by H. Beveridge [Edinburgh: Calvin Translation Society, 1844] vol. 1, 88f.). On the later evolution of his thought, see the commentary of A. GANOCZY, *Calvin . . .,* 253ff.

[20] For example, see *Confessio et expositio . . .,* cap. XVIII (*BKRK* 255.22ff.) (= COCHRANE 271, quoted by J.-J. von ALLMEN, *Le saint ministère . . .,* 55–57). In the same vein one thinks of the sermon on Psalm 110 preached by Martin Luther in 1535. There, basing himself on 1 Peter 5:1, he called the ministers of the Church (*Kirchendiener*) "servants" or "bishops," i.e., supervisors of those whom the apostles called presbyters, that is, the elders (". . . *und heissen jnn der Schrifft Diener, Bischove das ist: Auff seher odder, wie sie die Aposteln nennen, Presbyter, Seniores, das ist: Eltesten . . ."*). Their office is to be the servant of all, who are priests thanks to their baptism (". . . *Doch mus man aus dem gantzen hauffen etliche aus sondern und wehlen, denen solche Ampt befolhen werde, Und wer solchs füret, der ist nu nicht des Ampts halben ein Priester* [wie die andern alle sind] *Sondern ein Diener der andern aller . . .*"); see M. LUTHER, *6. Predigt über den 110. Psalm (9. Juni 1535),* no. 18, WA 41, 208.21–23 and 210.15–18 (= *LW* 13, 331 and 332). Do we detect the influence of St. Augustine in his *Sermo* 340, in which he distinguishes between the charge (*officium*) of his ministry and the grace of his baptism (*christianus)*?

[21] G. HAMMANN, *Entre la secte . . .,* 269. We recall the importance of Bucer for the entire development of the conception of ordained ministry, for he influenced

E. ESCHATOLOGICAL MEANING OF THE INDIVIDUAL MINISTRY

The recitation of the Our Father is interpreted as expressing the eschatological dimension of the act of ordination, and looks to the final coming of the Kingdom of God and salvation here and now. The principal functions of ministerial service are the public proclamation of the gospel, the administration of the sacraments, and the exercise

---

the traditions of the Lutheran, Reformed, and Anglican-Methodist communities. In his theology, the specific nature of the particular ministries resides in the special vocation received by certain members of the community, a vocation that is linked to the work of the Holy Spirit (the growth in the Church) and to the will of Christ; cf. M. BUCER, *Confessio Tetrapolitana* [1530], art. XIII (in German), 15 (in Latin), *MBDS* 3, 99 (= COCHRANE 69ff.); there he quotes 1 Corinthians 3:7 to show the cooperation needed between God and his ministers; God uses the ministers to carry out his plan and bring about the growth of the Church: *Furbereytung zum Concilio* [1533], *MBDS* 5, 301f., 329; *Bericht auss der heyligen geschrift* [1534], *MBDS* 5, 129ff., 168. On the role of the Holy Spirit in the ecclesiology of Bucer, see G. HAMMANN, *Entre la secte . . .*, 104–109. But Bucer is not alone in seeing this relationship between ministers and laity. In the same sermon of Luther quoted above, we read: ". . . Da mus zuvor ein jglicher ein Christen und ein geborner Priester sein, ehe er ein Prediger oder Bischoff wird, Und kan jn weder papst noch kein Mensch zum Priester machen, Wenn er aber ein Priester durch die Tauffe geborn ist, so kompt darnach das Ampt und machet einen unterscheid zwischen jm und andern Christen, Denn da mussen aus dem gantzen haussen der Christen etliche genomen werden, so da sollen andern fürstehen, Welchen denn Gott sonderliche gaben und geschickligkeit da zu gibt, das sie zum Ampt tügen, Als Sanct Paulus zun Epheser am vierden spricht: 'Etliche hat Er gegeben zu Aposteln, Etliche zu Propheten, Etlich zu Evangelisten, Etliche zu Hirten und Lerer, das die Heiligen' (das ist: die bereid zuvor Christen und getauffte Priester sind) 'geschickt seien zum werck des Ampts oder Diensts, da durch der Leib Christi' (das ist: die Christliche Gemeinde oder Kirche) 'erbawet werde' (Ep 4, 11s) . . ." (". . . Before anyone becomes a preacher or a bishop, he must first be a Christian, a born priest. No pope or any other man can make him a priest. But having been born a priest through Baptism, a man thereupon receives the office; and this is what makes a difference between him and other Christians. Out of the multitude of Christians some must be selected who shall lead the others by virtue of the spiritual gifts and aptitude which God gives them for the office. Thus St. Paul writes [Eph 4:11, 12]: 'And His gifts were that some should be apostles, some prophets, some evangelists, some pastors and teachers, for the equipment of the saints' (this means those who are already Christians and baptized priests), 'for the work of ministry, for the building up of the body of Christ' (that is, the Christian congregation or church)," M. LUTHER, *6. Predigt über . . .*, WA 41, 209.24–36 (= *LW* 13, 332).

of the keys, concrete and historical interventions of the means of grace within the heart of humanity whose purpose is to gather together and preserve the holy people until the end of time. This is the reason why the ministry is centered on the final coming of the divine Kingdom. Particularly in Lutheran tradition, but also among the Reformed communities, the prayer that follows and continues the petitions of the Our Father makes clear this eschatological dimension of the growth of the Kingdom:

"May the plan of *God* be revealed to us by the message of salvation, may the citizens of his Kingdom be prepared and assembled *for* him, may the glorification that is his due be given him by his creatures, may all that belongs to him since the beginning be restored to him and *offered*, through the service of the Word and the sacraments, this is the 'last end' of the apostolic ministry and what is unique to it."[22]

Another possible indication of the eschatological meaning of the ordained ministry is found in Bucer, when he writes, in the beginning of his *"Ratio ordinandi,"* of the reason why ordination takes place on Sunday: *"Tempus ille Dominicus dies deputatus est, **ut tota Ecclesia coacta**, ordinatio fiat . . ."*[270] This eschatological perception linked to the choice of Sunday for ordinations also creates the context of this event in the life of the Church. The convocation of the Church also gives special meaning to the conferral of ordination in the framework of this religious office, because the pastor has not only the care of the flock; he also has the task of gathering all the faithful together to hear the Word of God and celebrate the sacraments. However, the sense of this quotation of Bucer's could also refer to the necessary public aspect of ordination in a juridical sense.

A second image taken from Ephesians 4:10ff. is used in the offices of ordination. This evocation of the ministry of the apostles, the prophets, the evangelists, the doctors, etc., is very appropriately

---

[22] ". . . Daß **Gott** durch die Heilsbotschaft zu seinem Recht an uns kommt, daß **für ihn** die Bürger seines Königsreiches zubereitet und gesammelt werden, daß er zu der ihm gebührenden Verherrlichung durch die Kreatur kommt, daß ihm, was ihm vom Ursprung an gehört, als sein Eigentum vermittels des Dienstes an Wort und Sakrament zurückgegeben und **dargebracht** wird, das ist das 'Letzte' und das Eigentliche, worum es bei der Fortpflanzung des apostolischen Amtes geht," P. BRUNNER, "Beiträge zur Lehre . . .," 126.

chosen to characterize the gathering together of the scattered flock into the Church, and even to evoke the building up of the body of Christ. One very natural corollary is found in the metaphor of growth (the abundant harvest), which leads also to the image of the Kingdom of God, which has been inaugurated but which is still to be fully realized. Bucer—and the rituals that derive from his work—is definite on this point: it is for this that ministers are called to the ministry that Christ himself exercised on earth: "[I]t has pleased your mercy that we too should be brought and regenerated to you through your same Son, and by his same holy ministry, and should form this Church as it stands here before your holy face."[23] In this way the eschatological dimension of the ordained ministry is linked to the very mission of the Church, in which the dispersed flock is gathered together and waits for the final realization of the Kingdom of Christ. The individual ministry builds up the Church through preaching, teaching, and worship, so that she might accomplish her mission. In the sense in which the ministry is the continuation (in time and space) of the ministry of Christ who came to proclaim the Good News of the Kingdom of God, it participates in the ultimate realization of the plan of God in the world.

F. PNEUMATOLOGICAL MEANING OF THE ORDAINED MINISTRY: CHARISM AND FUNCTION

The election is a structural element of the entire process, present in all the rituals we have looked at. We have noted that this element

[23] Cf. *289; elsewhere Bucer says about the same thing: "The Kingdom of our Savior Jesus Christ is that administration and care of the eternal life of God's elect, by which this very Lord and King of Heaven by his doctrine and discipline, administered by suitable ministers chosen for this very purpose, gathers to himself his elect, those dispersed throughout the world who are his but whom he nonetheless wills to be subject to the powers of the world. He incorporates them into himself and his Church and so governs them in it that purged more fully day by day from sins they live well and happily both here and in the time to come," M. BUCER, *De regno Christi* (ed. F. Wendel) 54. ET: W. PAUCK (ed.), *Melanchthon and Bucer* (Philadelphia: Westminster [coll. "The Library of Christian Classics," 19] 1969) 225. On the development of eschatology and the mission of the Church in Bucer, see G. HAMMANN, *Entre la secte . . .,* 141–144. Cf. also *959, *966, *1561 A/B/C, *1589 A/B/C; the theme of growth is expressed by the preaching of the Word of God (the primary task of ministers), which grows and bears fruit for the perfecting of the Church: *295, *309/*322, *932, *975.

takes up more space and is given more importance than some other structural elements, especially in the rituals of the Reformed Churches. Might we ask ourselves why this should be so? The very fact of raising the question brings out the deep, underlying, significance of the absolute necessity for the election in the thinking of the Reformers of the time.

The answer to this question also reveals the pneumatological basis of the act of the faithful in the Church concerned in the ordination. Even keeping in mind the concept of the "interior vocation" which was so important in the thinking of Calvin, it is still by this act of election that the Reformers expressed their understanding of the exterior vocation, or call, of every minister. This act (which also strives to discern the interior vocation of the individuals who are to be proposed to the community) allows the process of ordination to proceed to the imposition of hands; it is through this act that the assembly recognizes the action of the Spirit in the chosen person, and understands that it, too, embodies the action of the Spirit. Moreover, we see the Church concerned receiving the minister as sent by God (the eschatological purpose); L. Petri himself calls the office of preaching a "gift of God."[24]

Even though the ideal of having the entire community participate in the choice of its ministers (as we see, for instance, in Łaski) could not be realized after the early years because of the complexity of its implementation, and due, too, to the growing number of the faithful in the Protestant congregations, the principle of the ancient right of the local Church to choose its ministers was revived by the Reformation. It is true that, both before and after the Reformation, election will continue to take place in the Catholic Church despite the Council of Trent and its prudent formulations (Sessio XXIII, ch. 4 [DS 1769])—and this, with a pneumatological basis for vocation and ordained ministry. Still, at the time under study, the participation in this election will gradually be reduced to a representation of the congregation, or a delegation of leaders/elders, or even, in the Anglican Church, to the (ecclesiastical) direction of the Church, which led to the indignant reaction of the Puritans which we saw above.

On the other hand, if this aspect is overemphasized, out of opposition to the almost total lack of participation of the Christians in the

[24] L. PETRI, *TSK* 139 (298).

Latin Catholic Church, the whole balance of the Protestant ritual process is threatened: the meaning of the imposition of hands and the prayer in their global context can be overlooked. The ordination proper could become merely an act of ratification of the vocation, instead of a true integration and accreditation of the brother who is *called* and *installed* in his office.[25] This did, indeed, sometimes happen, as we shall see in the third part of this study in the rituals of certain Churches.

The pneumatological meaning of the ordained ministry can, how-ever, be discerned in the imposition of hands and the prayer said for the ordinand. Even if the full meaning of this act may be eclipsed, we have seen that the meaning of this imposition of hands, in the rituals studied, is linked to the office in which the ordinand is being in-stalled. Except for Łaski, the imposition of hands is reserved for the installation of the minister in his functions (as pastor, minister of the Word, priest, elder [in the sense of presbyter], and superintendent or bishop).[26] This gesture is universally used, because of the weight of its biblical and traditional authority in the Church. However, the Re-formers did not agree on its interpretation.[27] But this gesture is linked

[25] On this point, cf. H. DOMBOIS, *Das Recht . . .*, 513f. (on vocation) and 533 (on the loss of meaning of the act of ordination, which becomes an "act of confirma-tion"). At this point in our study we cannot yet affirm that this is what happened, but a tendency in this direction is visible, except for the rituals of Bucer[290] and of Middleburgh.[975] We shall see in the third volume of the present study that, several centuries later, this phenomenon will reveal itself, more clearly in some thinkers than in others, regardless of the presence or absence of a pneumatology in the theology of the ministry and of the Church.

[26] In the case of Jan Łaski, we have seen that all ministers receive the imposition of hands (superintendent, minister of the Word, deacon, elder). In the Lutheran rituals, only pastors and bishops or superintendents receive it. In Bucer, deacons (where this office exists) also receive the imposition of hands. In the Reformed rit-uals, the imposition of hands as ritual of installation is used for ministers of the Word. Knox uses it also for the superintendent, and the rite of Middleburgh says explicitly that this gesture is not performed a second time when a minister changes parishes. In the case of the Church of England, the bishop imposes hands at the beginning of the office of ordination of a bishop, a priest, or a deacon. Lastly, Wesley's ritual uses that of the Anglicans (1662), with the result that the imposition of hands keeps its central place in the ritual.

[27] For example, Luther denied that the gesture of the imposition of hands was sacramental, while Bucer, and Calvin following him, qualified it as sacramental. For

to the communication of the gift of the Spirit or the gift of God. In almost all cases the gift of the ministry is described in terms of Ephesians 4:10ff., which links the ministry to the building up of the Body of Christ and the readying of the saints for their role in the Church.[28] In the Reformed, Anglican, and Methodist rituals, we see that entrance into a particular ministry is a specific gift of the Spirit or of God. This is less evident with the Lutherans, while Bucer links the imposition of hands very closely to the action of the Holy Spirit. The "Amen" with which the community recognizes and receives the minister that God is giving it is to be interpreted not as a human decision or mere act of approval, but as a sign that God is at work, with the Spirit, within the community, by enabling it to discern the spirits. In itself, the "Amen" is a beautiful act of witnessing to the sovereignty of God and his Christ over his people, the Church, and to his sollicitude for his flock. As the prayers for the elect show, the ultimate effect of this "Amen" given to the workings of the Spirit confirms not only the reception of the minister, but also the transmission of the gifts of strength, comfort, confidence, etc., all gifts of the same Spirit to the elect, enabling him to fulfill his mission of service in a specific community, a not insignificant aspect of the pneumatic dimension of the ordained ministry.

Another important aspect stands out from the rites we have examined: the communal aspect of the ordained ministry, expressed in terms of service, or *diakonia*, which characterizes every particular ministry in these Churches, as we saw above. Moreover, this dimen-

---

a comparison of the positions of Luther, Bucer, and Zwingli, see G. HAMMANN, *Entre la secte . . .,* 197–199; for the position of Calvin, L. SCHUMMER, *Le ministère . . .,* 22–29; and A. GANOCZY, *Calvin . . .,* 318–327.

[28] In the Lutheran group, we see that Luther and L. Petri do not use this quotation. However, they make the ministry dependent on the Holy Spirit;[247, 309] what is more, we saw in the quotation from a sermon of Luther that this is not unusual: cf. n. 21. In Bugenhagen[260] and Bucer[289-290] this interpretation of the ministry is clearly in evidence. In the Reformed group, with the exception of the ritual of Zurich, we find our quotation as well as the connection between installation in a particular ministry and the gift of the Holy Spirit: cf. Jan Łaski,[931] John Knox,[955-956] and Middleburgh,[966] where this connection is made in the address on the meaning of the ministry. The same is true in the Anglican and Methodist groups (same text as the *BCP* of 1662), which followed the ritual of Bucer: Anglican (and Methodist).[1560A/B/C, 1589A/B/C]

sion is present in the participation of several ministers in an ordination: often they are ministers from other Christian communities. To our way of thinking, this structure is faithful to what we have seen in the early Church: the local Church is conscious of needing the neighboring Churches with which it is in communion in order to proceed to the ordination of its ministers. This is an expression of communion, filled with pneumatological meaning: the ministers share in fraternal solidarity in the confession of faith of their Churches.

In all these actions the Spirit is at work:

—In the election: the community is a bearer of the Spirit; it mediates the call that comes from God (the vocation); the person concerned is recognized as having the aptitudes and the faith necessary to build up the Church; and all this comes from the Spirit;

—In the imposition of hands and the communication of the Spirit (or of the gift of God);

—In the gathering together of the Church and the establishment of close, communal ties with other congregations, seen in the presence of the other pastors and ministers (elders) of the Church;

—And, lastly, in the celebration of worship, in the course of which the acts of election, ordination, and installation in a particular congregation take place.

The participation of all the members of the Church (each in his or her place) also emphasizes the aspect of the particular ministry as a gift of God for his Church. This can be seen in all the prayers (both for the community and for the elect). In them the congregation prays God to help the community in its choice, to give his Spirit to the elect so that he might be faithful in his service and have at his disposal all that he needs to fulfill the responsibilities of his ministry. Lastly, nowhere do we read in the formularies that the pastor or the ordained minister is a delegate of the community: he is its servant,[29] like Christ who came not to be served but to serve, by giving his life for the flock of God.

---

[29] Even though he is their servant, the minister stands before the community of brethren with the authority of Christ, for his ministry is exercised as the actualization of the ministry of Christ, as we see in, for example, *CA* XXVIII, at lines 20–22 (in the Latin version): "He who hears you hears me, Luke 10:16" (*BC* 84); and also P. MELANCHTHON, *Apologia . . .*, VII.28 and VIII.47f. (*BSLK* 240 and 246 [= *BC*

G. THE QUESTION OF THE DIRECTION OF THE CHURCH

The image found most often in the rituals describes the ordained ministry as a pastoral charge or as a stewardship. The purpose of this ministry is the growth or the building up of the Church and her life of faith, so that she may fill the world with her witness to the gospel, and above all, the saving action of God in Christ, salvation offered by Christ to all who hear him as the living Word of God, and accept the grace that he offers. The ministry is thus seen as a gift which puts the minister at the service of "the good of all," as we read in the prayers for the elect as well as in the examination and the commitment of the elect to the Church in which he is about to serve.

---

173 and 177]). Just as an example, let us look at the first paragraph (*BSLK* 240 = *BC* 173): "Quare nos iuxta scripturas sentimus ecclesiam proprie dictam esse congregationem sanctorum, qui vere credunt evangelio Christi et habent spiritum sanctum. Et tamen fatemur multos hypocritas et malos his in hac vita admixtos habere societatem externorum signorum, qui sunt membra ecclesiae secundum societatem externorum signorum ideoque gerunt officia in ecclesia. Nec adimit sacramentis efficaciam, quod per indignos tractantur, quia repraesentant Christi personam propter vocationem ecclesiae, non repraesentant proprias personas, ut testatur Christus: Qui vos audit, me audit. Cum verbum Christi, cum sacramenta porrigunt, Christi vice et loco porrigunt. Id docet nos illa vox Christi, ne indignitate ministrorum offendamur" ("In accordance with the Scriptures, therefore, we maintain that the church in the proper sense is the assembly of saints who truly believe the gospel of Christ and who have the Holy Spirit. Nevertheless, we grant that the many hypocrites and evil men who are mingled with them in this life share an association in the outward marks, are members of the church according to this association in the outward marks, and therefore hold office in the church. When the sacraments are administered by unworthy men, this does not rob them of their efficacy. For they do not represent their own persons but the person of Christ, because of the church's call, as Christ testifies [Luke 10:16], 'He who hears you hears me.' When they offer the Word of Christ or the sacraments, they do so in Christ's place and stead. Christ's statement teaches us this in order that we may not be offended by the unworthiness of ministers"). Or again, with a slightly different nuance, *Confessio et expositio . . .*, cap. XVIII (*BKRK* 256.38–41 = COCHRANE 273): " In virtue of this power [the keys] the minister, because of his office, does that which the Lord has commanded him to do; and the Lord confirms what he does, and wills that what his servant has done will be so regarded and acknowledged, as if he himself had done it." Here, too, we see that the minister's office derives from the ministry of Christ, and he is in no wise a mere delegate of the congregation; within the Church he represents the Lord and the gospel (this authority was given him with the power of the keys). Lastly, see the commentary on this passage of J.-J. von ALLMEN, *Le saint ministère . . .*, 69–71.

In this context, it is only natural to see the pastoral ministry as being in a position to call together the community through the proclamation of the gospel, to lead the liturgical assembly, and in this way help prepare or form it for its mission in the world. This is precisely what we find in the lists of the tasks entrusted to the ordained minister. It is he who preaches the Word of God, presides over the Sunday worship, and administers baptism; it is he, too, who is to administer corrections, using his ministry of the keys and discipline, even to the point of excommunication in the case of truly grievous sin. It is he, too, who calls and sends out on mission the parishioners of the community (in the work of catechesis, the organization of charitable works in behalf of the poor, etc.). Lastly, he imposes hands in the ordination of other ministers. But the texts of ordination that we have studied show that he does not bear all these responsibilities alone: he carries them out with the fraternal help of other ministers (most often non-ordained), such as the elders and the doctors (in the case of the Reformed Churches), the deacons, and, in the Methodist Church, the lay preachers. So we see the collegial dimension, too, of the ministerial organization of these Churches.

The ministry of direction is more extensive in the case of the bishop or superintendent. We have seen that the theological interpretation of this office (where it exists) is not the same everywhere. For instance, in the structure of ordination in the Anglican Church we have noted that ordination by a bishop is considered necessary, while in the Churches of the Lutheran or Reformed type the episcopal function could well be exercised by another minister (very often one who exercised some *supra locale* responsibility himself). What is essential is that he be duly installed and authorized to carry out this function. It is also clear that the community or the local Church is not the whole Church: other Churches also bear responsibility for the gospel and the mission of the Church of Christ in the world. So we see in this ministry of direction on the regional level an interrelatedness that expresses the need for common obedience in Christ, the sole Lord, King, and High Priest of the Church.[30]

[30] Cf. the prayer of Jan Łaski."[931] Obedience to the Lord Christ and his presence in the Church through the indwelling of the Spirit is a theme in the writings of all the great figures of the Reformation; see M. LIENHARD, *L'Evangile . . .*, 135–148; H. STROHL, "La notion . . .," *RHPR* 16, 3–5 (1936) 265–319 (a comparison

Lastly, the way in which the pastoral ministry is exercised during an ordination demonstrates its collegial nature. Nowhere do we see the imposition of hands being conferred by the ordaining minister alone: it is the act of all the ministers present, an act of reception into the ministerial body, and the expression of solidarity in the responsibilities being assumed. The epistles from the New Testament show the young Churches' concern to exercise their ministry of direction in community, through decisions "reached together" for the good of the whole Church, through the resolution of tensions, through the aid given to the poorer communities, etc. In so doing the apostolic task of direction, consisting in finding the right way of ordering its ministry and organizing (building up) the Church for her mission in the world, does not devolve on a single minister acting alone, but on a community of ministers; the examples of Peter and Paul express this clearly.

H. STRUCTURING OF THE CHURCH AND ORDINATION

The study of the procedures of ordination allows us to identify certain ecclesiological models (cf. vol. I of the present study, ch. 2, H) which in turn reveal the underlying theological equilibria. In order to be able to compare the structuring of Churches of different confessions in the third volume of this study, it would be helpful to identify at this point a few ecclesiological models that can be seen in the first Reformed rituals of ordination. For all the models that we shall now look at, there are three elements that structure the process in every case: the *election (vocation)*, the *ordination*, and the *mission*.

---

between Luther, Melanchthon, Zwingli, Oecolampadius, Bucer, and Calvin); G. HAMMANN, *Entre la secte . . .*, 103–147, 288–291; J.-J. von ALLMEN, *Le saint ministère . . .*, 192–212; R. BORNERT, *La Réforme . . .*, 429–438.

Luther proposed a collegial government that could take the form of a "synodal-collegial episcopalism": "Consequently the church cannot be better governed and maintained than by having all of us live under one head, Christ, and by having all the bishops equal in office (however they may differ in gifts) and diligently joined together in unity of doctrine, faith, sacraments, prayers, works of love, etc. . . .," *The Smalcald Articles* [1537], IInd part, art. 4/9 (*BSLK* 430 = *BC* 300); cf. V. VAJTA, "Conception du ministère ecclésiastique selon Luther. Sa signification actuelle," in H. R. BOUDIN and A. HOUSSIAU (eds.), *Luther aujourd'hui* (Louvain-la-Neuve: Publications de la Faculté de Théologie, 1983) 190f.

Next we note that the entire process is understood as *communal (ecclesial), confessional, liturgical,* and *juridical.* It is **communal,** or **ecclesial,** because one of the actors in the constellation is the Church in which the ordination takes place, and all the members of the community are involved. It is **confessional,** because in this process the very identity of the Church is drawn into the action: the quality of its witness to the eternal gospel, the purity of its doctrine, and the continuity of its mission are all part and parcel of the process taking place, and reach their culmination in the office of consecration. It is **liturgical,** because it includes the imposition of hands and the epiclesis of the entire community, celebrated in a service of worship, in some instances, and the Eucharistic celebration, in others. Lastly, it is **juridical,** because a concrete charge is conferred by the ordination.

1. THE LUTHERAN-REFORMED MODEL

We have already seen the emphasis placed in these rituals of ordination on the election, in contrast to and reaction against the Catholic emphasis on ordination. The Protestant determination was to restore the Christian dignity conferred in baptism and to reaffirm that the entire Church is responsible for the gospel, and for the faith and the salvation that it preaches. Why was this reemphasis so important? Because it made it possible to overcome the divisions between Christians within the one Church, and to determine the right and proper nature of the pastoral ministry in relationship to the elements which make up the Church (the Spirit, the gospel, and the sacraments): the pastoral ministry is necessary, but it is always secondary in relationship to these major constitutive elements.[31] Accord-

---

[31] Confirmed by the confessional writings, as, for example, *CA* V (= *BC* 31); *Confessio et expositio . . .,* cap. XVIII (*BKRK* 253.19–47 = COCHRANE 268f.); and in the writings of Luther or Calvin, for example, *Von den Konziliis . . .,* WA 50, 632.3ff. (= *LW* 41, 154–156); IC (1560), IV.3.1 = OC 4, 615–617 (McNEILL 2, 1053f.). There still are important nuances between Luther's conception and Calvin's, regarding the basis of ordained ministry: ". . . Calvin does not derive individual ministry from the universal priesthood of all the faithful. Ministry is instituted by God to proclaim the Word and to administer the sacraments, but also to preserve the order God desires to govern his Church . . . The community and the ministry . . . face towards one another. Calvin can go so far as to say that the ministers represent the person of Christ. It is through human beings that heavenly wisdom is transmitted, and it is the shepherd who guarantees that mutual love will be

ing to this model, the ordained ministry is clearly in the service of those three principal elements, and is therefore part of the structuring of the Church.

The category of *diakonia* is given special importance: it is the service of the gospel, the building up of the Church through the preaching of the Word, the administration of the sacraments, and the exercise of the power of the keys. The ministry here is seen as the function of a shepherd who remains at the same time one of the flock. But the grace of the gospel endows the minister with a new personal relationship to his fellow Christians. These ministers stand facing the Church, for through them Christ speaks to his Church as her Lord. But the ministers are also members, subject like the rest of the flock to the judgment of God. Lastly, they exercise their ministry in the communion of the other charisms and ministries, and along with them. All these Churches are in agreement that the public or ordained ministry belongs only to the persons duly chosen and installed, and that if a minister changes parishes, the ordination is not to be repeated.

Luther fought to have Christ restored to his primacy as the sole Head of the Church in the mind of Christians: the attachment to Christ in faith should outweigh obedience to the pope or to the other ministers invested with apostolic authority. To bolster this conviction, Luther insisted that the Church is found everywhere the gospel is preached correctly and the sacraments are administered according to

---

preserved (IC IV, 3, 1) . . .": A. BIRMELE, "Le ministère . . .," 194. On the development of the use of the passage from Ephesians (Eph 4:10ff.) and the necessity for the ordained ministry in the thought of Calvin, see E. A. MC KEE, *Elders and the Plural Ministry. The Role of Exegetical History in Illuminating John Calvin's Theology* (Geneva: Droz, 1988) 133–136. Our research on the rituals of ordination surely substantiates this "face-to-face" aspect of ordained ministry in the Churches of the Reformed-Calvinistic tradition, but it is to be found also in the four examples from the Lutheran tradition that we have studied. In the same article (p. 193), Birmelé affirms the "bipolar" nature of the general conception of ministry in Luther (he draws on the theories of "delegation," and of "institution"), a state of tension that we have also emphasized, but in practice the rituals studied support rather the second theory. On a theological level, we must of course ascertain the gap between theoretical or theological discourse and actual practice. It is surely in the latter that we see the ways in which the gospel is grace, and how this truth structures the Church herself.

the command of God.[32] The personal position of the minister is relativized. The Church is not visible because of the presence of an
ordained minister, but because his ministry is exercised faithfully.

Another remark on the subject of the communion within the
Church is in order: this communion is restored within the local
Church (because of the reemphasis on the grace of baptismal priesthood). The role of the actors involved in the process shows that the
entire Church is responsible for the ministry entrusted to her by God.
The election takes place in common (the whole Church is involved,
either in the sense that all her members are present, or in the sense
that a group representing them and their leaders participates). The
imposition of hands and the epiclesis are carried out by several pastors, and sometimes by representatives of the elders. This fact could

[32] For example, *CA* VII (= *BC* 32); P. MELANCHTHON, *Apologia . . .*, VII and
VIII (*BSLK* 233–246 = *BC* 168–178); *Confessio et expositio . . .*, cap. XVII (*BKRK*
248.35–253.10 = COCHRANE 261–268); M. LUTHER, *Von den Konziliis . . .*, WA
50, 629.16–20 (= *LW* 149); J. CALVIN, IC (1560), IV.1.9 (OC 4, 576f.) (= McNEILL
2, 1023f.). For a discussion of this dimension of Luther's ecclesiology, see the article by V. VAJTA, "The Church as Spiritual-Sacramental Communio with Christ
and His Saints in the Theology of Luther," in P. MANNS and H. MEYER (eds.),
Luther's Ecumenical Significance. An Interconfessional Consultation, American trans.
of the German *[Ökumenische Erschließung Luthers. Referate und Ergebnisse einer
internationalen Theologenkonsultation]* (Philadelphia/N.Y./Ramsey, N.J.: Fortress
Press/Paulist Press, 1984) 112–121, with the responses of JOHN OF HELSINKI
(Orthodox) 137–139, G. WAINWRIGHT (Methodist) 139–149, and the conclusion
drawn by G. KRETSCHMAR (Lutheran) 155–158. On p. 157 Kretschmar has this
to say on the interpretations of Luther: ". . . If the visible side of the church is the
sign for its hidden essence, then there are, in spite of all ambiguity, nevertheless
valid structures of the historical church . . . ." A certain reservation regarding the
use of the couplet "visible Church"/"invisible Church" is found in A. GREINER,
"La notion d'Eglise dans la Confession d'Augsbourg," *Positions luthériennes* 29, 4
(1981) 314ff. There he prefers the couplet *"ecclesia coram hominibus"/"ecclesia coram
Deo,"* a concept that expresses better the relationship between article VII and article VIII of the *CA*. It would seem that the expression "hidden Church" (*Ecclesia
abscondita*) was preferred by Luther; see, for example, *Ad librum . . .*, WA 7,
722.1–12; *De Servo arbitrio* (1525), WA 18, 652.23f. (= *LW* 33, 88f.); *In epistolam S.
Pauli ad Galatas commentarius* ([1531] 1535), WA 40/II, 105f. = *Ecclesia occulta* (=
"Lectures on Galatians," *LW* 27, 83–85), and WA 7, 710.1–7 where it is a question
of the *Ecclesia invisibilis;* lastly, on the end of the primacy of the ministry (that is,
the unique importance of the pope and the episcopal hierarchy) and the use of
the thesis of the "invisible Church," see D. OLIVIER, "La question . . .," 94f.

be interpreted in this way: the local Churches are not all-powerful, wholly sovereign; they can only exist in connection with each other. Within this communion, this bond is seen in the expression of faith (the same confession of faith), in the same customs, and the same ministries. History prevented the Churches of the Reformation from receiving the episcopal ordination of the Catholic Church, and thus the communion of the Churches of the West was destroyed: the Protestants no longer celebrate their ordinations in communion with the local Latin Church, which no longer accepts their ordinations. A certain Catholic tendency to overemphasize the hierarchical, placing the accent on the *"traditio"* enacted by the imposition of hands by the bishops, and tending to ignore the *"communio"* within the local Church by reducing its role in the choice of its bishop, is henceforth faced with the opposite tendency on the part of the Protestants, emphasizing the local or regional *"communio"* at the expense of the *"traditio."*

This new emphasis on communion is reflected also in the exercise of the ministry. Installed as shepherd in a community, the pastor is never alone in the exercise of his responsibility. There are always others to share it with him, namely, the elders, or a council. On the regional level there is even a ministry that serves a number of parishes at once—the bishop or superintendent who supervises the quality of the preaching, the moral life of the communities, etc., and this also takes place in a collegial context, with the help of other pastors or a synod. Quite often this minister is installed in his functions in a process similar to that of ordination.

There is no need to comment on the necessity for the newly ordained to demonstrate correct faith and a highly moral life. But it is important to draw attention to the fact that these qualities were attested both by the Christians of the local Church, and by the imposition of hands conferred by the pastors of the neighboring communities. All the Lutheran and Reformed rituals mention the examination or scrutiny of each candidate, often carried out in the presence of the faithful, or at least of a group of their representatives. Quite often other ministers are present at this examination (pastors or elders, depending on the Church). The purpose of the examination is to ensure the continuity of apostolic preaching and the eternal mission of the Church, which is to be a faithful witness to the grace of God.

In a few cases we saw that the gesture of the imposition of hands was relativized (for example, in *The Buke of Discipline* of Knox; see *958, note 5), even though, as we have seen, these Churches did attribute great importance to the gesture. The imposition of hands was not considered sufficient in itself if other conditions were not met. This means that we are in the presence of an ecclesial process, for behind the rite stands always the reception of the Church, seen in the role of the other Christians during the entire process, in the election, and in the presence of other ministers from neighboring communities during the procedures of election, and sometimes in the imposition of hands. The ordained ministry is clearly integrated *into* the Church, which, moreover, confers the authority to be exercised by this ministry in her name.[33] However, we see that this reception will gradually supplant the *"traditio"* in the process of the institution of ministers.

2. THE ANGLICAN MODEL

We could call this model a "mixed model," for, as we saw above, it contains elements taken from the Lutheran-Reformed model (Bucer's, combined with Puritan influences full of Calvinistic ideas), and from the medieval model based on the late pontificals; this model will be adapted later by Wesley and his disciples. Certainly, the three structural elements (election, ordination, mission) are found here, but in a different pattern, which we shall examine with an eye to its originality and the ecclesiological equilibrium it embodies.

First of all, we see that the value of the *election* is diminished, for the *active* role of the people is reduced to a passive acceptance or rejection. But the role of the clergy has acquired greater importance. The community concerned in the ordination has little to do in the choice and examination of its future minister. We see, then, a weakening of the sense of the pneumatological foundation of the ministry, following the model of the late medieval Church.

The position of the episcopal ministry in the Anglican Church also shows a resemblance to medieval practice. We see in it the important, even capital, role reserved to the bishops in the continuity of the

[33] Luther offered a clear explanation of this when he stated that ministers exercise their office "for and in the name of the Church"; see *Von den Konziliis . . .*, WA 50, 632.2 (= *LW* 41, 154f.).

apostolic ministry and in the direction of the Church.[34] Despite the opposition of the Puritans, the necessity for episcopal ordination was maintained. The bishop also plays a very important role not only in choosing the new ministers, as we have seen, but also in the process of verifying their suitability and preparation during the examination. Thanks to the opposition of the Puritans, the pastoral aspect (the dimension of God as a kindly Father) of the episcopal ministry will gain in importance over time.

We must pause a moment to consider this conflict between the Puritans and the Anglicans, for involved in the whole debate was a long-standing issue that had been troubling the Christian Church since the Edict of Milan—namely, the relationship between Church and State. In the sixteenth century, Protestantism was not the only cause of the establishment of national Churches, but it was responsible for the normalization of this situation, especially with the Peace of Augsburg (1555) and the principle of *"cuius regio, eius religio."*[35] Where the pope used to exercise his authority (by divine right), now the prince took his place, often by divine right. In the Lutheran regions, even though the bishops—where there still were bishops—exercised government generally, the civil powers could always intervene to resolve problems of organization, discipline, and even doctrine. In England, as early as 1534, Henry VIII was named "supreme head on earth of the Church of England."[36] In order to preserve national unity the government sought to impose religious uniformity.

---

[34] The questions raised in the time of Henry VIII are quite revealing: "Is consecration necessary for a bishop? Or does the authority given him by the King suffice?", quoted by S. NEILL, "The Necessity of Episcopacy: Anglican Questions and Answers," *Concilium* 10, 8 (1972) 88.

[35] This principle is later than the Peace of Augsburg, which gave several practical rules for the resolution of the religious wars. For a historical overview, see J. LECLER, "Les origines et le sens de la formule: *cujus regio, ejus religio,*" *RechSR* 38, 1 (1951) 115–131. The equivalent, *"ubi unus dominus, ibi una sit religio,"* is used in the Peace of Augsburg.

[36] It was the "Supreme Head Act" of 1534 that recognized him as head of the Church of England with the power to define doctrine and to punish heresy: see J.R.H. MOORMAN, *A History of the Church in England,* 3rd rev. ed. (London: Adam & Charles Black, 1980) 168.

As for the debate between the Puritans and the Anglicans, the former maintained vehemently that Christ is the only head of the Church, which must remain free of the intervention of the State. For the Anglicans, an "Erastian"[37] solution was opted for. Even if the Act of Supremacy of Elizabeth I (1558) somewhat modified her father's enactment (instead of being the "head" of the Church, she called herself "supreme governor of the kingdom in spiritual or ecclesiastical,

[37] This was a theory attributed to a certain Erastus (born Thomas Lüber or Lieber in 1524 in Baden [Switzerland], died in 1583 in Basel), professor of medicine at Heidelberg. The roots of Erastianism can be found in the controversy between Erastus (a Zwinglian) and the Calvinist—later, Lutheran—party over the question of whether the ecclesiastical authorities had the right to excommunicate a member of the congregation in order to force such a person to conform to ecclesiastical discipline. After a thorough study of the biblical texts, Erastus concluded that all juridical power of coercion belongs to the magistrates alone. The main purpose of his position was not to increase the power of the State, nor to render the Church subject to the latter, but to establish the freedom of conscience of the individual. However, based on his theses nos. 73–75 ("Explicatio gravissimae quaestionis utrum excommunicatio, quatenus religionem intelligentes et amplexantes a sacramentorum usu propter admissum facinus arcet, mandato nitatur divino an excogitata sit ab hominibus" [Pesclavii, apud Baocium Sultaceterum, 1589 = London, Jacques Castelvetro, who had married the widow of Erastus]), the theory was propounded that the ecclesiastical order had no autonomous juridical ground, that only the State possessed and exercised jurisdiction; it was rather Grotius (born Hugo de Groot in 1583 in Delft, died in 1645 in Rostock), a Dutch jurist and diplomat, who elaborated—without mentioning Erastus—what today we call Erastianism. It was J. Whitgift (an Anglican) who disseminated and printed Erastus' theses in England, which explains their particular acceptance in Scotland and England. Erastianism reached its pinnacle of influence in the philosophy of Thomas Hobbes (1588–1679), especially in the 42nd chapter of *Leviathon* (1651) on ecclesiastical power, where he defends the absolute power of the State over the Church: read A. BONNARD, *Thomas Eraste (1524–1583) et la discipline ecclésiastique* (Lausanne: Georges Bridel, 1894); the two works of W. K. JORDAN, *The Development of Religious Toleration in England. T. 1: From the Beginning of the English Reformation to the Death of Queen Elizabeth*, 137–151 (Whitgift); T. 2: *From the Accession of James I to the Convention of the Long Parliament (1603–1640)* (London: George Allen & Unwin Ltd., 1932 and 1936) 453–491 (the Erastians); for the distinctions between the position of Erastus and the theory of Erastianism, see J. N. FIGGIS, "Erastus and Erastianism," *JTS* 2, 1 (1900/1901) 66–101. Lastly, for a brief historical survey of the part Erastianism played in the Church of England, see the article of J. Y. EVANS, "Erastianism," in J. HASTINGS (ed.), *Encyclopaedia of Religion and Ethics* (Edinburgh/N.Y.: T. & T. Clark/Charles Scribner's Son, 1912) t. 5, 358–366, esp. 364ff.

as well as temporal, matters"*[1604C]), Whitgift accepted the fact that the Queen's government controlled the Church. His responses to Cartwright were a sort of theoretical apologia for the State. For purposes of our study, it is important to see that the State was reconstructing the makeup of the Church in a form more favorable to its secular ends. The burden of maintaining a uniform form of worship and a system of support rested on the State: the established Church was not free in this context, and, as a result, it remained an instrument in the hands of the State. The protest of the Puritans bore on the fact that Christ was no longer the supreme head of the Church, and that the latter had lost Christ as her one Lord. The clergy in this state of affairs became a body of state bureaucrats. Quite often the bishops found themselves in London (in Parliament), rather than in their dioceses, while the priests exercised their spiritual ministry in a very lax fashion.

Indeed, this laxity in the exercise of both the episcopal and presbyteral ministries was one of the factors impelling Wesley to attempt to renew the Anglican Church spiritually from within.

It is clear that the episcopacy was a necessary element in the government of this Anglican model. Even though Wesley did not want to establish bishops in his "Methodist Societies" in England (we recall that he wanted them to continue as part of the Anglican Church), he saw their necessity for the organization of his "Societies" in North America, which until then had had no bishops because of the political conflict between the Anglican Church and its new communities in the colonies. Most likely the decision not to name a bishop (an Anglican bishop) for the young Churches of the New World was more the result of England's political policies regarding her rebellious colonies than it was a reflection of a theological stance. This was a good example of the Church's being incorporated into the State. Nevertheless, Wesley considered himself a "spiritual *episkopos*," and he carried out the prescriptions of Scripture to govern his Societies as a good father, a faithful steward, and a zealous missionary. He put into practice what the Church he loved professed in theory, a superintendency that was to provide a certain structure to the Methodist Churches in America. In place of the political pragmatism that from then on characterized the Church of England, it was theological concerns that motivated Wesley in the exercise of his ministry.

The affirmation of the principle of retaining the episcopacy in the Anglican model did not prevent these prelates from being in a dependent position vis-à-vis the State. The role of the monarch in election is attested in all the rituals we have studied, as well as in the oath of royal supremacy sworn by all ministers during the liturgical celebration of their ordination.[*1604A/B/C] Wesley kept his distance from this "Erastianism" in the practice of the Anglican Church; he gave the Methodist episcopacy its independence wherever it existed, affirming the Church's freedom to structure herself according to the demands of the gospel, according to her received graces and her mission in the world. The political situation in North America undoubtedly was a help to him in this.[38]

I. FRAMEWORK OF ORDINATION

In the early Church the ordained ministry was governed by a sacramental and Trinitarian ecclesiology, according to which ordination was presented as one of many communal, liturgical, and juridical actions by which the Church was built up. Over the centuries the ordained ministry became isolated from its ecclesial context (concrete and communal), and the process of ordination broke down and became less intelligible (which in turn led to the development of extraneous, "explanatory" rites). All this found an echo in the functioning of the ordained ministry in the Church: the aspect of power (jurisdiction) over the mystical Body of Christ was emphasized, along with—and this was graver still—the consecratory or sacrificial power of a few individuals for the whole of the sacramental Body of Christ—the multiplication of private Masses, the need for a juridical enactment for the exercise of certain functions of the ministry, etc. At the same

[38] The development of the concept of the Church among American Methodists is analyzed by E. W. GERDES, *Informed Ministry. Theological Reflections on the Practice of Ministry in Methodism* (Zurich: Gotthelf Verlag, 1976). In the third section of this work Gerdes shows how the Methodists' conception of the ministry differs from that of the national Churches of the monarchies. The model of the Societies founded by Wesley is the brotherhood ("fellowship") or *ecclesiola,* which corresponds to a political model of a democratic type (American context). The second model is that of the Anglican Church *(ecclesia),* which corresponds to the monarchical form of government. The way in which authority was exercised in each gives the following dichotomies: representative power vs. governmental power; consensus vs. imposition from above: cf. 76ff.

time the category of priesthood supplanted that of pastoral ministry, with the result that the aspect of *diakonia* or service was eclipsed in the theological thought of the late Middle Ages.

This was the context in which the Reformation erupted. The movement was critical of the then-current theology of the priesthood and the episcopacy, and of the differentiation between Christians that had evolved from this theology. In harmony with the main ideas of the Reformation applied to the realm of worship, the new rituals of ordination show a new balance in these matters. In this way the Christological, the pneumatological, and the eschatological find themselves in a new state of equilibrium, as regards vocation, the functions of particular ministries, and the mission of the Church. The communal and relational dimension of the Christian community is revitalized in the active role of the faithful and in the affirmation that all members are responsible for the life of the Church. The ordained ministries are reintegrated into the community, and their authority is exercised with and for the community in a more pastoral fashion. Yet while these positive changes were occurring, other aspects, troubling ones, also appeared.

The relationship between the local Church and the entire Church did not easily find a desirable balance, because of the hesitation to see the ordained ministry as the link between a given community and the other Churches. It is true that we note the presence of other ministers during the imposition of hands, but their presence seems to have a largely juridical meaning: they bear witness that the ordination is being carried out in due form, rather than being there as agents of the *"traditio/receptio"* of the early Church. We see the grave impact of this choice in the case of the installation of a bishop (or superintendent, or head of a local Church), for the apostolic nature of the ministry is lost from sight. We will recall that it was through this process that the faith of the local Church was received as sharing in the continuity of the faith of the apostles, and its ministry recognized as following in apostolic succession. Thus the minister who presided over this particular community belonged to the college of bishops as a brother, and the faith, the life, the customs, the ministries, etc., of this community were received as true to the apostolic legacy.

The overvaluation of the election at the expense of the *"traditio"* was a reinterpretation of the practice of the Latin Church against which the Reformers were reacting, but at the same time it introduced an imbalance in the entire process. The analysis of Dombois on this subject is particularly to the point: "The fact that ordination integrates and empowers the ordinand is lost sight of, giving way to the purely noetic distinction between *verbum internum et externum*. The inevitable result was the perception of the sacrament as an act of confirmation, or as simply a symbol."[39] The old tendency to think in terms of absolute ordination persisted. The Latin Church had overvalued the act of ordination, and the Reformed Churches have had the tendency to do the same thing for the act of election. In this way the process of admission to the ordained ministry as a link between the three structural elements breaks down.

One last aspect of the general framework of ordination in the Reformed world leads us to examine the true meaning of the ordained ministry in view of the fact that the celebration of the Eucharist was part of some of the rituals and not of others, which would have been out of the question in the early Church. The celebration of the Eucharist holds a place of prime importance in ordination, for it is in this act that we find the deepest realization of the true *koinōnia* between the triune God and the Trinitarian Church: the Christian brotherhood is gathered together into one place by the proclamation of the gospel, as the priestly people of God (1 Pet 2:5, 9), as members of the same body (of Christ) by their communion with the cup of blessing and the one bread (1 Cor 10:16f.) and the temple of the Holy Spirit (1 Cor 3:16f.; Eph 2:18-22). Now, the rituals studied see in the ordained ministry the role of shepherd/pastor, continually building up the Church through the proclamation of the Word of God, the celebration of the sacraments, the exercise of discipline, and even through the witness that the Christians' conduct bears to their faith. But if such is the case, why would the newly ordained not exercise this role during the liturgical part of the process of ordination, among his people, and at their head? And the third structural part of the process, the

---

[39] "Der einordnende und zuordnende Charakter der Ordination tritt gegenüber der noëtischen Unterscheidung von verbum internum und externum ganz zurück. Man kommt so zwangsläufig zu einem konfirmatorisch-signifikatorischen Sakramentsverständnis—oder setzt es stillschweigend voraus," H. DOMBOIS, *Das Recht . . .*, 533.

missioning, is also left in the shadows. We can surely ask the reasons why this should be so.

The *missio* was not immediately implemented in the rituals of ordination that we have looked at, probably because there persisted at the time some of the dominant scholastic theology that treated the ordained ministry as separate from the community. While the Catholics defined the priesthood and all ministries in terms of powers received, the Reformers reversed this concept and maintained the equality of all within the Church, which led to the inclusion of the new minister in the community at his ordination. The Latin Catholic Church had restricted the ministry to the concept of a priesthood linked to the power to offer the Eucharistic sacrifice and the power to forgive sins; the Churches of the Reformation did the same, while emphasizing the ministry of preaching, to which was added the administration of the sacraments. Neither side saw ordination as integrating the newly ordained into an organic, charismatic whole, because the structural role of the Spirit was forgotten, giving way to an almost exclusively Christological interpretation of ordination. Even though all the Churches that sprang from the Reformation were opposed to the practice of ordaining ministers without a concrete charge, they still continued to think of the ordained ministry in a unilateral fashion. We see this illustrated in the incapacity to understand the Eucharistic celebration as the locus of the gathering together of all the charisms that are rooted in the one ministry of Christ, with each member participating with the exercise of whatever charism he or she has received. So we see the Reformed Churches more and more ordaining men elected for a specific ministry, admitting them at the moment of their ordination to a pastoral body (a sort of ministerial accreditation) which is to install them in their local ministry.[40] Even in those cases

[40] This is the case for most Swiss Churches, the Church of the Channel Islands, and the Reformed Churches of France. This comment was taken from J.-J. von ALLMEN, *Le saint ministère . . .*, 50. See also J. AYMON, *Actes ecclésiastiques et civils de tous les Synodes nationaux des Eglises réformées de France* (The Hague: Charles Delo, 1710) t. 1, 246, 264, 307; and F. de SCHICKLER, *Les Eglises du refuge en Angleterre* (Paris: Fischbacher, 1892) t.3, 315. This tendency is also seen in the Lutheran Churches themselves; see the thesis of S. K. BOLES, *Lutheran Pastors in Ernestine Saxony and Thuringia, 1521–1546* (Ann Arbor, Mich.: University Microfilms International, 1971) esp. 185ff.

where the ordinand is installed in a particular community, he does not preside at the worship service that follows his installation.

The balance of the early Church is not preserved when the ordination does not end with the actual installation of the person in his function. Ordination is intended to enable the new minister to preside over the *ecclesia* as *koinōnia*, whereas, from then on, as in the late Middle Ages, another minister presides at the Eucharistic banquet or the worship service that follows. This fact reveals a profound imbalance in the real relationship between the ordained ministry and the cult, for the minister plays an indispensable role in the building up of the Church on the level of her worship (he puts the gift he has received at the service of others; cf. 1 Pet 4:10), and above all on the level of the continuation of her apostolic and eschatological mission (Eph 4:11-13)—in a word, the growth of the Kingdom (Mt 9:37f.).

Bibliography

1. ABBREVIATIONS

A. BIBLICAL REFERENCES
The Scripture quotations are from the New Revised Standard Version Bible, Catholic edition, © 1989 by the Division of Christian Education of the National Council of Churches of Christ in the USA. Used by permission. All rights reserved.

The following abbreviations are used for the books of the Bible:

Old Testament

Gen	Genesis	2 Chr	2 Chronicles	Dan	Daniel
Ex	Exodus	Ezra	Ezra	Hos	Hosea
Lev	Leviticus	Neh	Nehemiah	Joel	Joel
Num	Numbers	Esth	Esther	Am	Amos
Deut	Deuteronomy	Job	Job	Ob	Obadiah
Josh	Joshua	Ps	Psalms	Jon	Jonah
Judg	Judges	Prov	Proverbs	Mic	Micah
Ruth	Ruth	Eccl	Ecclesiastes	Nah	Nahum
1 Sam	1 Samuel	Song	Song of Solomon	Hab	Habakkuk
2 Sam	2 Samuel	Isa	Isaiah	Zeph	Zephaniah
1 Kings	1 Kings	Jer	Jeremiah	Hag	Haggai
2 Kings	2 Kings	Lam	Lamentations	Zech	Zechariah
1 Chr	1 Chronicles	Ezek	Ezekiel	Mal	Malachi

Apocryphal/Deuterocanonical Books

Tob	Tobit	Song of Thr	Prayer of Azariah and the
Jdt	Judith		Song of the Three Jews
Add Esth	Additions to Esther	Sus	Susanna
Wis	Wisdom	Bel	Bel and the Dragon
Sir	Sirach (Ecclesiasticus)	1 Macc	1 Maccabees
Bar	Baruch	2 Macc	2 Maccabees
1 Esd	1 Esdras	3 Macc	3 Maccabees
2 Esd	2 Esdras	4 Macc	4 Maccabees
Let Jer	Letter of Jeremiah	Pr Man	Prayer of Manasseh

New Testament

Mt	Matthew	Eph	Ephesians	Heb	Hebrews
Mk	Mark	Phil	Philippians	Jas	James
Lk	Luke	Col	Colossians	1 Pet	1 Peter
Jn	John	1 Thess	1 Thessalonians	2 Pet	2 Peter
Acts	Acts of the	2 Thess	2 Thessalonians	1 Jn	1 John
	Apostles	1 Tim	1 Timothy	2 Jn	2 John
Rom	Romans	2 Tim	2 Timothy	3 Jn	3 John
1 Cor	1 Corinthians	Titus	Titus	Jude	Jude
2 Cor	2 Corinthians	Philem	Philemon	Rev	Revelation
Gal	Galatians				

B. ABBREVIATIONS

AT
Apostolic Tradition, in W. A. JURGENS, *The Faith of the Early Fathers*, 3 vols., Collegeville: The Liturgical Press, 1970, vol. I; *La Tradition Apostolique de saint Hippolyte. Essai de reconstitution*. 5th improved ed. by A. Gerhards and S. Felbecker, Münster: Aschendorff (coll. "LQF," 39), 1989.

BC
The Book of Concord. The Confessions of the Evangelical Lutheran Church, trans. and ed. by T. G. TAPPERT, Philadelphia: Fortress, 1959.

BCP
Book of Common Prayer

BKRK
Bekenntnisschriften und Kirchenordnungen der nach Gottes Wort reformierten Kirche, W. NIESEL (ed.), Zurich: Verlag A. G. Zollikon, n.d. [1938].

BSLK
Die Bekenntnisschriften der evangelisch-lutherischen Kirche, 10th ed. [1st ed. 1930], Göttingen: Vandenhoeck und Ruprecht, 1986.

CA
Confessio Augustana [1530], Latin and German texts = *BSLK* 44–137; ET: *BC* 24–96.

COCHRANE
Cochrane, A. C. (ed.), *Reformed Confessions of the Sixteenth Century*, Philadelphia: Westminster Press, 1966.

The English Rite
BRIGHTMAN, F. E., *The English Rite Being a Synopsis of the Sources of the Book of Common Prayer with an Introduction and an Appendix*, reprint [2nd rev. ed. 1921], Westmead, Farnborough, Hampshire: Gregg International Publishers, Ltd., 1970, 2 vols.

IC	*L'Institution chrétienne* of John Calvin (cited IC [1560], IV. 3.10 = § 10 of ch. 3 of the IVth book of the *Institution chrétienne* of 1560) = *Institutes of the Christian Religion* (McNeill).
KO(s)	Kirchenordnung(en) (= church order[s]).
LW	*Luther's Works,* American edition, J. PELIKAN and H. T. LEHMANN (eds.), 55 vols., St. Louis/Philadelphia: Concordia Publishing House/Fortress Press, 1955ff.
MASKELL	MASKELL, W., *Monumenta Ritualia Ecclesiae Anglicanae. The Occasional Offices of the Church of England According to the Old Use of Salisbury the Prymer in English and Other Prayers and Forms with Dissertations and Notes,* reprint [1st ed. 1882], Westmead, Farnborough, Hampshire: Gregg International Publishers, Ltd., 1970, 3 vols.
MBSA	*Martini Buceri Scripta Anglicana,* C. HUBERT (ed.), Basel: Petri Pernae Officina, 1577.
MBDS	*Martin Bucers deutsche Schriften,* R. STUPPERICH (ed.), Gütersloh/Paris: Gerd Mohn/Presses Universitaires de France, 1960ff.
MBOL	*Martini Buceri Opera Latina,* vol. I published by C. AUGUSTIJN, P. FRAENKEL and M. LIENHARD (eds.), Leiden: Brill, 1982; vols. XV and XVbis published by F. WENDEL (ed.), Gütersloh/Paris: C. Bertelsmann Verlag/ Presses Universitaires de France, 1954–1955.
OC	*Iohannis Calvini. Opera quae supersunt omnia,* G. BAUM, E. CUNITZ and E. REUSS (eds.), 58 vols., Brunswick: C. A. Schwetschke et Filium (coll. "Corpus Reformatorum," 29–86/87) 1863–1900 (cited OC 4, 621 = col. 621 of the 4th volume of the *Opera*).
PRG	Romano-Germanic Pontifical of the Xth century, C. VOGEL and R. ELZE, *Le Pontifical romano-germanique du dixième siècle,* Vatican City: Bibliothèque apostolique vaticane (coll. "Studi e testi," 226, 227, 269), 1963–1972.
RICHTER	RICHTER, A. L. (ed.), *Die evangelischen Kirchenordnungen des sechzehnten Jahrhunderts,* anastatic reprint [1st ed. 1846], Nieuwkoop: B. Degraaf, 1967, 2 vols.
Sarum	= Pontifical Russell (ms of Cambridge Mm. iii. 21, XVth century), called "Sarum," coming from Salisbury or Lincoln; text of the Ordinal, MASKELL II, pp. 164–320.

SEA	*Statuta ecclesiae antiqua,* ed. Ch. MUNIER, *Les Statuta ecclesiae antiqua. Edition, études critiques,* Paris: Presses Universitaires de France (coll. "Bibliothèque de l'Institut de Droit canonique de l'Université de Strasbourg," 5) 1960, reprinted in *Concilia Galliae A. 314-A. 506,* Turnhout: Brépols, 1978 (= CC 148), pp. 162–188.
SEHLING	SEHLING, E. (ed.), *Die evangelischen Kirchenordnungen des XVI. Jahrhunderts,* anastatic reprint [1st ed. 1902–1913], Aalen, 1970, 5 vols., and Tübingen: J.C.B. Mohr, 1955ff., vols. 6–8, 11–15.
TSK	*Then Swenska Kyrkeordningen,* ed. E. FÄRNSTRÖM, Stockholm: Svenska Kyrkans Diakonistyrelses Bokförlag, 1932.
WA	Weimarer Ausgabe, *D. Martin Luthers Werke. Kritische Gesamtausgabe,* Weimar: Hermann Böhlaus Nachfolger, 1883ff.
WA Br	Weimarer Ausgabe, *D. Martin Luthers Werke. Briefwechsel,* Weimar: Hermann Böhlaus Nachfolger, 1883ff., 18 vols.

Collections

CC	*Corpus christianorum collectum a monachis O.S.B. abbatiae S. Petri in Steenbrugge, series latina,* Turnhout/Paris: Brépols, 1954ff.
SC	*Sources chrétiennes,* collection directed by H. de LUBAC and J. DANIELOU (then C. MONDESERT), Paris: Cerf, 1942ff.

Reviews and Periodicals

AAS	*Acta apostolicae sedis. Commentarium officiale,* Rome, then Vatican City: Typis Polyglottis Vaticanis, 1909ff.
ALW	*Archiv für Liturgiewissenschaff,* Regensburg: F. Pustet, 1950ff.
BLE	*Bulletin de littérature ecclésiastique,* Paris: Lecoffre, then Toulouse: Université catholique de Toulouse, 1899ff.
EL	*Ephemerides liturgicae,* Rome: Ed. liturgiche, 1887ff.
JLH	*Jahrbuch für Liturgik und Hymnologie,* Kassel: Johannes Stauda Verlag, 1955ff.
JTS	*Journal of Theological Studies,* London: Macmillan, then Oxford: Clarendon, 1900ff.
LMD	*La Maison-Dieu, Revue de pastorale liturgique,* Paris: Cerf, 1945ff.

LQF	*Liturgiegeschichtliche* (then *Liturgiewissenschaftliche*) *Quellen und Forschungen,* Münster: Aschendorff, 1919ff.
NRT	*Nouvelle revue théologique,* Tournai then Louvain: Casterman, 1869ff.
RDC	*Revue de droit canonique,* Strasbourg: Université de Strasbourg, 1951ff.
RechSR	*Recherches de science religieuse,* Paris: Bureau de la Revue, 1910ff.
RevSR	*Revue des sciences religieuses,* Strasbourg: Palais Universitaire, 1921ff.
RHE	*Revue d'histoire ecclésiastique,* Louvain: Charles Peeters, later Bureau de la Revue, then Université catholique de Louvain, 1900ff.
RHPR	*Revue d'histoire et de philosophie religieuses,* Strasbourg: Faculté de théologie protestante, 1921ff.
RSPT	*Revue des sciences philosophiques et théologiques,* Paris: Lecoffre, then Vrin, 1907ff.
ZKT	*Zeitschrift für katholische Theologie,* Innsbruck: Theologische Fakultät, 1877ff.

Churches and Ecclesial Organizations

SCM	Student Christian Movement Press
SPCK	Society for Promoting Christian Knowledge
UCC	United Church of Christ

Varia

col.	column
ET	English translation
fasc.	fascicle
L	Latin text
n. (nn.)	note (notes)
no(s).	number(s)
NS	new series
n.d.	no date
n.p.	no place
n.d.n.p.	no date, no place
t.	tome
vol.	volume

2. SOURCES

A. HISTORICAL AND LITERARY SOURCES: REFORMED SOURCES

ASBURY, F. *The Journal and Letters of Francis Asbury*. Eds. E. T. Clark, J. M. Potts, and J. S. Payton. London/Nashville: Epworth Press/Abingdon Press, 1958, 3 vols.

AYMON, J. *Actes ecclésiastiques et civils de tous les Synodes nationaux des Eglises réformées de France*. The Hague: Charles Delo, 1710, 2 vols.

BUCER, M. *Die Berner Disputation*, (*MBDS* 4, 31–154).

ID. *Bericht auss der heyligen geschrift von der recht gottseligen antsellung und hausshaltung Christlicher gemeyn, Eynsatzung der diener des worts Haltung und brauch der heyligen Sacramenten* (*MBDS* 5, 119–258).

ID. *Confessio Tetrapolitana* (*MBDS* 3, 35–185). ET: "The Tetrapolitan Confession of 1530," COCHRANE, A. C. (ed.), *Reformed Confessions of the Sixteenth Century*. Philadelphia: Westminster Press, 1966, 54–88.

ID. *Furbereytung zum Concilio wie alle recht Gotssfortigen von beden yetz fürnemmen theylen so man alt- und newgleubige, Bäpstische und Lutherische nennet, zu einigkeit Christlicher kirchen kommen und sich darin unbeuegt halten mögen; etlich freundiliche Gotsförchtige gespräch von fürnemmen stucken Christlichen lere, derenhalb man yetz im mißverstand ist* (*MBDS* 5, 270–362).

ID. *Grund und ursach auss gotlicher schrifft der neüwerungen an dem nachtmal des herren, so man die Mess nennet, Tauff, Feyrtagen, bildern und gesang in der gemein Christi, wann die züsammenkompt, durch und auff des wort gottes zü Strassburg fürgenommen* (*MBDS* 1, 194–278).

ID. *Der Kürtzer Catechismus 1543* (*MBDS* 6/3, 225–265).

ID. *Ein kurtzer warhafftiger bericht von Disputationem und gantzem handel, so zusuchen Cunrat Treger, Provincial der Augustiner, und den predigern des Evangelii zü Strassburg sich begeben hat* (*MBDS* 2, 37–173).

ID. *Martin Butzers an ein christlichen Rath und Gemeyn der statt Weissenburg Summary seiner Predig daselbst gethon* (*MBDS* 1, 79–147).

ID. *Ordenung der Kirchenübunge. Für die Kirchen zu Cassell 1539* (*MBDS* 7, 279–318).

ID. *De ordinatione legitima ministrorum ecclesiae revocanda* (*MBSA* 238–259). ET: "An Inquiry Concerning the Restoration of the Lawful Ordination of the Church's Ministers" = WRIGHT 254–283.

ID. *De Regno Christi* (*MBOL* 15). French trans.: *Du Royaume de Jésus-Christ, Edition critique de la traduction française de 1558*. Text established by F. Wendel

(*MBOL* 15bis). ET: "On the Kingdom of Christ," pp. 174–394 in PAUCK, W. (ed.). *Melanchthon and Bucer*. Philadelphia: Westminister (coll. "The Library of Christian Classics," 19) 1969.

ID. *Ein Summarischer vergriff der Christlichen lehre und Religion, die man zü Strasburg hat nun in die xxviii jar gelehret. Mit Einer antwoert der Prediger daselbet auff ein Lesterschrifft, in deren sie des Münsterischen geistes und lehre on einigen schein der warheit beschuldiget werden. Und Wem Reformation des eüsseren Ceremonischen Gotsdienste züstande* (*MBDS* 17, 121–150). French trans.: *Résumé sommaire de la doctrine et de la religion chrétiennes enseignées à Strasbourg depuis près de vingt-huit ans avec une réponse des prédicateurs de Strasbourg à un écrit diffamatoire les accusant, sans ombre de vérité, d'esprit et de doctrine anabaptistes et à qui il appartient de réformer les cérémonies extérieures du culte*, by F. Wendel, *Cahiers RHPR* 33, 1951. ET: *A Brief Summary of the Christian Doctrine and Religion Taught at Strasbourg for the Past Twenty-eight Years, together with a Reply from the Preachers of Strasbourg to a Defamatory Writing Accusing them without a Shadow of Truth of the Spirit and Teaching of Anabaptists; and [the question] Who is Competent to Reform the External Ceremonies of Divine Worship*, pp. 76–93 in WRIGHT, D. F., *Common Places of Martin Bucer*. Appleford: Sutton Courtenay Press (coll. "The Courtenay Library of Reformation Classics," 4) 1972.

ID. *De vi et usu sacri ministerii, explicatio* (*MBSA* 553–610).

ID. *Von der waren Seelsorge und dem rechten Hirtendienst, wie derselbige in der Kirchen Christi bestellet und verrichtet werden solle* (*MBDS* 7, 90–245).

CALVIN, J. *Articuli a facultate sacrae theologiae Parisiensi determinati super materiis fidei nostrae hodie controversis. Cum Antidoto* (1544) (= OC 7, 5–44). ET: "Articles agreed upon by the Faculty of Sacred Theology of Paris, with the Antidote," pp. 71–120 in *Tracts Relating to the Reformation*, trans. from the original Latin by H. Beveridge. Edinburgh: Calvin Translation Society, 1844, vol. I.

ID. *L'Institution de la Religion Chrétienne*, 1560 text. Geneva: Labor et Fides, 1955–1958, 4 vols. ET: McNEILL, J. T. (ed.). *Calvin: Institutes of the Christian Religion*. Translated and indexed by F. L. Battles. Philadelphia: Westminster (coll. "The Library of Christian Classics," 20, 21) 1960, 2 vols.

ID. *Ioannis Calvini. Opera quae supersunt omnia*. Eds. G. Baum, E. Cunitz and E. Reuss. Brunswick: C. A. Schwetschke et Filium (coll. "Corpus Reformatorum," 29–86/87) 1863–1900, 58 vols.

ID. *Projet d'Ordonnances ecclésiastiques* (1541) (= OC 10, 15–30). ET: *Draft Ecclesiastical Ordinances (1541)*, pp. 58–72, in REID, J.K.S. *Calvin: Theological Treatises*. Philadelphia: Westminster (coll. "The Library of Christian Classics," 22) 1954.

[THE CHURCH OF SCOTLAND]. *The Confession of Faith, Catechisms, Directories, Form of Church-Government, Discipline, etc. Of Public Authority in the Church of Scotland: Together with the Acts of Assembly, concerning the Doctrine, Discipline and Government of the Church of Scotland. Also a Collection of some Principal Acts and Ordinances of the Parliaments of Scotland and England, and of the General Assembly of the Church of Scotland, in favour of the Covenanted Reformation. To which is added the Form of Process in the Judicatories of the Church of Scotland, with relation to Scandals and Censures: Also several Acts and Overtures of the General Assemblies thereanent; with other things of a public and interesting nature.* Glasgow: John Byrce, 1785.

Confession de foi des Eglises réformées de France, called "Confession of La Rochelle" (1559); "Confession de foi faite d'un commun accord par les français qui désirent vivre selon la pureté de l'Evangile de notre seigneur Jésus-Christ" (*BKRK* 66–75) reprinted in FATIO, O. (ed.). *Confessions et catéchismes de la foi réformée*. Geneva: Labor et Fides (coll. "Publications de la Faculté de théologie de l'université de Genève," 11) 1986, pp. 111–127. ET: COCHRANE 144–158.

Confession de foi des Eglises réformées wallonnes et flamandes des Pays-Bas (approved by the Synod of Emden in 1571 and reworked by the Synod of Dordrecht in 1619); "La confession de foi des Eglises réformées wallonnes et flamandes des Pays-Bas," pp. 177–239 in *Le catéchisme de Genève par Jean Calvin en français moderne suivi de La Confession de foi des Eglises réformées de France et de La Confession de foi des Eglises réformées wallonnes et flamandes des Pays-Bas*. Published under the auspices of the Société calviniste de France. Paris: "Je sers," 1934. ET: "The Confession of Faith of the Reformed Church," pp. 189–219 in COCHRANE.

Second Helvetic Confession; *Confessio et expositio simplex orthodoxae fidei* (1566) = Confessio helvetica posterior (*BKRK* 219–275). *La Confession helvétique postérieure (texte français de 1566)*. Introduction and notes by J. Courvoisier. Neuchâtel/Paris: Delachaux & Niestlé (coll. "Cahiers théologiques de l'actualité protestante," 5/6) 1944, reprinted in FATIO, O. (ed.). *Confessions et catéchismes de la foi réformée*. Geneva: Labor et Fides (coll. "Publications de la Faculté de théologie de l'université de Genève," 11) 1986, pp. 179–306; ET: "The Second Helvetic Confession, 1566," pp. 224–301 in COCHRANE.

HITT, D., WARE, T. (eds.). *Minutes of the Methodist Conferences, Annually held in America; from 1773 to 1813, Inclusive*. N.Y.: John C. Totten, 1813, vol. I.

LUTHER, M. *Der 82. Psalm ausgelegt* (WA 31/I, 189–218). ET: *Psalm 82 = LW* 13: 41–72.

ID. *Die Schmalkaldischen Artikel* [1537/1538] (WA 50, 192–254 and *BSLK* 405–496). ET: *The Smalcald Articles = BC* 287–318.

ID. *De abroganda missa privata Martini Lutheri sententia* (WA 8, 411–476). ET: *The Misuse of the Mass* = LW 36:127–230.

ID. *De captivitate Babylonica ecclesiae praeludium* (WA 6, 497–573). ET: *The Babylonian Captivity of the Church* = LW 36:3–126.

ID. *Das ein christliche Versammlung oder Gemeine Recht und Macht habe, all Lehre zu urtheilen und Lehrer zu berufen, ein und abzusetzen, Grund und Ursach aus der Schrift* (WA 11, 408–416). ET: *That a Christian Assembly or Congregation has the Right and Power to Judge all Teaching and to Call, Appoint, and Dismiss Teachers, Established and Proven by Scripture* = LW 39:301–314.

ID. *An den christlichen Adel deutscher Nation von des christlichen standes besserung* (WA 6, 404–469). ET: *To the Christian Nobility of the German Nation Concerning the Reform of the Christian Estate* = LW 44:115–217.

ID. *Die deudsch Litaney* (WA 31/III, 29–36). ET: *The German Litany* = LW 53: 163–170.

ID. *Deutsche Messe und ordnung Gottes diensts* (WA 19, 72–113). ET: *The German Mass and Order of Service* = LW 53:61–90.

ID. *Epistola Lutheriana ad Leonem Decimum summum pontificem. Tractatus de libertate christiana* (WA 7, 42–73). ET: *The Freedom of a Christian* = LW 31: 329–377.

ID. *In epistolam S. Pauli ad Galatas commentarius* (WA 40/I and II). ET: *Lectures on Galatians* = LW 26/27.

ID. *Exempel, einen rechten christlichen Bischof zu weihen* (WA 53, 231–260).

ID. *De instituendis ministris Ecclesiae* (WA 12, 169–196). ET: *Concerning the Ministry* = LW 40:3–44.

ID. *Von den Konziliis und Kirchen* (WA 50, 509–653). ET: *On the Councils and the Church* = LW 41:3–178 (for this work only, pp. 148–164).

ID. *Eine kurtze Form der zehn Gebote, eine kurze Form des Glaubens, eine kurze Form des Vaterunsers* (WA 7, 204–229).

ID. *Latina litania correcta* (WA 30/III, 36–42). ET: *The Latin Litany Corrected* = LW 53:155–162.

ID. *Ad librum eximii Magistri Nostri, Magistri Ambrosii Catharini, defensoris, Silvestri Prieratis acerrimi, responsio* (WA 7, 705–778).

ID. *Luther an Ioh. Sutel in Göttingen* (WA Br 6, 43–44 [no. 1787]).

ID. *Luther an Ludwig Senfl in München* (WA Br 5, 639–640 [no. 1727]).

ID. *Luther an Nikolaus von Amsdorf in Zeitz* (WA Br 9, 609–611 [no. 3709]).

ID. *Von dem Papstum zu Rome widder den hochberumpten Romanisten zu Leipzig* (WA 6, 285–324). ET: *On the Papacy in Rome against the Most Celebrated Romanist in Leipzig* = LW 39:49–104.

ID. *Predigt am 21. Sonntag nach Trinitatis (16. Oktober)* no. 55 (WA 15, 716–721).

ID. *Predigt am Sonntag Quasimodogeniti im Hause (Bruchstück) (12. April 1534)* no. 30 (WA 37, 379–381).

ID. *Predigt am Sonntag Quasimodogeniti in Dessan gehalten (4. April 1540)* no. 26 (WA 49, 135–142).

ID. *6. Predigt über den 110. Psalm (9. Juni 1535)* no. 18 (WA 41, 204–215). ET: *Psalm 110 = LW* 13:329–334.

ID. *Predigt zu Vorma am Sonntag Misericordias domini (4. Mai 1522)* no. 24 (WA 10/III 120–124).

ID. *Predigten von 1519 bis 1521* (WA 9). ET: *Sermons from 1519 to 1521 = LW* 51: 51–61.

ID. *De Servo arbitrio* (WA 18, 600–787). ET: *The Bondage of the Will = LW* 33:3–295.

ID. *Aus das überchristlich, übergeistlich und überkünstlich Buch Bocks Emfers zu Leipzig Antwort. Darin auch Muranarrs seines Gesellen gedacht wird* (WA 7, 621–688). ET: *Answer to the Hyperchristian, Hyperspiritual and Hyperlearned Book by Goat Emser in Leipzig - including Some Thoughts Regarding his Companion the Fool Murner = LW* 39:137–224.

ID. *Unterricht der Visitatoren an die Pfarrherrn im Kurfürstentum Sachsen* (WA 26, 195–240). ET: *Instructions for the Visitors of Parish Pastors in Electoral Saxony = LW* 40:263–320.

ID. *Von der Winckelmesse und Pfaffen Weyhe* (WA 38, 195–256). ET: *The Private Mass and the Consecration of Priests = LW* 38:139–214.

MELANCHTHON, P. *Apologia confessionis Augustanae* (BSLK 141–404). ET: *Apology of the Augsburg Confession = BC* 97–285.

ID. *Confessio Fidei exhibita invictissimo Imperatori Carolo V. Caesari Augusto in comitiis Augustae Anno MDXXX* (BSLK 44–137). ET: *The Augsburg Confession. A Confession of Faith Presented in Augsburg by certain Princes and Cities to His Imperial Majesty Charles V in the Year 1530 = BC* 23–96.

ID. *Loci praecipui theologici von 1559 (2. Teil).* ENGELLAND, H. (ed.). *Melanchthons Werke.* Gütersloh: C. Bertelsmann Verlag, 1953, t. II/2.

ID. *De potestate et primatu papae (Tractatus)* (BSLK 471–498). ET: *Treatise on the Power and Primacy of the Pope = BC* 319–335.

The Second Book of Discipline; *The Second Book of Discipline.* With Introduction and Commentary by J. Kirk. Edinburgh: Saint Andrew Press, 1980.

WESLEY, J. *The Journal of the Rev. John Wesley, A.M. Sometime Fellow of Lincoln College, Oxford, England from Original MSS, with Notes from Unpublished Diaries, Annotations, Maps, and Illustrations.* Reprint [1st ed. 1909–1916]. Ed. N. Curnock. Standard Edition. London: Epworth Press, 1938, 8 vols.

ID. *The Letters of the Rev. John Wesley, A.M. Sometime Fellow of Lincoln College, Oxford.* Ed. J. Telford. Standard Edition. London: Epworth Press, 1931, 8 vols.

ID. *The Sunday Service of the Methodists in North America. With Other Occasional Services.* Reprint [1st ed. 1784]. Intro. by J. F. White. Bicentenary facsimile ed. Nashville: United Methodist Publishing House (coll. "Quarterly Review Reprint Series") 1984.

ID. *Wesley's Standard Sermons.* 4th ed. [1st ed. 1921]. Ed. E. H. Sugden. London: Epworth Press, 1955–1956, 2 vols.

ID. *The Works of the Rev. John Wesley, A.M. Sometime Fellow of Lincoln College, Oxford.* 3rd. rev. ed. Reprint [1st ed. 1829–1831]. Ed. T. Jackson. London: John Mason, 1856, 14 vols.

WHATCOAT, R. *Memoirs of the Rev. Richard Whatcoat Late Bishop of the Methodist Episcopal Church.* Ed. W. Phoebus. N.Y.: Joseph Allen, 1828.

B. LITURGICAL SOURCES

1. Lutheran Liturgy

First formularies:

"Das deutsche Ordinationsformular, 1535/1539": M. Luther, WA 38, 423–431. ET: *LW* 53, 122–126.

"Ordinatio Ecclesiastica Regnorum Daniae et Norwegiae et Ducatuum/ Sleswicensis/Holtsatiae etcet. Anno Domini M.D.xxxvij. Copenhague: Hans Vingaard" (= Copenhagen, Kgl. Bibliotek, LN 196): J. Bugenhagen. LAUSTEN, M. S. (ed.). *Kirkeordinansen 1537/39.* Copenhagen: Akademisk Forlag, 1989, pp. 93–149; FEDDERSEN, E. (ed.). "Die lateinisch Kirchenordnung König Christians III von 1537 nebst anderen Urkunden zur schleswig-holsteinschen Reformationsgeschichte," *Schriften des Vereins für schleswig-holsteinische Kirchengeschichte* 18 (1) 1934, pp. 1–93; and KIDD, B. J. (ed.). *Documents Illustrative of the Continental Reformation.* Oxford: Clarendon Press, 1967, pp. 330–334 (= only ordination).

"De ordinatione legitima ministrorum ecclesiae revocanda, 1549": M. Bucer. HUBERT, C. (ed.). *Martini Buceri scripta anglicana.* Basel: Petri Pernae Officina, 1577, pp. 238–259; and MESSENGER, E. C. *The Lutheran Origin of the Anglican Ordinal.* London: Burns, Oates and Washbourne, Ltd., 1934, pp. 15–27. ET: WRIGHT, D. F. *Common Places of Martin Bucer.* Appleford: Sutton Courtenay Press (coll. "The Courtenay Library of Reformation Classics," 4) 1972, pp. 269–283; and WHITAKER, E. C. *Martin Bucer and the Book of Common Prayer.* Great Wakering: Mayhew-McCrimmon, 1974, pp. 176–183.

PETRI, L. *Then Swenska Kyrkeordningen av år 1571.* Stockholm: A. Laurentzson, 1571. Ed. E. FÅRNSTRÖM, Stockholm: Svenska Kyrans Diakonistyrelses Bokförlag, 1932 (= The Swedish Church Order of 1571). ET: YELVERTON, F. F. *An Archbishop of the Reformation. Laurentius Petri Nericius. Archbishop of Uppsala 1531–1573. A Study of His Liturgical Projects.* London: Epworth Press, 1958, pp. 131–141.

2. Reformed Liturgy

First formularies:

"Züricher Prädicantenordnung, 1532": RICHTER, A. L. (ed.). *Die evangelischen Kirchenordnungen des sechzehnten Jahrhunderts.* Anastatic reprint [1st ed. 1846]. Nieuwkoop, 1967, t. 2, pp. 169f.; and DANIEL, H. A. (ed.). *Codex liturgicus ecclesiae universae in epitomen redactus,* t. 3, *Ecclesiae Reformatae atque Anglicanae.* Leipzig: T. O. Weigel, 1851, pp. 231–234.

"Forma ac ratio, 1550 (1565)": Ordinances of London, 1550: Joannes a Lasco, Forma ac ratio tota ecclesiastici Ministerii, in peregrinorum, potissimum vero Germanorum Ecclesia: instituta Londini in Anglia, per Pientissimum Principem Angliae etc. Regem Eduardum, eius nominis Sextu: Anno post Christum natum 1550. [Francofurti ad Moenam. Anno MDLV.] KUYPER, A. (ed.). *Joannis a Lasco. Opera tam edita quam inedita.* Amsterdam: Frederic Muller, 1866, t. 2, pp. 1–285. French trans.: La forme & maniere de tout le Ministere Ecclesiastique, obserué en l'Eglise des Estrangers, instituée a Londres en Angleterre, par le Roy *Edouard VI* de ce nom, Prince tres debonnaire du dict pays, lan 1550. Emden: Giles Ctematius, 1556. German translation: Kirchenordnung, wie die unter dem christlichen König auss Engelland, Edward dem VI. in der statt Londen, in der Niederlendischen Gemeine Christi, durch Kön. Maiest. mandat geordnet und gehalten worden, mit der Kirchendiener und Eltesten bewilligung, durch hernn Johann von Lasco, Freiherren in Polen, Superintendenten derselbigen Kirchen in Engelland in lateinischer sprach weitleufftiger beschrieben, aber durch Martinum Micronium in eine kurze Summ verfasset und jetzund ver deutschet. Gedruchtin der Churf. statt Heidelberg, durch Joh. Maner, 1565. RICHTER II, 99–115 and DANIEL, H. A. (ed.). *Codex liturgicus . . .,* t. 3, pp. 261–284.

"Liturgia Sacra, 1551–1555": Liturgia sacra, seu ritus ministerii in Ecclesia peregrinorum profugorum propter Evangelium Christi Argentinae. Adiecta est ad finem brevis Apologia pro hac Liturgia, Per Valerandum Pollanum Flandrum. Psalm 149, Laudem Deo canite in Ecclesia sanctorum. [Impressum Londini per Stephanum Mierdmannum. 23. Februar. AN M.DMLI.] For "De ordine ministrorum," cf. HONDERS, A. C. *Valerandus Pollanus. Liturgia Sacra (1551–1555).* Leiden: E. J. Brill, 1970, pp. 220–228. Same text for the refugees at Frankfurt, RICHTER II, 149–160. French trans.: L'Ordre des prières et ministère ecclésiastique avec la forme de pénitence pub. & certaines Prières de l'Eglise de Londres, Et la Confession de Foy de l'Eglise de Glastonbury en Somerset: Luc 21. Veillez et priez en tout temps, afin que vous puissiez eviter toutes les choses qui sont à advenir, et assister devant le Filz de l'homme. A Londres, 1552. For "L'Ordre des ministres ecclésiastiques," cf. HONDERS, A. C. *Valerandus . . .*, pp. 221–229.

"Genevan Service Book, 1556": Of the Ministers and Their Election. MAXWELL, W. D. *John Knox's Genevan Service Book, 1556. The Liturgical Portions of the Genevan Service Book, Used by John Knox While a Minister of the English Congregation of Marian Exiles at Geneva, 1556–1559.* London: Faith Press, 1965, pp. 165–169.

"The First Buke of Discipline, 1560": LAING, D. (ed.). *The Works of John Knox,* t. 2. Reprint [1st ed. 1895]. N.Y.: AMS Press, Inc., 1966, pp. 144–150; and *The First Book of Discipline*. With Introduction and Commentary by J. K. Cameron. Edinburgh: Saint Andrew Press, 1972.

"Book of Common Order, 1564": Of the Ministers and Their Election; The Form and Order of the Election of the Superintendent, Which May Serve in Election of All Other Ministers. SPROTT, G. W. *The Book of Common Order of the Church of Scotland, Commonly Known as John Knox's Liturgy.* 2nd ed. [1st ed. 1868]. Edinburgh: William Blackwood & Sons, 1901, pp. 13–27.

"A booke of the Forme of common prayers, 1586 (2nd ed. Middleburg)": Of Church Officers. Of the Pastors; Their Office, Election, and Ordination. HALL, P. (ed.). *Reliquiae Liturgicae.* Bath: Binns & Goodwin, 1847, t. 1, pp. 71–75.

"A booke of the Forme of common prayers, 1602 (4th ed. Middleburg)": The Manner of Ordaining Ministers of the Word, and Establishing Them in Their Churches. HALL, P. (ed.). *Reliquiae . . .*, t. 1, pp. 75–85.

"Scottish Ordinal, 1620": The Forme and Maner of Ordaining Ministers: and Consecrating of Archbishops and Bishops Used in the Church of Scotland. Edinburgh: Thomas Finlason, 1620. SPROTT, G. W. *Scottish Liturgies of the Reign of James VI.* Edinburgh: William Blackwood & Sons, 1901, pp. 111–129, 159–165.

3. Anglican and Episcopalian Liturgy

First formularies—The Book of Common Prayer (BCP):

The Book of Common Prayer of 1662 with Permissive Additions and Deviations Approved in 1927. London: Oxford University Press, 1927, pp. 334–346 (for the revision of the Ordinal).

CUMING, G. J. (ed.). *The Durham Book; Being the First Draft of the Revision of the Book of Common Prayer in 1661*. Reprint [1st ed. 1961]. London: Alcuin Club, 1975.

"The forme and maner of makyng and consecratyng of Archebisshoppes Bisshoppes, Priestes and Deacons." London: Hardus Grafton, 1549 [i.e., March 1550]. Ed. *The English Rite* II, pp. 921–1016.

"The fourme and maner of makynge and consecratynge, Bisshoppes, Priestes and Deacons." London: Edwarde Whitchurche, 1552. Ed. *The English Rite* II, pp. 927–1017.

"The Forme and Manner of Making, Ordeining, and Consecrating of Bishops, Priests, and Deacons, According to the Order of the Church of England." London: Printers to the Kings most excell. Majestie, [1661]. Ed. *The English Rite* II, pp. 927–1017.

4. Methodist Liturgies

First formulary:

"The Form and Manner of Making and Ordaining of Superintendants [sic!], Elders, and Deacons," WESLEY, J. *The Sunday Service of the Methodists in North America. With Other Occasional Services*. London, several editions, 1784. Ed. J. F. WHITE, *John Wesley's "Sunday Service of the Methodists in North America."* Nashville: United Methodist Publishing House, 1984, pp. 280–305.

3. STUDIES

A. REFORMATION (XVIth–XVIIIth CENTURIES)

Lutheran

AARTS, J. *Die Lehre Martin Luthers über das Amt in der Kirche. Eine genetisch-systematische Untersuching seiner Schriften von 1512 bis 1525*. Helsinki: Hämeenlinna (coll. "Schriften der Luther-Agricola-Gesellschaft," A 15) 1972.

BEINTKER, H.J.E. "Fortsetzung und Festigung der Reformation. Neuordnung in evangelischen Kirchen unter Bugenhagens Anleitung mittels seiner Braunschweiger Kirchenordnung von 1528," *Theologische Zeitschrift* 44 (1) 1988, pp. 1–31.

BOLES, S. K. *Lutheran Pastors in Ernestine Saxony and Thuringia, 1521–1546*. Ann Arbor: University Microfilms International, 1971.

BORNERT, R. *La Réforme protestante du culte à Strasbourg au XVIe siècle (1523–1598)*. Leiden: E. J. Brill (coll. "Studies in Medieval and Reformation Thought," 28) 1981.

BRUNNER, P. *Nikolaus von Amsdorf als Bischof von Naumburg.* Gütersloh: Verlagshaus Gerd Mohn, 1961.

BRUNOTTE, W. *Das geistliche Amt bei Luther.* Berlin: Lutherisches Verlagshaus, 1959.

DEWAILLY, L.-M. "Laurentius Petri et la Kyrkoordning de 1571," *Istina* 30 (3) 1985, pp. 228–245.

ID. "Petri (Olaus et Laurentius)," cols. 93–95, *Catholicisme*, fasc. 49, 1986.

ELERT, W. *The Structure of Lutheranism*, t. 1, *The Theology and Philosophy of the Life of Lutheranism Especially in the Sixteenth and Seventeenth Centuries.* Trans. of the German [*Morphologie des Luthertums*] by W. A. Hansen. St. Louis: Concordia Publishing House, 1962.

FÆHN, H. "Liturgiene ved preste- og bispevielse i Norge. Fra reformasjonen til Alterboken 1920," *Norsk Teologisk Tidsskrift* 85 (4) 1984, pp. 249–266.

FISCHER, R. H. "Another Look at Luther's Doctrine of the Ministry," *Lutheran Quarterly* 18 (3) 1966, pp. 260–271.

GLENTHØJ, J. "Amt und Ordination bei Bugenhagen in der Reformation der dänischen Kirche," *EVANGELIUM-'euaggelion'-GOSPEL. Zweimonatsschrift für lutherische Theologie und Kirche* 13 (1) 1986, pp. 12–28.

GRAFF, P. *Geschichte der Auflösung der alten gottesdienstlichen Formen in der evangelischen Kirche Deutschlands*, t. 1, *Bis zum Eintritt der Aufklärung und des Rationalismus.* Göttingen: Vandenhoeck & Ruprecht, 1937.

GREEN, L. "Change in Luther's Doctrine of the Ministry," *Lutheran Quarterly* 18 (2) 1966, pp. 173–183.

GREINER, A. "L'ecclésiologie de Martin Luther," *Positions luthériennes* 25 (3) 1977, pp. 156–168.

ID. "La notion d'Eglise dans la Confession d'Augsbourg," *Positions luthériennes* 29 (4) 1981, pp. 309–324.

HEUBACH, J. *Die Ordination zum Amt der Kirche.* Berlin: Lutherisches Verlagshaus (coll. "Arbeiten zur Geschichte und Theologie des Luthertums," 2) 1956.

HOLLOWAY, H. *The Norwegian Rite.* London: Arthur H. Stockwell, 1934.

KITTELSON, J. "Martin Bucer and the Ministry of the Church," pp. 83–94 in WRIGHT, D. F. (ed.). *Martin Bucer: Reforming Church and Community.* Cambridge: Cambridge University Press, 1994.

KRETSCHMAR, G. "Die Ordination bei Johannes Bugenhagen," pp. 357–384 in DE CLERCK, P., PALAZZO, E. (eds.). *Rituels. Mélanges offerts à Pierre-Marie Gy, o.p.* Paris: Cerf, 1990.

LECLER, J. "Les origines et le sens de la formule: *cujus regio, ejus religio*," *RechSR* 38 (1) 1951, pp. 115–131.

LIEBERG, H. *Amt und Ordination bei Luther und Melanchthon*. Göttingen: Vandenhoeck & Ruprecht, 1962.

LIENHARD, M. "La doctrine des deux règnes et son impact dans l'histoire," *Positions luthériennes* 24 (1) 1976, pp. 25–41.

ID. *L'Evangile et l'Eglise chez Luther*. Paris: Cerf (coll. "Cogitatio fidei," 153) 1989.

LINDHARDT, P. G. "Historisk om bispe- og præstevielsesritualerne," pp. 7–46 in KIRKEMINISTERIETS LITURGISKE KOMMISSION. *De biskoppelige handlinger: Præste- og bispevielse, provsteindsættelse og kirkeindvielse*. Copenhagen: B. Stougaard Jensen (coll. "Betænkning afgivet af Kirkeministeriets liturgiske kommission," 848) 1978.

LOHSE, B. "The Development of the Offices of Leadership in the German Lutheran Churches: 1517–1918," pp. 51–71 in ASHEIM, I., GOLD, V. R. (eds.). *Episcopacy in the Lutheran Church? Studies in the Development and Definition of the Offices of Church Leadership*. Philadelphia: Fortress Press, 1970.

ID. "Zur Ordination in der Reformation," pp. 11–52 in MUMM, R., KREMS, G. (eds.). *Ordination und kirchliches Amt*. Paderborn/Bielefeld: Verlag Bonifatius-Druckerei/Luther Verlag, 1976.

MANNS, P. "Amt und Eucharistie in der Theologie Martin Luthers," pp. 68–173 in BLÄSER, P., FRANK, S., MANNS, P. et al. *Amt und Eucharistie*. Paderborn: Verlag Bonifatius-Druckerei, 1973.

OLIVIER, D. *La foi de Luther*. Paris: Beauchesne (coll. "Point théologique," 27) 1978.

ID. "La question des ministères au sein des Eglises de la Réforme protestante durant la seconde moitié du XVIᵉ siècle," pp. 89–104 in VAUCELLES, L. de (ed.). *Eglises, sociétés et ministères. Essai d'herméneutique historique des origines du christianisme à nos jours*. Paris: Centre Sèvres (coll. "Travaux et conférences du Centre Sèvres," 7) 1986.

PAHL, I. (ed.). *Cœna Domini I. Die Abendmahlsliturgie der Reformationskirchen im 16./17. Jahrhundert*. Freiburg: Universitätsverlag (coll. "Spicilegium Friburgense," 29) 1983.

PARVIO, M. "The Post-Reformation Developments of Episcopacy in Sweden, Finland, and the Baltic States," pp. 125–137 in ASHEIM, I., GOLD, V. R. (eds.). *Episcopacy in the Lutheran Church? Studies in the Development and Definition of the Office of Church Leadership*. Philadelphia: Fortress Press, 1970.

PELIKAN, J. *Spirit Versus Structure: Luther and the Institutions of the Church*. N.Y.: Harper & Row, 1968.

PESCH, O. H. "Luther und die Kirche," *Lutherjahrbuch* 25, 1985, pp. 113–139.

PIEPKORN, A. C. "The Sacred Ministry and Holy Ordination in the Symbolical Books of the Lutheran Church," pp. 101–119 in EMPIE, P. C., MURPHY, T. A. (eds.). *Lutherans and Catholics in Dialogue*, vol. IV, *Eucharist and Ministry*. Reprint [1st ed. 1970.] Washington, D.C./Minneapolis: USCC/Augsburg Publishing House, 1979.

POLLET, J.-V. *Martin Bucer. Etudes sur la correspondance avec de nombreux textes inédits.* Paris: Presses Universitaires de France, 1958–1962, 2 vols.

PRAGMAN, J. H. *Traditions of Ministry. A History of the Doctrine of the Ministry in Lutheran Theology.* St. Louis: Concordia Publishing House, 1983.

REUMANN, J.H.P. *Ministries Examined. Laity, Clergy, Women and Bishops in a Time of Change.* Minneapolis: Augsburg, 1978.

RODHE, E. *Svenskt gudstjänstliv. Historisk Belyning av den Svenska Kyrkohandboken.* Uppsala: Ulmquist & Wiksells, 1923.

SCHLINK, E. *Theology of the Lutheran Confessions.* Trans. of the German [*Theologie der lutherischen Bekenntnisschriften*, 3rd ed.] by P. F. Koehneke and H. J. Bouman. Philadelphia: Fortress Press, 1961.

SCHULZ, F. "Evangelische Ordination. Zur Reform der liturgischen Ordnungen," *JLH* 17, 1972, pp. 1–54.

ID. "Die Ordination als Gemeindegottesdienst. Neue Untersuchungen zur evangelischen Ordination," *JLH* 24, 1979, pp. 1–31.

SIEGWALT, G. "Point de vue protestant sur le ministère d'unité," *Positions luthériennes* 25 (3) 1977, pp. 121–139.

ID. "Sacerdoce ministériel et ministère pastoral d'après les livres symboliques luthériens," *Verbum Caro* 22 (85) 1968, pp. 16–35.

SMITH, R. F. *Ordering Ministry. The Liturgical Witness of Sixteenth-Century German Ordination Rites.* Ann Arbor: University Microfilms International, 1988.

SPIJKER, W. van 't. "Bucer's Influence on Calvin: Church and Community," pp. 32–44 in WRIGHT, D. F. (ed.). *Martin Bucer: Reforming Church and Community.* Cambridge: Cambridge University Press, 1994.

ID. *The Ecclesiastical Offices in the Thought of Martin Bucer.* Leiden/N.Y./Cologne: E. J. Brill (coll. "Studies in Medieval and Reformation Thought," 57) 1996.

SPINKS, B. D. "Luther's Other Major Liturgical Reforms: 2. The Ordination of Ministers of the Word," *Liturgical Review* (Edinburgh) 9 (1) 1979, pp. 20–32.

STEPHENS, W. P. *The Holy Spirit in the Theology of Martin Bucer.* Cambridge: Cambridge University Press, 1970.

VAJTA, V. "The Church as Spiritual-Sacramental Communio with Christ and His Saints in the Theology of Luther," pp. 112–121 in MANNS, P., MEYER, H. (eds.). *Luther's Ecumenical Significance. An Interconfessional Consultation.* Trans. of the German *[Ökumenische Erschließung Luthers. Referate und Ergebnisse einer internationalen Theologenkonsultation, 1983].* Philadelphia/N.Y./Ramsey, N.J.: Fortress Press/Paulist Press, 1984.

ID. "Conception du ministère ecclésiastique selon Luther. Sa signification actuelle," pp. 185–196 in BOUDIN, H. R., HOUSSIAU, A. (eds.). *Luther aujourd'hui.* Louvain-la-Neuve: Publications de la Faculté de Théologie (coll. "Cahiers de la Revue théologique de Louvain," 11) 1983.

ID. *Luther on Worship. An Interpretation.* Trans. of the German *[Die Theologie des Gottesdienstes bei Luther]* by U. S. Leupold. Philadelphia: Muhlenberg Press, 1958.

VAN DE POLL, G. J. *Martin Bucer's Liturgical Ideas.* Assen: Van Gorcum & Comp., [1954].

VAN HAAG, T. "Die apostolische Sukzession in Schweden," *Kyrkohistorisk Årsskrift* 44 (1) 1944, pp. 4–168.

VOELTZEL, R. "Les ministères de direction dans les églises de la Réforme au XVIᵉ siècle," *Revue de Droit canonique* 23 (1–4) 1973, pp. 127–145.

WILKENS, T. G. "Ministry, Vocation and Ordination: Some Perspectives from Luther," *Lutheran Quarterly* 29 (1) 1977, pp. 66–81.

WRIGHT, D. F. (ed.). *Martin Bucer: Reforming Church and Community.* Cambridge: Cambridge University Press, 1994.

YELVERTON, E. E. *An Archbishop of the Reformation. Laurentius Petri Nericius, Archbishop of Uppsala 1531–1573. A Study of His Liturgical Projects.* London: Epworth Press, 1958.

Reformed

AINSLIE, J. L. *The Doctrines of Ministerial Order in the Reformed Churches of the Sixteenth and Seventeenth Centuries.* Edinburgh: T & T Clark, 1940.

ALLMEN, J.-J. von. *L'Eglise et ses fonctions d'après Jean-Frédéric Ostervald. Le problème de la théologie pratique au début du XVIIIᵐᵉ siècle.* Neuchâtel: Delachaux et Niestlé (coll. "Cahiers théologiques de l'actualité protestante," special number 3) 1947.

ID. "Ministry and Ordination According to Reformed Theology," *Scottish Journal of Theology* 25 (1) 1972, pp. 75–88.

ID. *Le saint ministère selon la conviction et la volonté des Réformés du XVIᵉ siècle.* Neuchâtel: Delachaux & Niestlé (coll. "Bibliothèque théologique") 1968.

BONNARD, A. *Thomas Eraste (1524–1583) et la discipline ecclésiastique*. Lausanne: Georges Bridel, 1894.

BRADSHAW, P. F. "An Act of God in the Church: A Reformation Understanding of Ordination," *Liturgy* (Washington, D.C.) 24 (3) 1979, pp. 22–24.

ID. "Ordination: Reformed Churches," pp. 331–341 in JONES, C., WAINWRIGHT, G., YARNOLD, E. (eds.). *The Study of Liturgy*. London: SPCK, 1978.

ID. "The Reformers and the Ordination Rites," *Studia Liturgica* 13 (2–4) 1979, pp. 94–107 (= VOS, W. & WAINRIGHT, G. [eds.]. *Ordination Rites*. Papers Read at the 1979 Congress of *Societas Liturgica*. Rotterdam: Liturgical Ecumenical Center Trust, 1980).

CLERC, F. *La Discipline des Eglises de la Souveraineté de Neuchâtel et Valangin (1712)*. Neuchâtel: Université de Neuchâtel, 1959.

CRESPY, G. *Les ministères de la réforme et la réforme des ministères*. Geneva: Labor et Fides, 1968.

DE CLERCK, P. "L'ordination des pasteurs selon quelques liturgies de consécration réformées," pp. 75–98 in *Mélanges liturgiques offerts au R. P. Dom Bernard Botte*. Louvain: Abbaye du Mont César, 1972.

DONALDSON, G. "Scottish Ordinations in the Restoration Period," *Scottish Historical Review* 33, 1954, pp. 169–175.

ID. *The Scottish Reformation*. Cambridge: Cambridge University Press, 1960.

EVANS, J. Y. "Erastianism," pp. 358–366 in HASTINGS, J. (ed.). *Encyclopaedia of Religion and Ethics*. Edinburgh/N.Y.: T. & T. Clark/Charles Scribner's Son, 1912, t. 5.

FIGGIS, J. N. "Erastus and Erastianism," *JTS* 2 (1) 1900/1901, pp. 66–101.

FRERE, W. H., DOUGLAS, C. E. (eds.). *LXXII Puritan Manifestoes. A Study of the Origin of the Puritan Revolt with a Reprint of the Admonition to the Parliament and Kindered Documents, 1572*. London/N.Y.: SPCK/E. S. Gorham, 1907.

GANOCZY, A. *Calvin, théologien de l'Eglise et du ministère*. Paris: Cerf (coll. "US," 48) 1964.

HAMMANN, G. *L'amour retrouvé. La diaconie chrétienne et le ministère de diacre. Du christianisme primitif aux réformateurs protestants du XVIᵉ siècle*. Paris: Cerf (coll. "Histoire": "Publications de la Faculté de théologie de l'Université de Neuchâtel [Suisse]," 13) 1994.

ID. *Entre la secte et la cité. Le projet d'Eglise du Réformateur Martin Bucer (1491–1551)*. Geneva: Labor et Fides (coll. "Histoire et société," 3) 1984.

HEYER, H. *L'Eglise de Genève 1535–1909. Esquisse historique de son organisation*. Geneva: A. Jullien, 1909.

HOPF, C. *Martin Bucer and the English Reformation*. Oxford: Blackwell, 1946.

JORDAN, W. K. *The Development of Religious Toleration in England*, t. 1, *From the Beginnings of the English Reformation to the Death of Queen Elizabeth*. London: George Allen & Unwin Ltd., 1932.

ID. *The Development of Religious Toleration in England*, t. 2, *From the Accession of James I to the Convention of the Long Parliament (1603–1640)*. London: George Allen & Unwin Ltd., 1936.

MAXWELL, W. D. *The History of Worship in the Church of Scotland*. London: Oxford University Press, 1955.

ID. *John Knox's Genevan Service Book. The Liturgical Portions of the Genevan Service Book, Used by John Knox While a Minister of the English Congregation of Marian Exiles at Geneva, 1556–1559*. London: Faith Press, 1965.

MC KEE, E. A. *Elders and the Plural Ministry. The Role of Exegetical History in Illuminating John Calvin's Theology*. Geneva: Droz (coll. "Travaux d'humanisme et renaissance," 223) 1988.

SCHICKLER, F. de. *Les Eglises du refuge en Angleterre*. Paris: Fischbacher, 1892, 3 vols.

SCHUMMER, L. *Le ministère pastoral dans l'Institution Chrétienne de Calvin à la lumière du troisième sacrement*. Wiesbaden: Franz Steiner Verlag (coll. "Veröffentlichungen des Instituts für Europäische Geschichte Mainz," 39) 1965.

STAUFFER, R. "L'ecclésiologie de Jean Calvin," *Positions luthériennes* 25 (3) 1977, pp. 140–154.

STROHL, H. "La notion d'Eglise chez les Réformateurs," *RHPR* 16 (3–5) 1936, pp. 265–319.

Anglican

BLUNT, J. H. (ed.). *The Annotated Book of Common Prayer Being an Historical, Ritual and Theological Commentary on the Devotional System of the Church of England*. London: Rivingtons, 1876.

BRADSHAW, P. F. *The Anglican Ordinal. Its History and Development from the Reformation to the Present Day*. London: SPCK (coll. "Alcuin Club Collections," 53) 1971.

CUMING, G. J. *A History of Anglican Liturgy*. London: Macmillan and Company, 1982.

ECHLIN, E. P. *The Story of Anglican Ministry*. Slough: St. Paul Publications, 1974.

FIRMINGER, W. K. "The Ordinal," pp. 626–682 in CLARKE, W.K.L., HARRIS, C. (eds.). *Liturgy and Worship: A Companion to the Prayer Books of the Anglican Communion*. London: SPCK, 1964.

GASQUET, F. A., BISHOP, E. *Edward VI and the Book of Common Prayer. An Examination into Its Origin and Early History, with an Appendix of Unpublished Documents.* [1st ed. 1890.] London: Sheed and Ward, 1928.

HATCHETT, M. J. *The Making of the First American Book of Common Prayer: 1776–1789.* N.Y.: Seabury Press, 1982.

MC GARVEY, W. *Liturgiae Americanae or the Book of Common Prayer as Used in the United States of America: Compared with the Proposed Book of 1786 and with the Prayer Books of the Church of England and an Historical Account and Documents.* Philadelphia: [Sunshine], 1895.

MESSENGER, E. C. *The Lutheran Origin of the Anglican Ordinal.* London: Burns & Oates and Washbourne, Ltd., 1934.

MOORMAN, J. *A History of the Church of England.* 3rd rev. ed. London: Adam & Charles Black, 1976.

PROCTER, F., FRERE, W. H. *A New History of the Book of Common Prayer with a Rationale of Its Offices.* Reprint [1st ed. 1901]. London: Macmillan and Company, 1965.

Methodist

BAKER, F. *John Wesley and the Church of England.* London: Epworth Press, 1970.

BRIGDEN, T. E. "Wesley's Ordinations at Bristol, September 1st and 2nd, 1784," *Proceedings of the Wesley Historical Society* 7 (part 1) 1909, pp. 8–11.

BURDON, A. "Ordination in British Methodism," *Studia Liturgica* 25 (2) 1995, pp. 151–173.

GEORGE, A. R. "Ordination," pp. 143–160 in DAVIES, R., GEORGE, A. R., RUPP, G. (eds.). *A History of the Methodist Church in Great Britain.* London: Epworth Press, 1978. 2 vols.

HARMON, N. B. *The Rites and Ritual of Episcopal Methodism with Particular Reference to the Rituals of The Methodist Episcopal Church and The Methodist Episcopal Church, South, Respectively.* Nashville/Dallas/Richmond/San Francisco: Publishing House of The Methodist Episcopal Church, South, 1926.

LAWSON, A. B. *John Wesley and the Christian Ministry. The Sources and Development of His Opinions and Practice.* London: SPCK, 1963.

MOEDE, G. F. *The Office of Bishop in Methodism: Its History and Development.* Zurich/N.Y./Nashville: Publishing House of The Methodist Church/Abingdon Press, 1964/1965.

OUTLER, A. C. (ed.). *John Wesley.* N.Y.: Oxford University Press (coll. "A Library of Protestant Thought") 1964.

ID. "The Ordinal," pp. 103–133 in DUNKLE, W. F., QUILLIAN, J. D. (eds.). *Companion to the Book of Worship*. Nashville/N.Y.: Abingdon Press, 1970.

SMITH, G. *History of Wesleyan Methodism*. London, 1872.

TIGERT, J. J. *A Constitutional History of American Episcopal Methodism*. 6th rev. and enlarged ed. Nashville/Dallas/Richmond: Publishing House of The Methodist Episcopal Church, South, 1916.

VICKERS, J. A. *Thomas Coke: Apostle of Methodism*. London/Nashville: Epworth Press/Abingdon Press, 1969.

B. XIXth–XXth CENTURIES

Latin Catholic Church

GANOCZY, A. *An Introduction to Catholic Sacramental Theology*. Trans. of the German [*Einführung in die katholische Sakramentenlehre*] by W. Thomas and A. Sherman. N.Y.: Paulist, 1984.

Lutheran Churches

BIRMELE, A. "Le ministère dans les Eglises de la Réforme," *Positions luthériennes* 29 (3) 1981, pp. 190–206.

BORREGAARD, S. "The Post-Reformation Developments of the Episcopacy in Denmark, Norway, and Iceland," pp. 116–124 in ASHEIM, I., GOLD, V. R. (eds.). *Episcopacy in the Lutheran Church? Studies in the Development and Definition of the Office of Church Leadership*. Philadelphia: Fortress Press, 1970.

BRUNNER, P. "Beiträge zur Lehre von der Ordination unter Bezug auf die geltenden Ordinationsformulare," pp. 53–133 in MUMM, R., KREMS, G. (eds.). *Ordination und kirchliches Amt*. Paderborn/Bielefeld: Verlag Bonifatius-Druckerei/Luther Verlag, 1976.

ID. "Salvation and the Office of the Ministry," *Lutheran Quarterly* 15 (2) 1963, pp. 99–117. Trans. of the German ["Das Heil und das Amt, Elemente einer dogmatischen Lehre vom Predigt- und Hirtenamt," pp. 293–309 in id., *Pro Ecclesia, Gesammelte Aufsätze zur dogmatischen Theologie*. Berlin: Lutherisches Verlagshaus, 1962] by P. D. Opsahl.

ID. "Ein Vorschlag für die Ordination in Kirchen lutherischen Bekenntnisses," *Theologische Literaturzeitung* 100 (3) 1975, pp. 174–187.

BURGESS, J. A. "What is a Bishop?," *Lutheran Quarterly* NS 1 (3) 1987, pp. 307–329.

ELLIOTT, J. H. "Death of a Slogan: From Royal Priests to Celebrating Community," *Una Sancta* (N.Y.) 25 (3) 1968, pp. 18–31.

220

FINCKE, E. "Le ministère de l'unité," pp. 63–156 in STÄHLIN, W. et al. *Eglises chrétiennes et épiscopat: vues fondamentales sur la théologie de l'épiscopat.* Trans. of the German by Sister Willibrorda. Paris: Mame, 1966.

GRAFF, P. *Geschichte der Auflösung der alten gottesdienstlichen Formen in der evangelischen Kirche Deutschlands,* t. 2, *Die Zeit der Aufklärung und des Rationalismus.* Göttingen: Vandenhoeck & Ruprecht, 1939.

LERCHE, J. H. "La charge épiscopale dans l'Eglise évangélique," pp. 29–61 in STÄHLIN, W. et al. *Eglises chrétiennes et épiscopat: vues fondamentales sur la théologie de l'épiscopat.* Trans. of the German by Sister Willibrorda. Paris: Mame, 1966.

MUMM, R., KREMS, G. (eds.). *Ordination und kirchliches Amt.* Paderborn/ Bielefeld: Verlag Bonifatius-Druckerei/Luther Verlag, 1976.

NELSON, P. R. *Lutheran Ordination in North America. The 1982 Rite.* Ann Arbor: University Microfilms International, 1987.

QUERE, R. W. "Ecclesiology and Ministry as Reflected in Contemporary Ordination Rites," pp. 83–114 in BROCKOPP, D. C., HELGE, B. L., TRUEMPER, D. G. (eds.). *Church and Ministry.* Valparaiso, Ind.: Institute of Liturgical Studies, 1982.

ID. "The Spirit and Gift are Ours: Imparting or Imploring the Spirit in Ordination Rites?," *Lutheran Quarterly* 27 (4) 1975, pp. 322–346.

Reformed Churches

ALLMEN, J.-J. von. "Le ministère des anciens. Essai sur le problème du presbytérat en ecclésiologie réformée," *Verbum Caro* 18 (71–72) 1964, pp. 214–256.

TORRANCE, T. F. "Consecration and Ordination," *Scottish Journal of Theology* 11 (3) 1958, pp. 225–252.

Anglican Communion

BUCHANAN, C. (ed.). *Modern Anglican Ordination Rites.* Bramcote, Nottingham: Grove Books Ltd. (col. "Alcuin/GROW Liturgical Study," 3; "Grove Liturgical Study," 51) 1987.

JASPER, R.C.D. *The Development of Anglican Liturgy 1662–1980.* London: S.P.C.K., 1989.

NEILL, S. "The Necessity of Episcopacy: Anglican Questions and Answers," *Concilium* 10 (8) 1972, pp. 87–96.

Methodist Churches

GERDES, E. W. *Informed Ministry. Theological Reflections on the Practice of Ministry in Methodism.* Zurich: Gotthelf Verlag (coll. "Studies in Methodism and Related Movements," 1) 1976.

GRABNER, J. D. *A Commentary on the Rites of "An Ordinal, The United Methodist Church."* Ann Arbor: University Microfilms International, 1983.

MATHEWS, J. K. *Set Apart to Serve. The Role of the Episcopacy in the Wesleyan Tradition.* Nashville: Abingdon Press, 1985.

Ecumenism

EMPIE, P. C., MURPHY, T. A. (eds.). *Lutherans and Catholics in Dialogue,* t. 4, *Eucharist and Ministry.* Washington, D. C.: USCC, 1970.

KASPER, W. "La 'Confessio Augustana' comme confession catholique et protestante," *Documentation catholique* 78 (8) 1980, pp. 381–384.

NEWBIGIN, L. *L'Eglise. Peuple des croyants, Corps du Christ, Temple de l'Esprit.* Neuchâtel/Paris: Delachaux & Niestlé (coll. "Taizé") 1958.

SCHULZ, F. "Documentation of Ordination Liturgies," pp. 35–87 in ROMAN CATHOLIC/JOINT COMMISSION. *The Ministry in the Church.* Geneva: LWF, 1982.

C. METHODOLOGICAL STUDIES AND HUMAN SCIENCES

DOMBOIS, H. *Das Recht der Gnade. Ökumenische Kirchenrecht, I.* 2nd ed. Witten: Luther Verlag (coll. "Forschungen und Berichte der evangelischen Studiengemeinschaft," 20) 1969.

IRWIN, K. W. *Context and Text. Method in Liturgical Theology.* Collegeville: The Liturgical Press/Pueblo Book, 1994.

D. GENERAL WORKS

ASHEIM, I., GOLD, V. R. (eds.). *Episcopacy in the Lutheran Church? Studies in the Development and Definition of the Office of Church Leadership.* English editon of the German *[Kirchenpräsident oder Bischof? Untersuchungen zur Entwicklung und Definition des kirchenleitenden Amtes in der lutherischen Kirche].* Philadelphia: Fortress Press, 1970.

CONGAR, Y. *L'Eglise de saint Augustin à l'époque moderne.* Paris: Cerf (coll. "Histoire des dogmes," III: Christologie-sotériologie-mariologie, 3) 1970.

COOKE, B. *Ministry to Word and Sacraments. History and Theology.* Philadelphia: Fortress Press, 1976.

ELLIOTT, J. H. *The Elect and the Holy. An Exegetical Examination of 1 Peter 2:4-10.* Leiden: E. J. Brill (coll. "Supplements to Novum Testamentum," 12) 1966.

ID. "Ministry and Church Order in the NT: A Traditio-Historical Analysis (1 Pt 5, 1-5 & plls)," *Catholic Biblical Quarterly* 32 (3) 1970, pp. 367–391.

GY, P.-M. "Ancient Ordination Prayers," *Studia Liturgica* 13 (2–4) 1979, pp. 70–93 (= VOS, W. & WAINWRIGHT, G. [eds.]. *Ordination Rites*. Papers Read at the 1979 Congress of *Societas Liturgica*. Rotterdam: Liturgical Ecumenical Center Trust, 1980).

IMSEN, S. *Superintendenten. En studie i kirkpolitikk, kirkeadministrasjon og statsutvikling mellom reformasjonen og eneveldet*. Oslo/Bergen/Troms: Universitetsforlaget, 1982.

KING, P. *An Inquiry into the Constitution, Discipline, Unity and Worship of the Primitive Church, that Flourished within the First Three Hundred Years after Christ*. Reprint [1st ed. 1691]. N.Y.: G. Lane & P. P. Sandford, 1841.

MAXWELL, J. M. *Worship and Reformed Theology. The Liturgical Lessons of Mercersburg*. Pittsburgh: The Pickwick Press (coll. "Pittsburgh Theological Monograph Series," 10) 1976.

MC KENZIE, J. L. "The Gospel According to Matthew," pp. 62–114 in BROWN, R. E., FITZMYER, J. A., MURPHY, R. E. (eds.). *The Jerome Biblical Commentary*, t. 2, *The New Testament and Topical Articles*. Englewood Cliffs, N.J.: Prentice-Hall, Inc., 1968.

OTT, L. *Le sacrement de l'Ordre*. French trans. of the German [*Das Weihesakrament*] by M. Deleporte. Paris: Cerf (coll. "Histoire des dogmes," 26; IV: Sacrements, 5) 1971.

SCHLINK, E. "La sucession apostolique," *Verbum Caro* 18 (69) 1964, pp. 52–86.

STILLINGFLEET, E. *Irenicum [Irenicon]: A Weapon-Salve for the Churches' Wounds or the Divine Right of Particular Forms of Church Government*. Reprint [1st ed. 1661]. Philadelphia: M. Sorin, 1842.

Index

Allmen, J.-J von, 76, 83, 90, 95, 102f., 104, 106, 109f., 171, 173f., 182, 184, 196

Amsdorf., N. von, 6, 14, 36

Asbury, F., 150, 156f.

Birmelé, A., 4, 186

Bradshaw, P. F., xxiii, 7, 11, 83, 90f., 93, 96, 103, 111–115, 117, 125, 127, 129, 131–133, 135–139, 143, 151, 155

Brunner, P., 6–9, 169, 176

Bucer, M., 4, 39–42, 44–46, 49–53, 56, 60, 64, 67, 75, 83, 88f., 92, 94f., 107, 112–118, 120, 124–127, 129, 145, 164, 172, 176f., 179f., 180, 184, 189

Bugenhagen, J., 30–39, 48, 64, 67, 164, 169, 180

Calvin, J., 40, 96, 103–107, 109, 117f., 170–174, 178f., 184–187

Coke, T., 150, 155, 157

Congar, Y., xvii, 19

Cranmer, T., 111–118, 120, 123–127, 153

DeClerck, P., 71, 74, 77, 84, 92

Dombois, H., 22, 27, 165f., 179, 195

Erasmus, D., 75

Flug, J., 6

Frederick, J., 5

Grabner, J. D., 152, 154f., 158

Jerome, xx, 20, 60, 127

Knox, J., 71, 83, 85f., 88f., 91f., 94–96, 100, 103, 107, 180, 189

Łaski, J., 44, 51, 71, 75f., 78, 81, 83f., 86, 88f., 92, 94–97, 99, 100, 102, 106, 110, 170, 179, 180, 183

Legrand, H.-M., xix

Luther, M., 4, 6, 9f., 14–23, 25, 28–33, 35, 39, 41, 44f., 52, 54, 64–66, 68, 163f., 169, 172, 174f., 180, 184, 186f., 189

Melanchthon, P., 18, 20, 75, 170, 181, 184, 187

Micron, M., 82

Nelson, P. R., 3

Olivier, D., 4, 187

Ott, L., 3

Pahl, I., 3, 7, 79

Pesch, O., 4

Petri, L., 4, 53, 56, 60–62, 67, 169, 178

Piepkorn, A. C., 8

Reumann, J.H.P., 3

Rörer, G., 4f.

Schulz, F., 13, 23–26, 33, 39, 44, 46, 51

Smith, R. F., 6

Spalatin, G., 6

Spinks, B., 3

Stein, N., 6

Stephens, W. P., 40f., 43–46, 52

Vasey, T., 150, 155f.

Wesley, J., 128, 147–151, 153–155, 158, 160f., 179, 189, 192f.

Whatcoat, R., 150, 155f.

Zwingli, U., 71, 75, 88, 96, 180, 184

* * * *

Agenda of Wittenberg, 4f., 23

Apostolic Tradition, 7, 125, 144

baptismal priesthood/common priesthood, 15, 21, 26, 67–69, 163–165, 168, 172–174

225

Biblical images, 12, 36, 47f., 57f., 74, 82, 92, 99f., 125, 127, 164

bishop/superintendent, xxi, 5, 9f., 14–16, 28f., 31–34, 37f., 49, 51, 53, 55f., 58–63, 76f., 79, 85, 94, 109f., 112, 119–127, 129f., 134, 139f., 149, 151f., 154–157, 159, 169, 174, 179, 183, 188f.

Book of Common Order, 85, 92f.

Book of Common Prayer, 40, 83, 96, 141, 151, 179
  Ordinal 1550/1552, 111–131
  Ordinal 1661, 131–141, 145, 151f., 154f., 159

Buke of Discipline, 85–95, 133, 170, 189

common priesthood. *See* baptismal priesthood

Confession of Augsburg, 5, 29, 168, 171, 181, 184, 187

Deacon, 75, 78, 86, 94, 102, 108, 112–114, 137, 143, 157

diakonia, 52, 164, 168, 172, 174, 180, 186, 194

Directory for Public Worship of God, 134

doctor, 80, 92, 102, 123, 126, 176

elder. *See* minister

epiclesis, 41, 44, 49, 80, 124, 145

episcopacy/superintendency, xx, 20, 53, 59, 67, 95, 108f., 118, 121, 129, 134–136, 140, 146

episkopē, 20, 63, 95, 108, 157, 174. *See also* episcopacy

Erastianism, 190–192

eschatology, 12, 48, 125, 175–178, 194, 197

eucharist. *See* Lord's Supper

examination, 72, 74, 78, 86, 88–90, 97f., 117f., 120f., 138–140

Forma ac Ratio, 71, 75–85

Formulary of Middleburgh, 95–102, 107, 133, 170, 179

Gelasian Sacramentary, 120

Genevan Service Book, 85f., 89, 96

gifts received by ordinand, 13, 37, 49, 58, 74, 81, 93, 100, 125, 127

God, 11, 13, 18, 22, 36, 45f., 49, 52, 55, 57–60, 62, 67, 69, 77, 90, 96, 98f., 117, 123, 140, 145

Holy Communion. *See* Lord's Supper

Holy Spirit, 9, 12f., 18f., 25–28, 32, 35, 38, 43, 45–47, 49f., 53, 55–57, 64–66, 72–74, 79, 98f., 104, 106–108, 116f., 122, 124, 126, 129, 137, 140f., 143, 145, 180, 186, 196

imposition of hands, xxii, 6, 9f., 14, 25–28, 31–33, 35, 38, 44–46, 51, 57, 60, 62, 69, 72f., 76, 79–82, 84, 86, 89–91, 93, 96–98, 103f., 113f., 116, 118, 129, 133, 143, 145, 158, 167, 179, 181, 188

Installation, 14f., 23–29, 32, 49, 67, 108, 167, 182

Jesus Christ, 11, 22, 36, 37f., 43, 46, 48, 53, 57, 67f., 79f., 89, 90, 97, 106, 123f., 140

Kyrkoordning, 53–63, 178

local church, 36, 41, 56f., 60, 65f., 79f., 86, 89, 91, 96, 98f., 105, 122, 144f., 176, 181, 194f.

Lord's prayer (Our Father), x, xii, 5f., 9, 11f., 32

Lord's Supper/eucharist/Holy Communion, 3, 6, 9, 32, 34, 41, 44, 59f., 63, 65, 68, 76, 84, 119, 122f., 137f., 149, 156–157, 160, 169, 195f.

minister/pastor/elder, 5, 10f., 15f., 23, 25, 28f., 31, 41, 53, 75f., 78, 86, 97, 102, 108f., 110, 112–119, 123–126, 130, 136–139, 152–154, 157

ministry:
  direction, 28, 53, 62, 97, 130, 140f., 160, 182–184, 190
  functions, 29, 35, 38f., 43, 46, 50, 53, 58f., 61, 63, 75, 77, 97, 101, 130, 141, 145, 160, 168–171

Ordinatio Ecclesiastica, 30–39

ordination:
  election, 6, 11, 14, 25, 27, 31, 34, 36, 41, 46, 54–56, 62, 64, 66, 72f., 74, 76f., 85–88, 94, 97, 102f., 108, 115, 142, 167, 181, 184, 187, 189, 195

mission, 6, 38, 44, 65, 94, 105, 144, 183f., 196f.
structure, 27, 32–34, 38f., 41, 51f., 54, 62, 68, 118, 184, 193
ordination as:
ecclesial act, 64, 69, 184, 193
juridical act, 26, 39, 69, 184, 193
liturgical act, 39, 69, 184, 193
ordination prayers, xxii, 11, 28, 32f., 35f., 38, 44–47, 56f., 60, 73, 80f., 91, 98f., 103, 113, 116, 122–127, 155, 158, 179
De Ordinatione Legitima, 39–53
pastor. *See* minister
pneumatology, 10, 27, 177–181, 189, 194
preaching, 15, 28f., 60f., 74–76, 88, 97, 103, 105, 118, 121, 123, 157, 165, 171–174, 183, 186
presbyterian, 76, 83, 85, 93, 95, 133, 141, 142
Puritans, 71, 93, 100, 102f., 129, 132–137, 142f., 146, 178, 189–192
rites:
Anglican, 111–146, 164, 167, 171, 177, 189–193
Lutheran, 3–69, 115, 167, 177, 179, 183, 185–189
Methodist, 147–161, 167, 171, 177, 192f.

Reformed, 71–110, 170, 177, 183, 185–189
role of:
civil authorities, 72
congregations, 7, 10, 18, 27, 35f., 45, 55, 59, 62f., 65, 69, 74, 87f., 97f., 105, 116, 189
heads of neighboring communities, 67, 108, 181
neighboring bishops, 146
Romano–Germanic Pontifical (=PRG), 122
Sarum Pontifical, 114, 120, 123, 125, 128, 138
Second Helvetic Confession, 104, 106, 110, 163, 171, 173f., 182
Sint speciosi, 122, 126
structure of the Church, 74f., 83f., 94, 100f., 128–130, 141, 159f., 184–193
Sunday Service of the Methodists in N. America, 147–161
superintendency. *See* episcopacy
superintendent. *See* bishop
teacher, 76, 80, 91, 97, 102, 121, 153
Trinitarian theology, 45, 52, 193, 195
vocation, 27, 38, 88, 94, 106, 117f., 178f., 184, 194
Vollzugsformal (formula of transmission), 5, 24f., 41, 56, 65
Zürichter Prädicantenordnung, 71–75, 170